Kate Howarth was born in Sydney in 1950 and grew up in the suburbs of Darlington and Parramatta, and far western New South Wales. She was forced to leave school at fourteen and an eclectic career followed; she has been a factory worker, an Avon lady, corporate executive and restaurateur, to name a few. At the age of fifty-two she began writing her memoir, *Ten Hail Marys*, which in 2008 was shortlisted for the David Unaipon Award for Indigenous Writers. In 2010, it was shortlisted for the Victorian Premier's Literary Award for Indigenous Writing and won the *Age* Book of the Year for Non-fiction. Kate is proud of her connection to the Wiradjuri and Wonnarua people of New South Wales.

kate howarth

SETTLING DAY

UQP

First published 2015 by University of Queensland Press
PO Box 6042, St Lucia, Queensland 4067 Australia

uqp.com.au
uqp@uqp.uq.edu.au

Cover design by Christabella Designs
Cover photograph by Archangel
Typeset in 11/16.5pt Janson by Post Pre-press Group, Brisbane
Printed in Australia by McPherson's Printing Group, Melbourne

This project has been assisted by
the Commonwealth Government through
the Australia Council, its arts funding
and advisory body.

Cataloguing-in-Publication Data
National Library of Australia Cataloguing-in-publication data is available at
http://catalogue.nla.gov.au

ISBN 978 0 7022 5005 7 (pbk)
ISBN 978 0 7022 5240 2 (pdf)
ISBN 978 0 7022 5241 9 (epub)
ISBN 978 0 7022 5242 6 (kindle)

For my children and grandchildren

My son, Adam, aged eighteen months.

1

He'll get over it

'Where to, love?'

My mind was blank as I stared through the wire mesh screen. The ticket seller at Lidcombe Station repeated his question, drumming his fingers impatiently on the counter.

'Central Station, please,' I mumbled, slipping a two dollar note into the brass metal tray.

'Single or return?'

'Single, thank you.'

Sydney's Central Station isn't so much a destination as a hub for interstate and suburban trains and buses to converge. I'd think about where I was going when I got there. As I waited on the platform I noticed a man standing nearby reading a newspaper. The front page spread featured a beachscape with the headline: 'Prime Minister Harold Holt, disappeared presumed drowned.'

It had only been four weeks since I'd left my husband, John McNorton, but being separated from my infant son, Adam, whom I couldn't take with me, made it seem like an eternity. I hadn't gone far in that time, just two suburbs in fact, but without my son it may as well have been to the ends of the earth. Not an hour had gone by when I didn't think about the last time we had been together, his angelic face turned up to mine. I had stood next to his cot and promised that I'd be back as soon as I found a job and was settled. I'd found a job within the month, but without Adam I was never going to be settled.

A few days earlier I'd called John at work and told him that I wanted to meet. If necessary, I was prepared to go down on my knees and beg him to take me back. If that wasn't possible I was hoping to arrange to see Adam every weekend.

We met under the Lidcombe railway bridge, a short walk from where I was staying. John drove a distinctive Volkswagen and was waiting for me. 'Hello, John,' I said, getting into the passenger seat. He looked straight ahead as he lit up a cigarette. As trains roared overhead and monster trucks rocked us from side to side in the slipstream, my fate and that of my one-and-a-half-year-old son was decided.

'It's that Peter guy isn't it?'

'No,' I said, unable to look at him.

'Yes it is,' he grinned.

'Please John, let me come home,' I begged. 'Or at least let me see Adam. I'm going insane.'

'No way,' he replied, smugly.

A freight train rumbled overhead. My mind raced in all directions. *How did he know about Peter?* Then it struck me. John's father had very good connections with the Parramatta police. On the night I had left John I caught a taxi to Peter's flat in Lidcombe. A couple of weeks later two uniformed coppers had knocked on the door wanting to speak with a Kay Howarth, in connection to stolen goods. Surprised and intimidated, I stood back and let them into the flat, eager to cooperate and establish my innocence. They made a thorough search of the bedrooms and enquired after the males occupying the premises. It wasn't until after they'd gone that I wondered how they knew my name.

Sitting in the car next to John I felt my anger rise. I'd been a sixteen-year-old unmarried mother when my son was born. For five months, during my confinement at St Margaret's Home for Unwed Mothers, I'd fought the nuns to prevent my son being taken for adoption. 'You can't afford to keep this child,' I was told time and time again, 'we have a wealthy family waiting to take him.'

It was true my family had abandoned me and I had no means of support. But I was sixteen and coming from a very primal place with regard to my baby. It was the first time in my life that I had any power and I was going to use it to stop them taking him. How would we live? I had no idea. All I knew for sure was that no one would love my son as much as I did and I didn't care how wealthy they were. Every night I got down on my knees and prayed to the Virgin Mary to send us some help.

John and his family had known I was at St Margaret's. They too had expected me to give up my baby for adoption, and never hear from me again. At the eleventh hour and, it seemed, by divine intervention, my Aunty Daphne had heard of my plight and intervened. It was quite ironic that the one person in my family with the least capacity to help was the only one who reached out. But Daphne's situation was very complicated and there was a limit to how much assistance she could provide in the long term.

In order to keep my son I was railroaded into marrying John. I soon discovered the haste to get us to the altar had been motivated by a threat of carnal knowledge, being brought against John by my grandmother, a crime which carried a three-year prison term. After the police interviewed me and learned of our plans to marry we heard no more of it.

During the twenty months we were together, John and I had lived in a rough industrial suburb, with no phone, no transport and

I didn't have enough money to dress myself or my son. I had felt isolated and was struggling to cope, while my husband, seemingly oblivious to my circumstances, squandered his money on various hobbies. At one time he purchased a second car, an FJ Holden, and while he tinkered in the garage with his mate Graham, I made clothes for our baby with material cut from his old clothes.

John sat with the cigarette clamped between his teeth, blowing smoke in my face. 'I need to get back to work,' he said, bringing me back to the present.

'What about Adam?' I pleaded. 'He needs his mother.'

'He'll get over it,' he said, starting up the engine. As I turned and opened the passenger door, he added, 'And don't think of going to Aunty Daphne or Uncle Stan, they want nothing to do with you.'

'Please, John,' I sobbed, 'if you let me explain what really happened, you will understand why I had to go.'

He shook his head and revved the motor. As he drove away I felt as if the lifeblood was being drained from me. A truck roared past and the male passenger in the car behind whistled as the wind caught my skirt sending it flying up over my knees. I felt as putrid as the filth being kicked up from the road, with my grandmother's prophecies ringing in my ears. *You'll go onto the street and hawk your fork, just like your mother.*

Enraged that he could threaten to take my son, I made an appointment in my lunch hour to see a solicitor in Rydalmere who left me in no doubt about where I stood. As I took a seat, I glanced at the statue of the Virgin Mary on his desk, lined up next to the photographs of his children.

'Your husband can turn you out with just your clothes and, if you have one, your sewing machine,' he told me, dismissing the notion

4

that I had a leg to stand on when I revealed that after leaving my husband I had been living in a flat with two men – Peter Ashton, a former boyfriend who had helped me to get away, and his good mate Deanie.

In 1967 this was precisely what the law allowed when women found themselves in my position.

When Peter got home that night I told him about the meeting with the solicitor. His reaction wasn't unpredictable, although I still wasn't prepared for it. 'You've lost your son. Get over it. You can have more children.'

I flew at him, unleashing a torrent of rage. 'None of you know what I went through to keep my son. I'll never get over losing him!'

Peter took his clothes out of our wardrobe, packed his bags and left the next morning.

Living so close to Adam, and not being able to see him, was going to tear me apart and perhaps drive me to desperation. I thought about just going and taking him. John's mother wouldn't have been able to physically stop me. But take him where? With no family support or child care agencies operating at the time, at least none that I knew of, who'd look after him while I had to work? Prostitution, it seemed, would have been my only option and my son deserved a better life than that. By leaving him with his father, I reasoned, he would at least be safe. He'd be taken care of. I felt that my circumstances had come about because of mistakes I'd made and my son shouldn't have to suffer because of them. Perhaps John was right. Adam was so young; he might get over losing me.

'You can stay here,' Deanie offered, putting his arm around me as I packed my suitcase for the ninth time in less than three years. The warmth and compassion from someone showing me sympathy caused me to collapse into a blubbering mess. He held me until I was cried out and able to catch my breath. 'It's alright, I've got another jumper,' he chuckled tenderly, wiping himself down and handing me a towel.

'Thank you Deanie, but it's killing me not being able to see Adam. It's best if I go away.'

'I'll walk you to the station,' he said, picking up my sewing machine. We didn't talk on the way. There was no need to explain anything. Deanie was now my only friend in the world and leaving him with no idea of when, or if, we'd meet again would have been painful in ordinary circumstances. On that day, however, circumstances were anything but ordinary.

'Please don't wait with me,' I told Deanie, numbly, when we reached the station. 'I'll be stronger on my own.'

As I watched him walk away he turned and waved one last time. Even at a distance I could see he was crying. Standing on Lidcombe Station, surrounded by nameless strangers, my whole life flashed before me. At seventeen I couldn't self-analyse or make any sense of the rollercoaster ride that had seen me lose my family, all hope of an education, and now my son, with the passing of only four years.

What would they tell him? I wondered. *How would they explain my absence?*

It took all my strength to pick up the Singer, which weighed more than my suitcase, and jostle for space on the train with standing room only. I placed the machine between my legs and with no handrail to steady myself I lurched from side to side, banging into other passengers. After a while it seemed pointless apologising. I felt numb, like someone picking over the blackened ashes of a house that had burned to the ground, searching for something to salvage. After all I'd been through, my son was the only real family that was truly mine and now he was gone. John and his family had no clue what we'd been through at the hospital.

Would they let him know what a good mother I was, and how much I loved him?

Little did I know it would be another fourteen years before I had an answer to this question.

'This bus terminates here, love,' the driver said, pulling hard on the handbrake and reaching behind his seat for a newspaper.

'Where am I?' I asked, checking to see if I still had my suitcase and the Singer. I'd been so entranced in my own thoughts I'd not paid any attention when I got to Central and had jumped on the first bus passing by.

'This is Bondi Beach,' he said, shaking his head, clearly bemused that I didn't recognise one of Australia's most famous landmarks.

As I stumbled from the bus I felt condemned, sentenced to a life without Adam. I wandered aimlessly with no idea where I was, or how I had gotten there. Perhaps I'd been subconsciously drawn to the sea where, like Prime Minister Harold Holt, I could dis-appear without trace.

As my head cleared I became aware of two young men walking towards me on the pedestrian crossing. One smiled shyly and whispered something to the other. His mate looked me up and down. 'Yeah, but it's a pity about the dress,' I overheard him say, with a chuckle.

His friend looked embarrassed but said nothing.

This seemed an odd comment to make. I was wearing what I thought was a nice dress. I'd made it myself and it fitted perfectly.

A short time later two girls, about my age, walked past. They too looked me up and down, before giggling behind their hands. They were wearing mini-skirts and suddenly I saw the joke. Having lived in the western suburbs most of my life, and in almost total isolation for the past two years, I was way out of touch with the fashion trends of the cosmopolitan eastern suburbs beaches.

The aroma from the cafés along Campbell Parade reminded me that I hadn't eaten since lunchtime the day before. A blackboard menu at the front of Enid's Café caught my eye: 'Tea and raisin toast $1.00'. As I waited for my order to arrive I picked up a copy of the newspaper.

Looking at the *Sydney Morning Herald* jobs vacant advertisements, I wasn't sure what I was even qualified to do. I didn't type forty-five words per minute, and I couldn't present the Intermediate Certificate, both of which seemed to be minimum requirements for most of the clerical work going. I circled an ad for a job as a trainee at a film-processing laboratory in the city. I knew nothing about processing film, but I did have some experience working as a laboratory assistant. After I finished my meal I left the café, found a public telephone and got an appointment for an interview.

That night I slept in a cheap hotel a block back from the beach. The single bed, which sagged in the middle, was as comfortable as a collapsed banana chair, and between that and the noisy drunks stumbling up and down the stairs I hardly got a wink of sleep. The next morning I got up early enough to adjust the hem of my skirt. Even if I felt like Tess of the D'Urbervilles I didn't have to look like an outcast.

2

A little respect

The pungent stench of cat pee and piles of rotting waste assaulted my senses as I picked my way down a lane off Pitt Street. Once inside, the photo lab was surprisingly trendy, with black shag-pile carpet, red vinyl chairs, chrome and laminated office furniture. Framed photographs of half-starved fashion models with gaunt expressions lined the felt-covered walls. A pretty young woman seated at reception, painting her fingernails, looked up at me and smiled.

'Hello, I'm Jenny,' she shouted, trying to be heard above Aretha Franklin's big voice blaring from hidden speakers, that all she wanted was a little 'R–E–S–P–E–C–T!'

'Hello, I'm Kathy McNamara. I have an interview for the position vacant.' The name had just popped into my head. This was the beginning of my new life, a clean slate, a chance to start again; I thought I may as well have a new name.

Jenny pressed the button on the intercom.

'Robbo, the applicant for the job is here.'

'I'll be right there, honey.'

A short, pudgy man wearing a purple paisley shirt, opened almost to the waist, gyrated to the beat of the music as he approached. He grinned, exposing a mouth full of nicotine-stained teeth. A shiver of revulsion swept over me.

'Sock it to me! Sock it to me!' he sang along with the tune as he danced around, looking me over as if I was a piece of livestock.

'I'm Robbo,' he said, 'when can you start?'

My urge was to leave, but I needed the job.

'Today?' I replied, forcing a smile.

Jenny, whom I soon learned was from New Zealand, was on a working holiday with two girlfriends, Shirley and Cheryl.

'We're looking for someone to share our house in Bondi,' Jenny told me later that afternoon when she saw me looking for rooms to let. I moved in that night.

Jenny, Cheryl and Shirley were from Gisborne, which sounded like an idyllic seaside village on New Zealand's north island. They'd known each other since they were kids. Shirley and Cheryl were hairdressers, but were working as barmaids in Kings Cross. I tried not to show surprise. Barmaids were not highly regarded in those days and both Shirley and Cheryl seemed so prim and proper.

'So, where are you from Kathy?' Shirley asked.

I hesitated. I didn't want anyone making a connection between me and the ghosts of my past, so I made the story up as I went along. 'My family's from the bush. I ran away when I was fourteen and haven't been back,' I said. Their eyes bulging at this reply, I couldn't imagine how they'd react to the truth about me. I felt a deep shame, as if it was my fault in some way, that I'd lost my family and that I didn't have an education.

After paying for my share of the rent and food and putting aside money to get to work, I had just enough left over to buy some material to make a new dress. Cut to a modest two inches above the knee it was just long enough to conceal my stocking tops and suspenders. Pantyhose hadn't hit the market yet and the more liberated young women were taking the lead from English fashion model, Jean Shrimpton, who'd shocked the country by appearing at the Melbourne Cup, with bare legs and no hat or gloves.

Not surprisingly, my new boss turned out to be a total sleaze. The first time he brushed up against my breasts in the darkroom I accepted that it was accidental. When it became routine it was impossible to dismiss. He'd been giving Jenny the same man-handling, grabbing her on the bum thinking it was a great joke. Jenny and I quit on the same day and went for interviews at the Chevron Hotel in Kings Cross. Barmaids needed to be at least twenty-one and I knew if they asked for proof-of-age I was sunk. I needn't have worried; as it turned out, a pretty young woman with no experience could get a job as a barmaid with very few questions asked.

The first day in the Quarterdeck bar thirsty men, ten deep, tapped the counter with silver coins anxious to get as many schooners into themselves as they could during their lunch break. The experienced barmaids, who could pull schooners and top them up without turning off the fixed tap, attracted most of the customers and consequently most of the tips. Even after months of practice all I could manage was four at a time, yet my tip jar was always full. I suspect my youth and long black hair, which I could almost sit on, gave me an edge.

Working in a public bar was a real eye opener and the irony of my situation wasn't lost on me. In an office job, a female could be groped and was expected to tolerate obscene language and sexual innuendo, but it was still considered a more respectable way to earn a living than a job as a barmaid, where the customers showed us the utmost respect.

By 1969 the number of Australian soldiers who had been killed in Vietnam hit triple digits and the government was still refusing to call it a war. Baby-faced American soldiers, with spiky crew-cuts and pockets bulging with cash, poured into Kings Cross on rest and recreation leave. They were extremely polite and left enough tips in one night to equate to a week's pay. The downside of all this overpaid testosterone in uniform was the number of unmarried, pregnant girls that were left in their wake, many of whom suffered a dreadful fate in a society that promoted free love while denying unmarried women access to abortion or the contraceptive Pill. This period in Australian history stands out as producing what has become known as a 'bumper crop' of adoptions.

One night the banquet manager asked me if I'd do a shift in the ballroom. The Chevron was the first international-style hotel to open in Sydney. It was overtaking the old Trocadero as the preferred venue for shindigs organised by Sydney's high-society ladies, who got dressed to the nines and drank champagne, all in the name of raising money for children's charities.

When I arrived that evening there were more bums on seats in the ballroom than there were plates to serve them. Floor staff had to hover, ready to pounce on an empty plate, then race back to the kitchen to get it washed and ready for another meal to go out.

'I don't want that!' a woman snapped, bumping my hand as I passed behind her. The sloppy concoction of canned peaches and pink junket that I had been holding quivered and splashed over the side of the bowl, slipping silently into the vortex of her massive beehive hairdo. I froze, expecting a reaction. When she didn't flinch I realised she was wearing a wig, and discreetly kept moving.

A young man about my age, who'd been complaining all night, was getting up to leave. His table looked like a pigsty.

'Waitress,' he said, clicking his fingers in the air.

'Yes, sir,' I smiled, walking over to the table.

'Here's your tip,' he chortled, slapping a twenty cent coin into my hand.

Several of his companions laughed.

'Buy a book on table etiquette,' I said, placing the coin on the table. The laughing stopped as I abruptly turned and walked away. It would be over three decades, and in vastly different circumstances, until our paths would cross again.

3

Come where?

We were both clutching Joni Mitchell's debut album *Song to a Seagull* as we waited to be served at the record shop in Bondi Junction. 'Isn't she wonderful?' he said, smiling and tapping the cover of the LP. We struck up a conversation and he told me his name was Danny Frawley.

'What are you reading?' he asked, motioning to my basket, which contained a stack of books I'd just picked up from the library.

'It's a bit of an eclectic mix, Charles Dickens and some text-books on business strategy,' I said, thumping through the pile that was weighing down one arm.

'*Advanced Accounting and Business Management?*' Danny asked quizzically, running his finger along the spine of one of the books.

'I think it would be a good skill to have if I hope to succeed in business, don't you?' I smiled.

He nodded. 'Would you like a coffee?'

'Thank you,' I said, pleased that our conversation wouldn't end in the store.

'Here, let me take that for you,' he said, reaching down to help me with my basket. Over coffee we discovered that we had many interests in common. He invited me to listen to a live band at the Royal Hotel in Bondi. I told him that although I worked in a bar, it was a means to an end. I tended to steer clear of pubs after work. I didn't drink alcohol and I had no tolerance for drunken behaviour.

'Come on Kathy, Jeannie Lewis is singing, you'll like her,' he pleaded. I really liked live music and Danny was a big strapping lad whom I felt sure would stand between me and any troublemakers.

The pub was packed when we arrived. The stares from the blokes leaning against the bar seemed to strip me naked as we pushed and shoved our way through the crowd to where Danny's friends were sitting.

'Kathy, this is Jack Gazzard,' Danny said, introducing me to a mate of his, who was sitting with a woman brandishing a diamond engagement ring.

'Hello Jack,' I smiled, offering my hand.

Jack took a firm grip and his eyes bore into me as if he wanted to see right into my soul.

Once our eyes met, neither of us wanted to break the connection. Danny broke the spell. 'You can't keep her mate,' he said, nodding to Jack's hand that was still holding mine.

The next time I saw Jack was at the City versus Country rugby league match. The City team was thrashing the boys from the Country and Danny was screaming himself hoarse with excitement. 'Go the City!' Danny yelled, across the pavilion.

Jack was sitting a few rows in front of us and kept turning around trying to catch my attention whenever there was a break in the game. Even before the referee blew the whistle at half-time, Jack was on his feet and making his way over to where I was sitting.

'Miss World,' he said, reaching out to touch my hair. This comment appeared flippant and annoyed me. I didn't see myself as being particularly beautiful.

'Thank you, but you're engaged,' I said, rather curtly, stepping back and flicking my hair over my shoulder.

The following week the Bondi Royal football team won their final match and were celebrating at the pub. Jack was the captain of the team so I knew he'd be there. Danny didn't have to plead this time. Jack smiled when he saw me. His fiancée was nowhere to be seen.

'I broke off the engagement. I haven't been able to get you out of my head,' he said, smiling. That night he drove me home and we kissed goodnight. He asked me out to dinner the following week.

'I'm sorry Jack, I'm going to Queensland with my girlfriends on Sunday morning,' I said, feeling as disappointed as he looked. 'But, we're having a farewell party on Saturday night, if you'd like to come?'

A house party at Bondi was always a risky business. The word would go round the local pub that it was 'on' at a certain address and anyone carrying a guitar or grog could get in. The parties usually ended in drunken brawls. We needed to get our bond back, so our party was by invitation only, and we'd asked two giant Maoris to watch the front door and persuade gate crashers to leave. Jack arrived with his mate, Richard, who was already staggering and looking for a fight. I suggested to Jack that he take Richard home. 'I'll come with you if you like,' I offered.

We took Richard home and instead of going back to the party we parked at Bondi Beach. The full moon lit up the water like a cosmic spotlight.

'You're so beautiful,' Jack said, pulling me across the bench seat of his FJ Holden.

'Everyone looks beautiful in the moonlight,' I said, snuggling into his arms. This was the first affection I'd had in a while and I struggled to hold in my emotions as I recalled the last time I'd felt Adam's small arms around me. On the last day we'd spent together I had been sobbing and Adam had pressed his soft face against mine, his tiny lips quivering, 'Mum Mum', as he stroked my hair.

'I don't want you to go,' Jack said, burying his face in my neck and sucking in a deep breath. 'You smell so good.'

'I have to Jack. It's all arranged and besides, after today I have nowhere to live.'

Jack got a travel rug from his car and we lay on the beach until dawn. I wasn't popular when I got back to the house, but passionate kisses and watching the sun rise with Jack was worth the cold stares from the girls who were in the yard bagging piles of bottles and tinnies and looking the worse for wear. Cheryl had a shiner; she'd stepped between two drunks going at each other. Inside, the house looked like a tsunami had swept through it. *There goes our bond*, I thought, picking up broken glasses and cigarettes that had been stubbed out on the carpet.

Everything I owned still fitted into one suitcase, with room to spare, but the other girls had twelve pieces of luggage between them, which didn't improve the grumpy disposition of the coach driver taking us to Queensland. Four barmaids, three with funny accents, arriving in a country town expecting to find work at the local pub was an ill-conceived plan. Standing by the side of the road with thirteen suitcases and a sewing machine, trying to hitch a ride south must have amused the locals no end. We got lucky when a transport truck heading to Sydney gave us a lift. When he realised that none of us was going to put out for the ride he dumped us just outside Surfers Paradise. We hung around there for a few months, but work was spasmodic, and we all agreed to head back to Sydney. We got our jobs back at the Chevron just in time to watch the first moon landing on the 17-inch black-and-white television above the bar. A cheer went up as Neil Armstrong took a giant leap for mankind. I was cleaning the bar when Jack walked in.

'Hello, Jack. It's nice to see you. I'm sorry, but the bar's closed,' I said, trying to sound casual.

'I haven't come for a drink. Richard and I have been to every bar in Sydney trying to find you,' he said, pushing a mop of hair back from his forehead.

Jack drove me home that night, and every night after that. Upon our return to Sydney the girls and I had rented a house and as I was sharing a room with Jenny, intimacy with Jack wasn't possible. After a couple of weeks he was getting frustrated and hinted that we get into the back of his car one night. I bridled at the suggestion.

'I'm sorry, you're right. Would you like to go away for a weekend? The Newport Arms has a good restaurant with a sunset over the water.'

We got to the Newport Arms in the afternoon. It was still a bit cold for a swim for my liking, but the day was warm so we lay around the pool reading until it was time to get dressed for dinner. This was the first time Jack had seen me without clothes on. He was wearing his swimmers and I tried not to be obvious as I checked him out. Jack used to run and work out every day. Where his fitness was concerned he was borderline obsessive, I just wished he didn't smoke. But in those days it seemed that everyone but me smoked and I had to suffer in silence.

I sat between his legs with my hair pulled over my shoulders, shivering with pleasure as Jack's hands massaged my back and neck. Wearing only his thin Speedos I could feel his erection pushing against the cheeks of my bum. Suddenly he jumped up and dived into the icy cold pool.

'It's not too bad,' he said, when he surfaced.

'Enjoy your swim,' I laughed. 'I'm going to take a hot shower.'

At dinner Jack pulled out my chair and I was trying to act grown up as the waiter handed us menus.

'What would you like?' Jack asked.

There was nothing on the menu that I even recognised.

'Lobster mornay, thank you,' I said, taking a punt and hoping it would be like eating a giant prawn.

'Good choice,' he said. 'I'll have the same.'

When the lobster arrived, in its shell, topped with a bubbling cheesy concoction, I kept my cool and followed Jack's lead. He ordered wine and I tried not to screw my face up at the bitter taste. After dinner we moved across to the comfortable lounge chairs by the window while Jack had a cigarette. It was too dark to see across Pittwater, but the luxury boats rocking hypnotically on the marina of the Royal Prince Alfred Yacht Club gave a feeling of being at an exotic holiday destination, light-years away from the world I grew up in.

'Would you like a coffee and liqueur?'

'Yes, thank you,' I said. I'd never had a liqueur in my life, but thought it was time I became a bit more adventurous.

'Tia Maria, with cream, is that alright?' Jack asked, motioning to the waiter.

I nodded politely, hoping I looked more worldly than I felt.

Two tiny glasses, barely a mouthful, arrived with a thin layer of cream floating on the top. *Do I drink it in one go? Or sip it?* I wondered. We chinked glasses and Jack took a sip.

'I could learn to like that,' I said, with an urge to tilt the glass right back to savour the last drop.

'Good, I'll get you another one.'

After the second glass of liqueur, on top of two glasses of wine, my face felt flushed and the dread I'd been feeling about what was to follow, lessened. Perhaps that was Jack's intention.

Wanting this night to be special I'd splurged almost a week's pay on a white lace and chiffon negligee set. It looked nice, but I had no idea what feeling sexy was all about, I just wanted to get it over with.

'Am I hurting you?'

'No,' I smiled, and for the next few minutes I thought, *please hurry up*.

As Jack rolled off me he asked, 'Did you cum?'

Come where? I had no idea what he meant.

'Yes,' I said, hoping that would be the right answer.

Jack lit a cigarette. With his free hand he ran a finger along my profile. 'God, Kathy, you're so beautiful. I love you so much,' he said.

'Jack, my name is Kay,' I said, feeling rather stupid that we'd just made love and I hadn't told him my real name.

Jack and I hadn't discussed contraception and I was never more pleased to see my period. I made an appointment with a general practitioner at Bondi Beach, who was well known for dispensing prescriptions for the Pill without asking too many questions. Some Catholic doctors wouldn't prescribe the Pill but this man was a flamboyantly homosexual Jewish doctor, who chain-smoked, fainted at the sight of blood and drove a convertible Rolls Royce, all without having to pull on a rubber glove. I had to wait for my period to finish before I could start taking the Pill, and then allow fourteen days before having sex. Meanwhile, I tried to get Jack to wear a condom. 'That's like taking a shower in a plastic raincoat,' he laughed.

4

It's time

Jack was still living at home, and probably because I refused to
have sex in the car, he suggested that we get a flat together, split-
ting everything fifty-fifty. We found a nice unfurnished flat above
a supermarket on Bondi Road. The outgoing tenants wanted to
sell all of their furniture, including a teak stereo record player. I
did the haggling and we bought the lot for under $100.

The domestic arrangements for men and women living together
seemed to be set in stone. Jack made himself scarce while I did all
the housework – cooking, washing and ironing – and tried not to
turn into a nag to get him to remember to take out the garbage.
I considered myself fortunate that Jack didn't leave the bathroom
looking like a cat had been shaved in the hand basin and picked his
clothes up from the floor and put them into the laundry basket.

Jack never enquired about any of my previous relationships.
There wasn't much to tell. Even though I'd been married and had
a child I remained as naive as anyone could be about sex. Any
notion that I would derive any pleasure from the act was far from

my thinking. One afternoon we made love on the lounge-room floor, in broad daylight, which was daring for me. Jack knew I was shy and blushed easily.

'Say "fuck",' he teased, smiling down at me.

'Jack, stop it. I can't say that word.'

'Well say "cunt",' he said, with a wicked laugh.

'Jack!' I slapped his chest. 'Stop that. I *can't* say those words.'

'She's a strange woman, my mother,' Jack commented, as we drove over to Bronte for me to meet his mother for the first time.

Mrs Gazzard was a Catholic and Jack said she wasn't impressed that we were living in sin. Most of Jack's friends were Catholic and looked down their noses at Jack and me living together without being married, while they had sex in the back of their boyfriends' cars. Every now and then one of the girls from our group of friends would disappear to 'visit an aunt in the country'. It was an expression I knew all too well. I didn't want anyone preaching good old Christian values to me.

Jack's parents had only recently separated after thirty years of what Jack claimed was a loveless marriage. He was their only child. His mother was the deputy matron at Waverley Hospital and she was the model of lickety-split efficiency. Numerous school portraits of Jack, a Waverley College Old Boy, and holy pictures of the Sacred Heart lined the walls. Statues of Our Lady and St Anthony shared shelf space with porcelain dogs, miniature shoes and Toby jugs of all shapes and sizes.

'So, Kay, where are you from?' Mrs Gazzard started her grilling as she placed covers onto the lounge before we sat down.

'My family are from Nyngan, but we also lived in Parramatta,' I replied.

'Oh,' she said, pulling her mouth into a disapproving pout,

making me glad that I hadn't mentioned Herne Bay, the hostel where immigrants, displaced persons and Aboriginal families like mine went when they had to wait for government-assisted housing.

Throughout the meal Mrs Gazzard watched me like a hawk. I was grateful for Aunty Daphne, who'd been a stickler for good table manners. 'People will judge you by the way you behave at the table,' she'd warned, showing me how to break, rather than cut, a bread roll.

After the meal I helped with the dishes while Jack packed some personal things from his room. Mrs Gazzard continued her interrogation and seemed to relax once it was established that I was Catholic. Her acceptance of me was sealed when I told her I'd made the outfit I was wearing.

In spite of Jack's dire warnings with regard to his mother, I sensed that behind the exaggerated attention to social graces, beat the warm heart of a mother who adored her son. 'Thank you for a lovely meal Mrs Gazzard,' I said, as she walked us to the car.

'Please call me Peggy,' she said, leaning forward to kiss my cheek.

'Well you were a big hit, she's never done that before!' Jack chuckled as we were driving away.

'She wasn't so bad,' I said, 'she does love you, you know.'

'She's got a funny way of showing it.'

Jack's mother kissed him and called him 'Pon', which she explained was short for Johnnie Pon, a nickname she'd given to him when he was a baby. His bedroom was immaculate and there wasn't a speck of dust on his football trophies. She'd cooked us a wonderful meal and slipped an envelope containing some cash into his hand as we were leaving. I wondered what Jack was expecting from his mother. This was evidence of affection I couldn't even relate to.

As I got to know Peggy I could see that she had a very complex personality. She was agoraphobic, xenophobic and more super-stitious than my grandmother, which I wouldn't have thought possible. She had a bogeyman for every occasion and opening her front door was like trying to break into the Royal Mint. Surprisingly, one thing she loved to do was swim, and on her days off she took a dip at Bronte Beach.

'So you're not concerned about sharks?'

'I swim in the bogey hole, sharks don't get in there,' she said.

When we dropped Peggy home after a swim one day I asked Jack where his Aboriginal connection came from.

'We don't have any boong blood as far as I know,' he said. 'Mum's often made cracks about her black gin legs, but always said she had Irish heritage.'

Jack wasn't racist; his language was just typical of the insensi-tivity and ignorance with regard to Aboriginal people at that time, and it wasn't unusual for people of Peggy's era to conceal their Aboriginal heritage if they could get away with it.

'I've sold the car,' Jack announced, walking through the door carry-ing a motorcycle helmet. As Jack only had a learner's permit and couldn't take a pillion passenger I decided to get a motorcycle of my own. Not since the day that I got my first bicycle had I experienced the exhilaration and independence that I felt riding away on my brand new Honda 125. Pretty soon most of our friends, including Danny, had motorcycles and we'd get away on trail rides along the back roads of Wisemans Ferry. In those days it was unusual to see a female with her own bike. People would gawk in amazement when I pulled off my helmet, shook out my hair and unzipped my leather jacket, exposing an 'It's Time' t-shirt, worn without a bra, in support of the election of Gough Whitlam. The dashing leader of the Labor

Party would soon put an end to twenty-three years of conservative government; the impending election was to be the first time I would vote, following the 1967 Referendum that gave Aboriginal people across Australia the right to vote. For me it also represented a personal power that no one could deny me, and I took it very seriously.

Life with Jack had evolved into a comfortable routine. We never squabbled over money or argued about trivialities. He taught me to play chess and it was a challenge to beat him at Scrabble. We shared similar views with regard to politics and human rights, and we both loved books, art, animals, music, political satire and Edna Everage, whom Jack reckoned was a send-up of his own mother. And it was true; the genius of Barry Humphries was that he captured a little piece of every Australian suburban housewife, including my own grandmother who had a penchant for plastic gladioli and 'manners' on the street.

Underscoring this outwardly blissful existence was an inner turmoil, which kept me on tenterhooks, inhibiting me from going to certain places for fear I might meet someone from my past. I was pleased that Jack had no interest in the Royal Easter Show or motor sports, where I'd have more of a chance of bumping into someone who knew me.

It was a Sunday in July 1973 when my two lives intersected irretrievably. Outside the wind was howling and the rain pelted down, drowning out the record player. It was a good day to be indoors reading the newspapers. An article caught my eye. It wasn't headline news, nor was it bad news, but it had a profound impact on me. The Whitlam government had introduced the Supporting Mother's Benefit. Prior to this announcement it was the absence of financial support that facilitated thousands of babies born to unmarried mothers being surrendered for adoption.

Suddenly I was overcome with thoughts of how different my life, and that of my son, would have been if this support had been available when we needed it. A flood of scalding tears rolled down my face, dropping from my chin onto the newspaper, causing the ink to run down the page. Jack was absorbed in his book and didn't notice. I went to the bathroom and when I came back he looked up and out of the blue asked, 'What would you say to us having a baby?'

We'd been together about four years by this time and hadn't even discussed getting married, much less having a child.

'Jack, we aren't married.'

He laughed out loud. 'What's being married got to do with anything?'

This was the day I had been dreading, when I'd finally have to come clean and tell Jack the truth.

'Jack, there's something I have to tell you,' I said nervously, taking his hand.

'You've had a baby who died. Yes, you've told me,' he said.

'No Jack, I have a son, Adam. He's seven years old and lives with his father,' I could feel my bottom lip quivering. I hadn't talked about Adam with anyone in my new life.

Jack sat, expressionless, as I told him the story. He stared at me for a long time before he spoke.

'I don't want another man's child. I want you to have my children. You lost your son, now move on.'

'This isn't just another man's child,' I was almost shouting. 'Adam is my son. I'll never move on without him. I'll never have another child until we've been reunited!' I picked up my helmet and keys and without stopping to get into my wet-weather gear I stumbled out the door and rode down to North Bondi. I parked on the headland overlooking the Little Mermaid, a bronze sculpture sitting on the rocks off the point. I faced off against the blustering southerly, as an icy tempest of salt spray, wind and pelting rain hammered down on me like a thousand sharp knives cutting me to the bone. White-capped waves rose high into the air before crashing down on the Little Mermaid. I felt a strange empathy with that lone figure taking a pounding from the elements, but standing her ground, refusing to be dragged from the rocks into the raging sea.

'Adam!' I cried, a desperate chant swallowed by the wind. I needed to say my son's name out loud, to hang onto him in any way I could.

The moment Jack suggested that I forget my son and move on, I knew our relationship was over. Yet I couldn't bring myself to leave immediately. I was hoping that when he had time to process the situation he would change his mind. He didn't. The push I needed came a few months later when Jack's mate, Bruce Cornwell, moved into our flat. One day Bruce brought his girlfriend back to the flat. She had a vaguely familiar face. He introduced her as Carol, but as we got talking I came to know that Carol's stage name was Carlotta, the hostess of the famous Les Girls' all-male revue at Kings Cross. One of my best friends growing up was a male called Ray, who liked me calling him Rhonda. We used to dress up and sing Judy Garland songs. The boys in our area treated him pretty rough, and he took some savage beatings. Talking with Carol I realised how brave she was to live her life honestly in a society that still upheld laws against sodomy, and where poofter bashing was considered a sport.

More and more our flat became the party venue, where I worked to prepare enough food and make the place nice, only to have everyone get drunk, or stoned, and leave me to clean up the mess. To top it off, Jack and Bruce started going out through the week and not inviting me. Jack always came back stoned. He'd started to let himself go. He gained weight and grew a scraggly beard that reeked of a sickly mix of tobacco and marijuana. His hair, parted in the middle, fell to his shoulders. I woke up one morning and realised I was living with a bloated, hairy, dope-smoking hippy who never remembered to take out the garbage.

'Here, buy yourself something nice,' Jack said one night, pushing a wad of cash across the table. At a glance I could see the bundle contained mostly fifty dollar notes, which had only recently gone into circulation and had a distinctive colour.

'Where did this money come from?' I asked.

'Don't be like that. It wasn't stolen. We've been selling weed in the wine bars,' he said casually, as if living with a drug pusher was something that I shouldn't be concerned about.

'Jack, this has to stop or I am out of here,' I said, before going to bed.

It didn't stop. Jack was hooked in more ways than one.

Riding a motorcycle meant I couldn't take everything with me when I moved out, and I had to make several trips back to the flat. On my last trip back to pick up my sewing machine Jack looked sheepish when he answered the door.

'Do you have another woman here already?'

'Of course not,' he said standing aside to let me in.

Bruce Cornwell and two rough-looking characters I'd never seen before were standing around the dining table. Pretending not to notice the white powder in plastic bags and a set of scales, I picked up the sewing machine and left without a word. Jack followed me down the stairs.

'Kay, please come back, I love you,' he said, reaching out for my arm.

'Do you think I didn't see what's going on up there?' I said, pulling away and strapping the machine onto the luggage rack of my bike. I caught a glimpse of him in the rear-view mirror as I rode away.

5

Dressed to impress

My leaving Jack coincided with Danny wanting to move out of home. We decided to find a place together and settled on a nice house in Bronte. When I arrived home from work one evening three motorcycles were parked in the driveway. One Husqvana was Danny's and the Kawasaki belonged to Myles Stivano. The other bike, a brand spanking new Huskie, I'd never seen before. The laughter, and the smell, was coming from the kitchen. Danny and Myles were sitting on the floor giggling like schoolgirls. This was how they introduced me to Noel Christensen. Between them, they'd blackened every pot and pan and splattered spaghetti sauce up the walls and over the venetian blind, but still hadn't managed to make something to eat.

'Katie, cook us some dinner, we're starving,' Danny badgered, with the stupefied grin of someone who'd just smoked a joint.

After I knocked them up a simple meal I started to clean up the mess. Our landlord lived downstairs and was always popping in unannounced. He was a fastidious man who'd probably have freaked out to had he seen the state of the kitchen.

'Man, that was sensational,' Myles said, wiping his plate clean.

'She's a great cook,' Danny said.

'Yeah, just like my Aunty Flo,' Noel chimed in.

The nickname stuck. It was shortened to Flo, but Danny and Noel never called me anything else after that. To Myles I remained 'The Princess'.

'Myles Carson Stivano, that's a pretty fancy name for a black-fella. Where's your mob?' I asked.

'My mob? Oh no, I don't have a mob,' Myles said, with a nervous laugh. 'See that?' he went on, pushing up his sleeve, 'white skin, like my arse.'

'Thousands might believe you Myles,' I teased.

We'd been living at Bronte a few months when an old school mate of Jack Gazzard, with close connections to the local police, called to ask if I knew where Jack and Bruce were. 'If you see Jack, tell him to get going. The cops are looking for him.' I didn't have Jack's phone number, but I found out where he was living and passed on the message. Many years later I read that Bruce 'Snapper' Cornwell went on to become the largest importer of heroin in Australia. He was convicted and sentenced to twenty-four years in prison.

I maintained my friendship with Jack's mother, Peggy, and although she must have been broken-hearted when Jack just dis-appeared and didn't even bother to say goodbye, she never spoke of it. I had more empathy for her loss than I could afford to express.

She called me at work one day to tell me that her mother had passed away. It was the first funeral I'd ever been to, and remains one of the saddest, with only me, Peggy and her sister at the grave-side. They stood apart as Peggy quietly cried. I put my arm around her and tried to imagine what it must feel like to have had a loving mother and to watch her coffin being lowered into the ground. It's a pain I was spared, but strangely, I envied it.

Myles Stivano had recently become engaged. His fiancée's sister, Christine, was looking to share a house. Danny and I had a chat with her, and agreed that we'd find a bigger house to accommodate the three of us. We found a four-bedroom place in Rose Bay. The parties were endless and Christine and I were always left to clean up afterwards. Danny and I clashed over this and I told him I wanted to break the lease. We had to go to a solicitor to sort out the details, and when the paperwork was completed, Danny pushed past me and left without a word.

To lose Danny's friendship was devastating. I remained friends with Christine, Myles and Noel. I'd affectionately dubbed them and others in the gang the Lavender Hill Mob – not unlike the characters of the British film by the same name – but even so, after the fall-out with Danny I felt that I needed to get away for a while.

I'd quit bar work a few years before and was working as a book-keeper with a freight forwarding company in the city. I was almost going out of my mind with boredom. A friend had recently gone to work as the bar manager at a pub in Coffs Harbour. He said their books were in a dreadful mess and asked if I would come up and sort them out. The job was asking for more practical experience than I had at the time, but I'd continued to study through the library and had gained a theoretical understanding of advanced accounting. The job in Coffs would give me an opportunity to put the theory into practice. It took about three months to straighten out the books, but when they offered me a permanent job I declined. Instead, I moved back to Sydney and found a flat in Centennial Park.

By this time I was twenty-four years old and still trying to get a foothold on an opportunity to develop a career. My motivation was not about money or status for its own sake, I was driven by the need to make something of myself. I was determined to become someone my son would be proud of when we were finally reunited. If we had to be separated, I wanted to make sure some good came out of it.

Scanning the positions vacant advertisements in the *Sydney Morning Herald* was a ritual. Formal Wear Hire Service was advertising again for an assistant to the accountant. They were looking for a man, but I didn't let that stand in my way. I'd applied for the same job about a year earlier but was unsuccessful and I think I knew why. Females were expected to wear dresses, stockings and carry handbags, whereas I had worn slacks, a leather jacket and carried a motorcycle helmet into my interview. This was too liberated at the time, even for a trendy company like Formal Wear that was at the cutting edge of hiring the suits and gowns for weddings and other formal occasions. They'd recently won a prestigious marketing award and with a network of retail outlets Australia-wide, I felt that the company may have the career prospects I was seeking.

'Hello, I'm Ross, darling,' the receptionist introduced himself after replacing the receiver. Ross had the most engaging blue eyes and a mass of golden curls framing his face, reminiscent of an Italian Renaissance painting. It was unusual for a male to be handling reception duties in 1974 but Formal Wear Hire Service was an unusual company. For starters, it was owned and operated by a woman.

'Hello Ross, darling, I'm here for an interview.'

The company's general manager, Oliver Whitehouse, was

just as I remembered him but after my makeover I bore little resemblance to the person he'd interviewed previously. The long black hair had been left on the cutting-room floor; a set of falsies concealed the badly chewed fingernails. The slacks, leather jacket and helmet were replaced with a smart outfit from Maria Finlay's Double Bay boutique, teamed with a pair of Pierre Cardin shoes and matching handbag. I'd cleaned out my bank account to get this job.

When I arrived for my interview, Oliver was taking a phone call and motioned for me to take a seat. His body groaned with effort as he reached across the desk to retrieve a small pair of scissors from an onyx ashtray to snip the end of his cigar.

'Yes, yes,' he spoke to the caller, not shifting his eyes from me.

Oliver's head looked like a jack-o'-lantern plonked onto the shoulders of his massive frame, flattening any neck he may have had. Thick rippling waves of oiled, silver hair glinted like a corrugated iron roof in the bright sunlight streaming through the window. Furrowed lines of concentration ran in parallel tracks across his wide brow, and laugh lines around his mouth and eyes indicated he was a deep thinker with a robust sense of humour. The food stains on his necktie, draped over a wide girth, suggested a man who liked his tucker. After he finished the call he perused my resume. I felt myself blushing, fearing that he'd seen through the disguise.

'What makes you think you can do a man's job?'

That was a relief and a question I'd anticipated.

'Mr Whitehouse, as I understand it, the job is for an assistant to the accountant. There's no heavy lifting involved so I don't see how any man could do a better job than I could, just because he's a man.'

Grinning, with the cigar clamped between his teeth, he pressed the intercom on his desk.

'Peggy, I have someone I'd like you to see,' he said. Things were looking up. Last time I hadn't been invited to see Mrs Levy, the company's founder and CEO.

Mrs Levy's office didn't have a desk; it was more like a sitting room. Several comfortable chairs were placed around an ornate coffee table, stacked with fashion magazines and a vase of fresh flowers.

Mrs Levy checked me over from head to toe. After a few perfunctory questions she offered me the job. Perhaps she appreciated my audacity to apply for a position that advertised for a male, or maybe the Norma Tullo suit worked in my favour.

'Hello, I am Rebecca, darling,' an exquisite redhead in a figure-hugging dress greeted me when I arrived for work on my first day. The eyes gave him away. No two people would have eyes like that. The transformation from Ross to Rebecca was otherwise seamless.

I reported to Oliver Whitehouse and he spent some time with me going over the company's recent history. He also told me that Mrs Levy's husband, Warwick, had cancer and didn't have long to live. Although Mr Levy didn't play an active part in the company, he came to the office when he could and was always in good spirits.

Mrs Levy seemed to surround herself with homosexual men, whom she called her 'boys' and whom she treated like children. Unfortunately, some of the boys took advantage of her trust. I'd only been with the company a few months when I discovered that the invoices from the dry-cleaning service exceeded the sales dockets from the stores. This meant that more suits, or bridal gowns, were being hired each week than were showing in the sales figures. From what I could see, it involved a number of branches. I told my boss, the accountant, about these discrepancies.

Early next morning Mrs Levy's booming voice echoed off the

rafters of the converted warehouse offices. 'Get out of my sight, you fucking idiot! You're fired!'

My boss had made the mistake of mentioning my findings to Mrs Levy, also taking the credit. Perhaps he'd expected her to be pleased to know that the people she loved and trusted were robbing her blind; this information would have broken her heart.

It was very disconcerting to see a grown man cry as my manager packed his bag to leave. I was promoted to his position, which I thought was a great joke when I realised that anyone with advanced bookkeeping skills could do the job that came with an executive salary and a company car.

Dealing with threatening letters and harassing phone calls from creditors soon consumed much of my day. I'd only been in the new job a week when it became clear that the company was in trouble, the biggest unpaid creditor being the Australian Taxation Office. Even a total revamp and weeding out the thieves may not save it. It was annoying that I'd been given this appointment when the senior management must have been aware of the situation, but I played Mrs Levy's game, each morning presenting her with the sales figures bound in the suede leather journals.

Meanwhile, I quietly scouted around for another job. I felt a bit guilty about this as I'd recently poached Vicki, the marketing manager's secretary. Vicki had been with the company for a week before we actually got to speak. We met in the ladies room one morning and she told me she liked working with Formal Wear but didn't have enough to do. She had previously been a court stenographer, took shorthand verbatim and typed 120 words per minute. Her boss, Chris, just wanted a pretty face sitting outside his office to make him cups of coffee and fetch his lunch. When I told Oliver that we'd lose this brilliant young woman if we didn't give her more work, he gave me the go-ahead to let Chris know that he was losing his tea lady.

'Peggy won't stand for this!' Chris said, storming off. That was the last I saw of him.

Vicki and I hit it off from the outset. She wanted to relocate to the eastern suburbs and we decided to find a house to share. We found a delightful colonial sandstone cottage in Bondi. It was the beginning of a lifelong friendship. Two mature women living together is pretty easygoing after living with men. Women understand why we put the toilet lid down and no one has to nag about the garbage going out. Vicki and I never had a problem keeping our working relationship separate from our friendship, but as her friend I felt obliged to level with her.

'There isn't a great future for anyone at Formal Wear. If a good job comes your way, I'd take it if I were you.'

'I'll stay as long as you need me,' Vicki said, loyally squeezing my hand.

One morning I was going through the job ads in the *Sydney Morning Herald* when Oliver called me into his office.

Here it comes, I thought, *the gig's up.*

'Please take a seat, Kath.'

He took a deep drag on a cigar and tilted his head back, sending billowing clouds of smoke into the air. He didn't seem to be in any hurry to put me out of my misery.

'I'd like to recommend you for the position of National Sales and Marketing Manager,' he said, finally.

This offer of a promotion, although flattering, was the last thing I was expecting. There didn't seem to be any point beating around the bush. 'Oliver, I am very pleased that you have this confidence in me, but I have to ask, why are you offering a promotion when the company may not exist long enough to get my name onto the business cards?'

When Oliver laughed all of him had a good time. Cigar ash went everywhere as he tried to regain his composure. 'That's what I like about you – you see through the bullshit and cut right to the chase,' he said, sweeping the ash from the desk with his hand. Then he leaned forward, whispering, 'I have a plan,' before leaning back and taking another drag on his cigar. It was going to take something very innovative to salvage the company which, from what I could assess, was already insolvent. He went on to explain the concept of franchising to me, an idea imported from the United States. While multinationals such as McDonald's and Kentucky Fried Chicken had started a trend, it was yet to take hold in Australia.

'Before I put you forward for a promotion I'd like to send your personal details to a man called Haigwood Masters,' Oliver went on. 'He'll be able to tell me if my instincts about you are accurate.'

'What kind of personal information do you require?' I asked, suspiciously.

'This may sound strange, but I need two photographs – one in profile and one of your face – and three samples of your handwriting.'

If Oliver had a plan to save the business and needed me to pull it off, I was in. I agreed to have my photograph and handwriting sent to Haigwood Masters for an assessment. *After all, what could anyone learn about me from a photograph and some handwriting?*

I called my friend Noel Christensen, who took the photographs at his office on Bronte Road.

6

'Mind if I call you Kate?'

'Haig's given you a glowing recommendation for the promotion.'
Oliver sounded pleased as he handed me a large sealed brown
envelope a couple of days later. 'He asked me to give you this
separate report. It's of a personal nature.'

When I got back to my office and read the report I was
sceptical. The comment about my ability and potential, albeit
complimentary, seemed a bit far-fetched: 'Your skills and life
experiences uniquely equip you for the personnel industry. If you
ever decide to make a career in that field you will rise quickly
to the top and will go forward to manage and perhaps own a
successful company.'

He's got to be joking! Personnel? I was about to dismiss the whole
report when I got to the part that said: 'You have never experienced an orgasm.' I stared at this line in total amazement. How
could anyone tell that from a photograph and my handwriting?
But it was true. As far as I was concerned the notion of the female
orgasm was a male fantasy. Haig outlined my whole life on the

page. He said that I was 'accessible' to his treatment and he'd be willing to see me.

'You lucky, lucky girl, Haig never agrees to see anyone he can't help.' Oliver beamed when I told him about Haig's report, having omitted the more personal comments.

Haig had included a note with his professional fees, which amounted to a staggering $1000 per hour. For me, he was prepared to reduce his fee by half, which was still almost two weeks' salary. If this man could really help me to realise my full potential, as he claimed he would be able to do, and if a female orgasm wasn't a myth, as I'd supposed, I was prepared to give it a go.

When I called to make an appointment, Haig asked me to bring a photograph of my grandmother, and one of my son, to our consultation. Oliver drove us out to Haig's property at Oakdale, where he lived with his wife, Josephine, who was an artist as well as an organisational psychologist like her husband.

'Not bad for a bloke in his seventies,' Oliver said, as Haig unlatched the gate and waved us through.

At twenty-four I wasn't good at guessing ages but I'd never have put Haig in his seventies. Although balding on top, he was a blood-nut with hardly a hint of grey. A ginger cat, I thought, as his sleek body, all muscle and sinew, stalked rather than walked towards us. After an exchange of pleasantries Oliver disappeared to join Josephine, while Haig and I got down to business. There was no plush-pile carpet in Haig's consulting room and no couch to lie on; instead we strolled around his secluded property on the edge of the Burragorang Valley, pausing here and there to sit on a bush rock or a fallen tree. Overhead, the gnarly branches of the Angophora, twisting and weaving towards the light, provided shelter and shade for the ever-present Xanthorrhoea, congregating in clusters like close-knit families.

'Do you mind if I call you Kate? Kathy doesn't suit you and Kay was a name given to you.'

'I quite like Kate, my family used to call me Katie.'

'Before we begin, may I ask who took these photographs?' He was referring to the original photos Oliver had sent that Noel had taken of me.

'A friend of mine, he's a professional photographer.'

'He is an outstanding photographer. He has managed to capture the true essence of your personality.'

Haig started our session by assessing my grandmother's photograph. 'Your grandmother was a monster,' Haig said, after examining her photograph with a magnifying glass.

The only photograph I had of my grandmother, who I called Mamma, was taken at her wedding to Frank Hadlow. She was squinting into the sun, and in the photograph her face was no bigger than a pea. Maybe that gave a distorted impression. Although Mamma was a paradox of inconsistencies, I never knew anyone to work as hard as she did, taking care of her aged, and later dying, parents and all of us kids, and I felt the need to defend her.

'No, Haig. There was a lot of good in Mamma,' I said, hoping he wouldn't be annoyed by the contradiction. He smiled and repeated what he'd said.

Haig studied Adam's photograph for a long time before speaking. 'You were a good mother, this is a healthy, happy baby,' he said.

'I love my baby with all my heart, he was my world,' I replied, feeling the tears starting to well.

'Because of shared experiences during the pregnancy and up until the time you and Adam were separated you formed a very strong bond.'

'During my pregnancy?'

'Oh, yes. The unborn can hear everything going on around them; they can sense a mother's emotions. Children from conception to seven-year-olds absorb everything. To quote a Jesuit maxim: "Give me the boy until he's seven and I'll give you the man."'

'Losing you the way he did will have caused your son to shut down his emotions,' Haig continued. With a deep sadness in his voice he explained what he termed the 'abandoned child syndrome', a behavioural or psychological condition that results from the loss of one or both parents. Hearing how Adam would likely internalise his loss was too much; I put my head into my hands and wept.

'I didn't abandon my son,' I wailed, my face flushed with anger as I recalled the events of nearly seven years before.

'Your decision to leave your son in a safe environment was the best decision for him,' Haig said, with a note of tenderness that had me fighting back a fresh bout of tears. In my heart I always felt this was true but hearing these words from someone else was like a cool, soothing balm on open wounds.

Haig suggested that we break for lunch and join Oliver and Josephine at the house. The modest timber cottage, painted gum-leaf green, was perched on the edge of a ravine and blended perfectly with the environment. Kangaroos hopped through the garden, scratching and stretching, unperturbed by visitors. A wombat, with an air of indifference, snatched a carrot from the tray of vegetable scraps under the tree. The wide entrance hall resembled an art gallery. A sideways glance through an open door revealed a mattress on the floor, with books towering up on each side. Around three walls in the living room were floor-to-ceiling bookcases, catalogued and stacked as neat as a library. The waxed timber floors were bare, except for a large jade-green Oriental carpet. The back wall of the cottage had been removed and replaced with a single sheet of glass, creating a spectacular living space. The furnishing was sparse, and eclectic, and included a grand piano positioned off to the side of the glass wall, so as not to obstruct the view down the valley.

Josephine Masters was a striking woman. Not in a glamorous way, but for her individuality. A good bit taller than Haig, she was pencil thin with her jet-black hair cropped short and a straight fringe spanning a wide forehead. There was a vintage look about her, like she'd just stepped out of a 1940s movie set. Half expecting Haig and Josephine would be vegetarian I was surprised when a steaming platter of corned silverside, cabbage and mashed potatoes was placed on the table. It was a delicious, nostalgic meal, reminding me of happier times in my childhood and causing me to wonder just how clever Haig was at getting inside someone's head.

'Haig, I sometimes get a feeling about people I meet for the first time. Is that something psychic, or something subconscious?' I asked during the meal, struggling to find the right words to express myself. I also asked him to explain how handwriting analysis worked.

Haig explained that because of my unusual early life and the necessity to read people, especially Mamma, I had a highly developed intuitive skill, which is particularly attuned to what people say and their tone of voice. Haig said that what I sensed about people couldn't be taught, it came with experience. He went on to say that handwriting analysis could be learned, and I'd be able to learn the technique very quickly, but that it would take many years of study and application to become proficient.

'Will you teach me to read handwriting?' I asked him.

Haig gave me the titles of books on handwriting analysis he wanted me to study before our next session. Then he offered me a word of warning: 'Handwriting analysts have the ability for great good and also great harm. You can be right a thousand times, but the one time you are wrong could affect another person's life in a profound way. Don't dabble with handwriting until you have a proper understanding of the responsibilities and the consequences.'

After lunch Haig concentrated on things I needed to focus on to realise my potential in other areas. He set me exercises and gave me assignments to bring back to our next session.

'How can you see so much potential in someone who left school at fourteen?' I asked him at the end of our appointment.

He smiled. 'Kate, your natural aptitude and hunger for knowledge are greater than most people's, even those with multiple qualifications. You will be able to achieve anything you put your mind to.'

Oliver knew I wasn't in the mood for conversation on the drive home. My brain felt ready to explode, but I wanted to go over everything that had happened. At $500 an hour, I didn't want to waste a minute.

Haig had told me that to abreact the stored grief and emotion associated with my past I needed to go back.

'Go back where?' I'd enquired. There was nowhere to go back to.

'Everything you've experienced is stored in your body. Take your mind back,' he told me.

That night, too churned up to sleep, I lay in bed trying to recall snippets from my past, as far back as I could remember. Names of places like Raglan and Abercrombie streets in Darlington came into focus. I recalled a two-storey terrace house with a factory on the corner that smelled of dead animals, and me, as a very small child, drawing on a path in the back garden with charcoal from the wood-fire stove in the kitchen. These images were so vivid; I felt they had to be real and not figments of my imagination. When I spoke to Haig about it he suggested that I go down to Abercrombie Street and walk around the area to see if any other memories would surface.

'This may be a very difficult experience for you. Do you have someone who could go with you?' Haig asked.

Although I wasn't ready to make a full confession of my past to Vicki, I told her I was retracing my footsteps back to my family of origin. Vicki drove us to Darlington. As we turned onto Abercrombie Street my head was spinning like a gyrocompass, trying to get a bearing. 'There it is!' I said excitedly, pointing to the street across the road. Raglan Street had a look of desperation about it. The University of Sydney seemed to be eating into the neighbourhood like a ravenous beast. Along the other side of the street was a row of what would have been grand Victorian terrace houses. All but one was completely derelict and boarded up.

'I think I'll get out and walk around. Maybe that'll jog something,' I said to Vicky.

'Look!' I called out, when I spotted what would have once been the entry and exit to the laneway that ran behind the house in my vision. I was drawn to the row of terraces. The blue house hadn't seen a coat of paint in many years, but it looked occupied. On a hunch I walked over and knocked on the door. A stooped, white-haired lady answered.

'I'm sorry to bother you Ma'am, but I'm trying to trace a family I believe lived in this street when I was a baby. Their name was Gresham?'

'Betty!' The woman called up the stairs.

I felt my heart race.

'Your name isn't Betty Burgess is it?' I asked the woman who slowly made her way down the stairs.

'Yes,' she replied, looking startled.

I recalled Aunty Daphne mentioning Betty Burgess, the sister of Ray Burgess, the man I'd once been told was my father, but whom I'd never met. I reached out to take her hand.

'I'm Phyllis's daughter, Katie,' I said, hoping that would mean something to her.

'My goodness! You're the spit out of her mouth,' Betty said, throwing her arms around me. 'I'll put the kettle on,' she said, wiping her eyes with the hem of her apron.

As I hadn't seen any member of my family for many years, I couldn't share much information with Betty, and I only told her the good stuff about Aunty Daphne; that she had three beautiful children. I didn't tell her about the life of drudgery and nightly beatings from Uncle Jack. But Betty was able to tell me a great deal about my grandmother, and my mother and her siblings, when they had lived across the street twenty-four years ago. My recollection of our house was spot-on, right down to the spiked iron fence below the upstairs balcony, and the back laneway where the coppers bundled Fred, my grandmother's second husband, into the back of a Black Maria after a drunken rampage one time.

Conscious that Vicki was waiting in the car and that I'd crashed into these people's lives uninvited, I finished my tea and left.

'You look like you've seen a ghost,' Vicki said, when I got back to the car.

'I think I just met my paternal grandmother and Aunt Betty,' I explained.

After that meeting, many more people, places and events came flooding back into focus. Working on another hunch I called St Benedict's Church, on the corner of Broadway and Abercrombie Street, and enquired about obtaining a baptism certificate. The day I held that piece of paper in my hands was the first documented evidence that someone had cared enough about me to have the original sin washed from my soul. That person would have been Uncle Stan.

A few weeks after these extraordinary events, I looked down

at my hands. I'd stopped biting my fingernails, which had been chewed to the quick for as long as I could recall. I went out and bought my first manicure set.

It was about 7 am and I was having breakfast when the phone rang. It was Oliver. 'Warwick Levy died last night,' he said, delivering the sad news.

Oliver explained that Mrs Levy and Mr Klein, a silent partner, had been at odds over the idea of franchising, which to me was understandable, she'd built Formal Wear from nothing and she knew that franchising would result in major staff cuts. Mrs Levy was one of the few successful business people I've ever met who cared about the people who worked for her, and I admired her for it. Mr Klein was a personal guarantor against the massive debts of Formal Wear, and franchising was the only hope there was of turning things around. Mrs Levy was an obstruction, and didn't return to the company.

There was no farewell party and no gold watch, and personally, I felt cheated that I didn't get to tell Mrs Levy how much I'd enjoyed working for her. As a woman she'd been a great role model and it seemed an abrupt end for someone with the creative genius to have built an innovative company, long before the term 'glass ceiling' was even coined.

Mr Klein, the founder of Anthony Squires menswear, which at the time was considered to be the most elegant menswear label in the country, took over the running of the business. From his slicked-down silver hair to his immaculate shoes he was all class. On his first day at the helm, he introduced himself and shook the hand of every member of staff, from the youngest worker in the warehouse right up to management. I knew right away I'd enjoy working with him.

December 1974 was the start of a scorching hot summer, and the Christmas party at Formal Wear was one to remember. Mr Klein, looking as dashing as ever, welcomed guests at the door upon arrival. One after the other a string of tall, elegantly dressed females arrived, extending a gloved hand to Mr Klein and winking at me before tottering off on four-inch stilettos. Rebecca, aka Ross, made a grand entrance, kissing and hugging everyone in sight, and calling them 'darling'.

'Rebecca, you must be sweltering in this,' I said, stroking the white mink jacket.

'Darling, I'd never allow the weather to dictate style!' he said, flouncing off.

Pretty soon the place resembled the backstage at Les Girls. Mr Klein leaned over and whispered, 'Where did all these lovely ladies come from, and when are the men expected to arrive?' He left before the five o'clock shadows started poking through the pancake make-up and Danielle, aka Daniel, mimed Shirley Bassey's 'Hey Big Spender' with so much gusto his wig flew off. By midnight, the masks and mascara had completely melted. The floor was strewn with sequins and false titties, which had been discarded in the heat, and numerous pairs of shoes with snapped heels.

'Now there's a market waiting to be explored,' I noted, motioning to the shoes. 'Ladies shoes for men,' I grinned.

After months of hard negotiations a franchising agreement was being finalised with Waltons, a major retailer with ninety-six outlets across Australia. The intention was for Waltons to operate a franchise of Formal Wear within their retail outlets, limited to male suit hire, with Formal Wear operating a central warehouse to supply the suits.

Oliver also struck a deal with Mr Klein so that he and I would each get a bonus on the signing of the franchising agreement. We'd stay to see the company make the transition, and when that was effective, we'd resign. The deal was sealed on a handshake.

Over the next few months Oliver worked on the nuts and bolts of the franchise agreement while I travelled all over the country with Mr Klein, talking with other prospects, which included specialist 'gentlemen's outfitters' who were interested in increasing their bottom line with no major stock outlay. It wasn't a difficult concept to sell.

A phone call from Oliver on 1 August 1975 brought everything unstuck. 'Lou Klein died last night, a heart attack.'

The news hit me with an unexpected wave of emotion. Mr Klein had been a mentor, whom I admired and respected. He had inspired and encouraged me to challenge myself. He'd often ask my opinion on something or other, providing a huge boost to my confidence. I once overheard him say, 'If you want something done, give it to Katie, she's like a dog with a bone.' Mr Klein also gave me some good advice: 'Success in life is determined by how many good decisions one makes over how many bad.' It left no place for blame when life didn't turn out as one hoped.

As I'd never been to a Jewish funeral I called a friend who filled me in on the appropriate etiquette.

'You're invited to a sitting shiva for Lou Klein?' he asked. 'I'm impressed.'

Mr Klein's funeral saw the largest gathering ever seen at the Sephardi Synagogue in Woollahra. The eulogy was read by the recently elected Lord Mayor of Sydney, Leo Port, and the who's-who of Sydney's most influential and wealthy businessmen came to pay their respects.

In time, Mr Klein's son and brother-in-law took over the running of the company. Oliver called me to his office. He was packing up his desk. 'The new management aren't going to honour the deal we made with Lou,' he said, wrapping the onyx ashtray in some newspaper and putting it into his briefcase.

Oliver and I left together.

.

7

Small steps

'Where am I going to get a dildo?' I asked, not expecting an answer.

'The same place I got mine,' Vicki smiled, putting on the kettle.

I screeched with laughter. Vicki was a diminutive blonde who giggled behind her hand if someone told a mildly risqué joke. I'd never have imagined that she'd possess a dildo. I thought only lesbians needed such things.

Haig Masters had phoned to say that he was going to some 'black-tie' do in Sydney; he was staying at the Boulevard Hotel at Kings Cross and could give me an hour session. I still hadn't found a job and had to think hard about spending $500.

'There's something I'd like you to bring to our next meeting,' Haig said. At first I thought I'd heard him incorrectly when he mentioned a vibrator and he had to repeat himself.

There were several adult shops to choose from at Taylor Square, in Darlinghurst, but the thought of going into any one of them caused me to break into a cold sweat. Vicki came along to hold my hand.

'Good grief!' I gasped when I saw the glass-fronted cabinet displaying devices in all sizes and colours; some had pearls wrapped around the shaft while others had ticklers sticking out like weedy sea urchins. The black leather pants with the back cut-out left little to the imagination. Whips, spurs, spiked paddles and assorted objects for drawing blood and inflicting pain hung from the walls. The nipple clamps with tiny sharp teeth made my eyes water just thinking about them.

'That looks interesting,' Vicki said, nudging me in the ribs and pointing to an item in the glass cabinet.

'That would need to be kept in a cage and fed twice a day,' I said, pulling her away, as we both collapsed into fits of giggles. In the end I settled for a plain plastic apparatus, bearing little resemblance to a penis, and we left the shop grateful for the brown paper bag.

It felt odd meeting Haig in a hotel room. Josephine was nowhere to be seen.

'This session we are going to release your sexual inhibitions,' he said.

My mouth went dry and I wanted to run.

'Kate, you've been sexually abused as a young person,' his voice was both tender and concerned.

This shocked me. Haig had always been spot on, but this time I felt he was wrong. 'Surely I would remember such an event?'

He smiled, taking my hand again. Haig had never touched me before and in this setting I didn't feel comfortable. Suddenly all of my defence mechanisms came into play and I felt myself stiffen at his touch.

'You have, at some time, been sexually abused. When you are ready to deal with this it will come out,' he said to me. 'Now, did you bring the item I asked for?'

51

'Yes,' I said, handing him the bag, which he promptly handed back.

'It's not for me. Please take the item from the bag,' he said, kindly.

The bag hadn't been opened since I left the adult shop. Looking at the ceiling, I fumbled around trying to locate the vibrator. As I pulled it out and placed it on the table I grew increasingly fearful of where this might be going. Haig started reading aloud from a medical journal, choosing his words carefully as he gave me explicit instructions, which were far too explicit for my liking. Then he clenched his fist with his thumb sticking up in the air. He asked me to pretend that his thumb was a penis and to put it into my mouth. I froze in disbelief. But then like an obedient child, afraid of being punished if I didn't do as I was told, I took his hand and guided it towards my mouth. As the tip of my tongue touched his warm skin I almost gagged. 'No!' I said pushing his hand away, shivering with revulsion.

'You have made a huge step forward today,' he said, smiling at me. *A huge step forward to what?* I wondered. I felt humiliated and couldn't even look at him. I left without saying a word, and when I got home I took a scalding shower and some Panadol and lay on my bed, clutching my stomach. I felt as though I had a great big worm squirming around inside trying to get out. The dildo went into the bottom drawer; I just couldn't bring myself to experiment.

My feelings of betrayal were exacerbated a few weeks later. After leaving Formal Wear Oliver purchased a small employment agency in Crows Nest and wanted me to go and work with him. He felt let down when I told him that I wanted to find a job with greater prospects. We agreed to stay in touch, which pleased me as Oliver, who was about twenty-five years my senior, had become somewhat of a father figure to me. One night we had dinner at Eliza's restaurant in Double Bay. Oliver had a few beers and started to talk to me in a way he'd never done before. For instance, he was curious about whether or not I had a boyfriend, which I thought was odd. I didn't really want to talk about my private life with him to that extent, and indicated that I was ready to leave. He drove me home and when he pulled up he turned off the engine. I reached out to shake his hand and thank him for the nice evening. He grabbed me and pulled me to him. I could feel his erection and struggled to break free. He reached out and caressed my breast. 'Stop, Oliver!' I said, slapping his hand away. He looked deeply embarrassed and I got out of the car. After that, we didn't see each other again.

In the space of a few months three of the most influential people in my life, men whom I'd trusted and had come to rely on for friendship, guidance and advice, were gone. I felt bereft. For the first time in years I was unemployed with no idea what direction to take next.

Fortunately, I had managed to save some money and felt that a holiday would give me time to take stock and formulate a new plan. I needed to get back on track so that I could work my way closer to Adam, which had been my motivation since the day I left. I booked a ten-day holiday on South Molle Island in the Whitsundays.

Unfortunately, my trip coincided with a used-car salesmen's convention from Brisbane. Ten days stuck on an island with a communal dining room full of drunken louts who thought they were God's gift to women was heavy going. Topless sunbathing was illegal in Queensland but I managed to find a quiet, remote corner of the island where I could go topless and think about my career.

I'd been giving some thought to Haig's comments about my potential in the personnel industry. Although I had no experience with personnel agencies, the perception was they were unprofessional. Still, I had nothing to lose by checking them out, so I decided that when I got back to Sydney I'd line up some appointments.

It was 11 November 1975 when I left the island. It was late when I got back and Vicki was watching the ten o'clock news. She looked up when she heard me come in. 'Look at you. God I wish I could tan as quickly as you do,' she said, turning off the television.

'I do have a bit of a head start!' I laughed.

'Did you hear about Whitlam? He's been sacked.'

Even in transit it had been impossible to miss the buzz in the air on that historical day. I'd grabbed a newspaper at the airport, with the headline announcing that the Governor-General, Sir John Kerr, had dismissed the democratically elected Whitlam government. The photograph of Whitlam on the steps of Parliament House showed a man feeling terribly betrayed, but holding his dignity.

8

I, Elizabeth Barrett

Following several interviews with companies in the personnel industry, I concluded that none of them had what I was looking for, so I took a job as the general manager of a newly formed customs agency. With spacious offices at Circular Quay, it had all the outward trappings of a successful operation and I was hopeful, and enthusiastic, about helping them make a success of the business. It only took two days to work out they were dipping into the freight trust accounts to cover salaries and operating expenses. It would only be a matter of time before it caught up with them. Meanwhile, the executives, who took extended lunch breaks, had their heads in the sand and their hands on the arse of every female who walked past. I quickly resolved myself to the fact that this wasn't going to be a career opportunity, but for the moment it paid a good salary and provided a company vehicle.

Meanwhile, when our lease expired, Vicki and I decided to go our separate ways. There was no disagreement over anything; Vicki had a new man in her life and I think it suited them both for

Vicki to be living alone. She rented a flat in Paddington, I moved to Bellevue Hill, and we made a pact to meet at The Bourbon and Beefsteak in Kings Cross every second Thursday. We sat in Ronnie's quiet back bar, away from the disco, where we could talk.

It was on one of these nights that I first set eyes on Karl. Even in the dimly lit bar I could see that he was breathtakingly handsome. But there was more than physical appeal; he had an air of authority that set him apart from the men he was with. We'd eyed each other up for several hours before he made his move. After establishing he was the captain of a cargo ship from Germany, I gave him my business card and asked him to call.

'You are big head?' he said, in a thick German accent.

After some frustration I realised he meant 'big wig'. He was impressed to meet a woman who had a business card.

Karl called the next day and I was pleased he couldn't see my face flush with excitement at the thought of seeing him again. We met on the forecourt of the Sydney Opera House and had dinner at Bennelong Restaurant.

'Would you like to see my ship?' he asked.

On his ship it was obvious Karl was king. His crew stepped aside, some even bowing, when he passed. He took me into his quarters, which was like a small apartment with permanent water views and a manservant catering to our every need. Karl wasn't pushy, and I'm sure that if I'd said I wanted to go home he wouldn't have objected.

I hadn't made much headway in the pleasure department since my session with Haig Masters at the Boulevard Hotel. Although time and distance had allowed me to see that in spite of the confronting methods, Haig's intentions were to help me unlock deep-seated sexual repression, I still remained a closed book as far as sex was concerned, the pages fused together with a mixture of fear and dread. Not wanting Karl to feel there was anything amiss,

I moaned and groaned and faked an orgasm as I'd always done.

The next morning, as he walked me down the gangway, some of his crew were hanging around having cigarettes, smiling and nudging each other as they shared in the knowledge the captain had scored. I felt myself blushing to be leaving the ship after spending the night with a man I hardly knew, and wasn't expecting to hear from again.

Later on that evening when the phone rang I was startled. *Who calls at this hour unless there's been an accident?* I thought, with some trepidation as I picked up the receiver. There was a strange signal, as if someone was trying to tune into a radio station, then I heard Karl's voice. He'd called ship-to-shore as he was going out through the Heads to say *auf wiedersehen*.

Karl had been gone about four weeks when a parcel post-marked from Hong Kong arrived. Fumbling like I had ten thumbs in rubber gloves I ripped the package open. It contained a lovely topaz bracelet, a letter and a photograph of Karl standing at the bow of the ship with his shirt off, against the backdrop of Hong Kong's harbour. Around midnight he called to say his ship was only an hour away from Sydney. I got dressed, grabbed a torch and sped through every orange traffic light along New South Head Road. My heart was pounding as I stood at the edge of The Gap in Watsons Bay, a high point on South Head with a sheer drop to the rocks below that was also an infamous suicide spot. A local man who'd seen me standing at the fence approached to ask if I was alright.

'Yes, thank you, I'm just waiting for my boyfriend's ship,' I said, feeling a bit of a tragedy to be standing at The Gap in the middle of the night. Satisfied that I wasn't going to jump to my death he said goodnight and walked away, shaking his head.

When I saw the navigation lights of the ship I flashed the torch three times, as Karl had asked me to do. When a light flashed back

I thought I was going to melt over the side of the cliff. As Karl's ship passed through the Heads I raced back to my car and drove slowly along New South Head Road, stopping at every vantage point to watch him guide the ship down the harbour. I knew Karl would be busy after docking so I went home, feeling like a kid waiting for Christmas morning.

The next day, I was sitting in my office having lunch and daydreaming about Karl, when a buzz on the intercom jolted me back to reality.

'There's a handsome man here to see you,' the receptionist informed me, with a slight chuckle.

Karl was shown into my office. Calling him handsome was an understatement; he was six-foot-one with a crown of gold where other people had hair, and sapphire-blue eyes. When he smiled, I needed to steady myself.

'*Guten tag liebling*,' he said, lifting me clear off the floor.

We crammed as much as we could into the next six days and because Karl's English wasn't fluent he had to communicate his feelings in other ways. This was when I came to understand that love isn't what we say, it is what we do, and Karl just couldn't do enough for me. If I opened my mouth and said I liked something, he'd want to go off and get it.

On Karl's third trip back to Sydney I called in sick and went cruising with him on his ship down the coast to Melbourne. We spent a couple of days sightseeing and walking around the Royal Botanic Gardens eating ice cream. Sitting on a bench, watching the ducks, he proposed and I said yes. He was embarrassed that he didn't have a ring and wanted to take me straight to a jewellery store. We only had two hours before I had to catch my plane back to Sydney and I didn't want to waste it shopping.

'When you come, we get diamond,' he said, pulling me close to him.

I felt like I'd been cast into a modern version of a Victorian love story. He was Robert Browning and I, Elizabeth Barrett, bewildered that such a wonderful man would love me with so much passion. As soon as I got home I applied for a passport and arranged to have my vaccinations. I was going to live with Karl in Germany.

'I need my husband's signature to get a passport?' I enquired of the woman checking my application.

'Yes, you do,' she said, handing me back the incomplete paperwork.

It had been nine years since I had spoken with John McNorton. It was humiliating having to write to him to get permission to leave the country. He sent back the signed documents and attached divorce papers listing me as a 'deserting wife and abandoning parent'. Infuriated, I spoke to a solicitor friend of mine who told me not to worry about it. 'It's just legal terminology,' he assured me. But to me it was a lie. I had never abandoned my son, and the injustice of this statement, in black and white, on a document that could never be altered, really burned me up.

John, or perhaps his mother, enclosed a small photograph of Adam. I couldn't tell how long ago it had been taken, but he looked about eight years old. He was wearing a Parramatta Rugby jersey and clutching a football. I was immediately struck by how much he looked like me at the same age. He was almost too pretty to be a boy. I fell onto my bed, staring at the familiar face, with a sweet shy smile. As I stared at his image it jolted me back to reality like a thunderclap. For months I'd been swept up in the whirlwind of an incredibly romantic relationship with Karl. Looking at the photograph of Adam I suddenly felt ashamed to realise that days had passed when I hadn't even thought about him.

Karl had made me forget that I'd had a past and for a short time I'd let myself imagine a different future. It was wonderful while it lasted, but a future without Adam was something I couldn't contemplate. Although all I had at that point was a hope that I'd get Adam back, I knew that I had to do everything I could to keep that hope alive. Of course, I could write to Karl and come clean. But that wouldn't help. Karl had a son from a previous marriage and I could no more expect him to leave Germany, and his son behind, than I could leave Adam.

'Dearest Karl,' I started to write, but the words wouldn't come. *How could my life be explained in a letter?* I decided not to write at all. I'd rather he thought of me as being fickle than an abandoning mother.

The night was warm. I'd taken a shower and was lying naked on my bed, clutching the photographs of the two people I loved most in the world. I groaned out loud, torn by the realisation that I couldn't have either of them in my life.

Tossing and turning, I relived the nights I had spent with Karl, rolling on the waves and making love with the moonlight streaming through the porthole of his cabin. I had never fantasised about sex or lusted longingly after a man before. Usually when I was with a man I play-acted in bed and couldn't wait for the intercourse to be over to get to the best part, the cuddling and going to sleep in each other's arms. Caressing my naked body, aching to feel the weight of Karl's body over me and inside me, I started to feel aroused. I remembered the dildo, which was still in its original bag in my bedside drawer. I turned off the light; I didn't want to see it in case it put me off. Letting my imagination roam freely, I explored myself in a way I'd never dared to before. As the euphoria subsided I rolled onto my stomach and buried my face into a pillow to contain the deep racking sobs that flooded through me.

The next morning I took out all of Karl's letters and photographs and tore them into tiny pieces and burned them in the kitchen sink. I wouldn't need anything to remind me of what Karl had meant to me. I drove up to The Gap and threw the topaz bracelet he had given me into the sea. That way, I'd always know where it was.

9

When can you start?

'Why do you want to enter the personnel field?' John Plummer, the owner of Centacom Personnel, asked after reading my resume.

'I heard there's money in it,' I said bluntly, knowing that would kick the door open.

'When can you start?'

Centacom's head office in the city was like a factory processing line. No training was offered to new staff and very little instruction was given. Their offices were filled with a steady stream of applicants clutching typing test results and anxiously waiting to be called forward for an interview. From day one I was making a placement a day and Mr Plummer rewarded me with a promotion to Head Personnel Consultant; a vanity promotion that meant nothing, although it seemed to bother some of the branch managers who'd heard about my placement rate and felt threatened. Not without good cause; I was after one of their jobs.

'I've seen these superstars come and go,' the manager from the

Double Bay office remarked sarcastically as she walked past my desk on her way to a meeting with Mr Plummer.

If making money had been my sole motivation for working, staying at Centacom would have been a good decision. John Plummer was generous to his top producers but there was no scope for advancement unless a branch manager died or resigned, and Mr Plummer was an astute businessman who made sure his best people didn't resign. It wouldn't take long for word to get out that I was scouting around for another position so I came clean and gave him my notice. Mr Plummer gave me a written reference and wished me well.

'I've lined up an interview with Manpower Personnel, what can you tell me about them?'

'They're not a major player,' Mr Plummer said, perhaps puzzled that I would resign from his well-established company to consider a competitor who wasn't even on the radar. 'They deal with temps and unskilled labour,' he added.

The advertisement had asked for a 'self-motivated person to work with complete autonomy' to set up a permanent placement division for office services. That had a lot of appeal. I was looking for a position where I could create my own opportunities, to see what I could do, rather than slot into a position where there was no scope, or encouragement, to think outside set parameters.

'I really don't know how a person who isn't self-motivated could work with complete autonomy,' I said to Vicki when I called her to discuss the position. Vicki thought employment agencies were parasites and wasn't offering any encouragement, but in spite of her negativity and my reservations, I called the number and was surprised when a man on the other end answered, 'This is Mr Norman speaking.'

This seemed a tad arrogant. Still, there was something about Mr Norman that piqued my curiosity.

Manpower's office was located on the second floor of a late-Victorian building on Hunter Street, sandwiched between two massive buildings under construction. There was no lift in the building and by the time I reached the second floor landing my ears were ringing from the jack hammers and drills vibrating on all sides, filling the stairwell with a fine white powder. A thick blue haze of cigarette smoke engulfed me as I opened the glass door. The heel of one of my stilettos got caught on the torn carpet and I stumbled towards the reception desk.

'Hello, I'm Jan, how may I help you?' the receptionist shouted to be heard above the din shaking everything not fixed to the floor.

'I'm Kate McNamara,' I coughed, brushing the dust from my jacket. 'I have an interview with Mr Norman.'

'Please take a seat and complete this application form,' she said, handing me a clipboard and pen, ignoring my offer of a folder containing a resume.

As I waited, I sat between two unshaven men, reeking of body odour. They were both smoking and dropping ash everywhere. My interview with Manpower almost ended there. I leaned forward to pick up my bag to leave.

'Kate?' Like a perfectly tuned guitar, his voice sent a ripple through me. I looked up to see a breathtakingly handsome man; tall, slim, with dark wavy hair and a drop-dead gorgeous smile. He reminded me of someone, a movie star, but I couldn't put a name to it.

'I'm Mr Norman,' he said, leading me to his office.

He ignored the handwritten application and gave my resume a cursory read before closing the folder.

'You're a widow?'

'Yes,' I replied, twisting my wedding ring, which I'd started wearing again after I ended it with Karl. I found it was a great deterrent for unwanted attention.

'Tell me, in your own words, what is your background?'

'I can only answer in my own words, Mr Norman,' I replied, a little sardonically.

He listened attentively as I outlined my relevant work experience.

'Do you have any questions about the job?' he asked.

'Yes, thank you, I do have a few.'

Mr Norman placed his hand over his mouth and coughed when I asked him to outline the history and current financial status of the company in Australia. His response was hesitant but I got the gist of it. The company was a franchise of an American operation that had tried to make a go of it in the early 1970s and failed. Rather than be made redundant, Mr Norman took up the offer to take over the Sydney franchise. The state of the office and the absence of telephone activity suggested that business wasn't exactly booming.

'What's the company's turnover?'

'That's a rather impertinent question,' he said, fiddling with his pen.

'Mr Norman, you are looking for someone to help you grow this company, so I am trying to gauge a starting point.'

Dodging my question, he explained that the core business was temporary help, mostly in industrial servicing, and he was looking to start a new division for permanent placements in office services. The retainer and commission he was offering was in line with what Centacom, an established agency, paid. Working at Centacom I had made good commissions from a constant flow of jobs hitting my desk every day. At Manpower, I'd have to drum up the business before there'd be any jobs to fill.

We both agreed to think about it for a few days.

*

That night I told Vicki about the interview and gave her my assessment of the company and Mr Norman, who seemed to be asking a lot and not offering much in return. 'How they are doing any business out of that dump is a mystery to me. The whole place needs a good scrub,' I said. 'But Mr Norman does look like the actor Robert Taylor,' I piped up, suddenly recalling why he had seemed so familiar. 'You know, the 1930s Hollywood heart-throb, "the man with the perfect profile".'

'*Whooo hooo!*' Vicki squealed, whistling down the phone.

'He's not wearing a ring, and there are no family portraits on his desk, but I bet he's married,' I said, feigning disappointment.

The next morning Mr Norman called to offer me the job. I told him I would take the position on the understanding that I receive ten per cent for all permanent placements. He baulked, saying that was double the commission paid by other agencies.

'Mr Norman, at the moment that is ten per cent of nothing.' I had no intention of backing down. If I didn't get the job I wouldn't lose any sleep over it. As I saw it, he needed me more than I needed the job he was offering.

'When can you start?' he finally asked.

My first day of work coincided with Mr Norman's thirty-ninth birthday. The staff had bought him a cake and we all sang happy birthday, while he pretended not to enjoy the fuss. Mr Norman was a real charmer and every female in the office, including me, had a crush on him.

I'd been with the company about three months when Mr Norman came to my office, grinning and shaking his head.

'What's so amusing?' I asked.

'How do you do it?' he asked, handing me a cheque.

'How do I do what?' I replied, looking at the tidy commission I'd made that month.

'Come on. What's your secret? I've never seen anyone make so many placements with no fall-out.'

'I read handwriting.'

'That's mumbo jumbo, you must have something else,' he probed.

'Would you like to submit to the test?' I challenged.

'Sure, I'm game,' he laughed.

When I finished my assessment and gave him my feedback he wasn't laughing and I thought I may have gone too far. To lighten things up I said, 'A perfect gift for you Mr Norman, would be a book on sailing boats.' Then, doing precisely what Haig Masters had warned me against, I gave him some advice. 'Mr Norman, when you sign your name, instead of cancelling yourself out by drawing a line through, stop and put the line under your signature, with a full stop at the end.'

'What will that do?' he asked.

'It will make a big statement about who you are.'

Mr Norman practised his signature and soon had a new rubber stamp made for the purpose of signing pay cheques when he was out of the office.

One morning, he gave me the handwritten application of a candidate by the name of Angelo Angeledes, whom he was considering referring for a second interview with a high-end accounting practice. They were seeking a driver for a senior partner.

'This man's an assassin,' I said, handing back the form, thinking that should be all he'd need to know.

'He was in the secret police in Cyprus,' Mr Norman said, looking somewhat startled by my quick summary of the applicant.

'That doesn't surprise me, he's a cold-blooded killer, and if he was ever caught he'd take his own life rather than face justice,' I declared.

Mr Angeledes wasn't referred on.

A week or so later Mr Norman handed me a large brown envelope. 'Will you take a look at this for me?'

The envelope contained a letter from one of our industrial clients, enclosing several examples of handwriting for an employee they were considering for a promotion to sales manager. The position involved working with a team of women. There was nothing to indicate the gender of the applicant.

'I'll charge them $500,' he said, 'does that sound reasonable?'

The next day I handed the analysis back to Mr Norman.

'This man isn't suited to work with a team of women. His management style is too autocratic. He'd be well suited to sports media.'

Mr Norman was intrigued that I could see that the candidate was a male and told me his name. He was already a controversial figure in the sports industry. He didn't get the promotion but went on to become a sports media celebrity. I hoped I'd done him a favour.

After that I told Mr Norman that I wasn't confident providing handwriting analyses for candidates I'd not interviewed. It also irked me that he was charging a fee amounting to five times my weekly retainer without cutting me in on the deal.

Carole, the new bookkeeper, had been with us for a few months when she started flaunting expensive jewellery. She claimed her boyfriend gave it to her. I paid little attention to this, beyond commenting 'that's nice'. In the meantime, so I could stay on top of my workload, Mr Norman had agreed to give me a key to the office so I could work late and come in on weekends. One Saturday morning in the office I happened to look through the temporary payroll records, curious to know how that division had grown since I had joined the company. It struck me that the wages we were paying amounted to more than the invoices being charged for labour. It was an easy job to audit the names on the payroll against the completed work orders. I was left with ten people who were getting paid and for whom no work order existed.

The next week Carole turned up showing off a Rado watch. She didn't strike me as a woman who'd have a boyfriend who could afford a $3000 trinket for no special reason. I got the feeling that the watch, and other jewellery, may have more to do with the anomalies on the payroll than a generous cashed-up boyfriend.

'Nice watch. Your boyfriend bought you this?'

'Yes,' she said, pulling her arm away.

Mr Norman came into the office shortly after and I showed him what Carole had been up to. His nostrils flared as he slammed his fist onto the desk.

'How dare she steal from me? I'll have her sent to prison!' he ranted, reaching for the phone to call the police.

'Mr Norman, the pay cheques are signed with a rubber stamp. A clever defence would be able to establish that anyone could have issued those cheques and cashed them, even you,' I said.

He thought about this for a moment and put down the receiver. He called Carole into his office and, in front of me, ripped strips from her, dismissing her on the spot.

'A bookkeeper's in a position of trust. I shouldn't have to protect myself against the possibility that she might steal from me.' He was still seething days later.

10

Hand on the Bible

'Goodnight Mr Norman, I'll see you tomorrow,' I said, popping my head into his office around 7 p.m. It was most unusual for Mr Norman to work late.

'I'm just leaving too. Would you like a lift home?'

'No, thank you – it's out of your way.' Mr Norman lived in Kirrawee, which was in the opposite direction.

'It's no bother, really,' he said, grabbing his jacket.

While Mr Norman went to get his car I waited at the front of the building. Before long a two-door orange and black Ford coupe with tinted windows pulled up at the kerb, a real hoon's car. The Ford tooted. I ignored it. Then the passenger door opened.

'What are you waiting for?'

'I took you for a Renault man,' I said, getting into the car.

He laughed.

We made small talk on the drive to my place. As I turned to get out of the car he reached over and touched my shoulder. 'Can we talk for a while? I hardly know anything about you.'

We talked. As usual, I was guarded, not wanting to give too much away or start telling lies I may need to later retract. Mr Norman went home around 10 p.m.

The next morning Jan called me on the intercom: 'Mrs Norman's here to see you.'

Through the glass partition of my office I could see a strikingly beautiful woman and she didn't look happy.

'Please take a seat Mrs Norman. How may I help you?' I asked politely.

She ignored my offer to be seated. 'How long have you been having an affair with my husband?'

'I beg your pardon. I am not having an affair with your husband,' I said, astounded by the accusation.

'You're a liar!'

I stood up to indicate the conversation was over. She burst into tears.

'My husband said he's in love with you.'

I sat down again. 'Mrs Norman, I promise you we are not having an affair.'

'Would you swear to that on the Bible?'

'Yes, I would.'

With that, she reached into her handbag, pulled out a Bible and placed it on the desk. A bit stunned that she seemed to have come prepared, I took the oath.

She wrapped her arms around me and thanked me. I asked Jan to make Mrs Norman a cup of tea, and when she'd collected herself she left.

Totally flabbergasted, I told Jan what Mrs Norman had said. She didn't seem at all surprised and told me about the time the staff had bought Mr Norman a tie for Christmas. Thinking it was a gift from a woman he was having an affair with, Mrs Norman got up in the middle of the night and shredded all of his ties.

This was too bizarre and I wasn't interested in seeing where it might be going. I packed up my desk and wrote a letter of resignation.

As I waited for Mr Norman to come into the office I had plenty of time to mull over the events of the previous six months. There was nothing in his manner towards me that could have prepared me for the visit from his wife.

'Mr Norman, I'm resigning, effective immediately,' I said, handing him the letter before he'd had time to remove his jacket.

'Why, what's wrong?'

'Your wife came to see me this morning.'

'Oh,' he said, biting his cheek.

'Why would you tell your wife that you are in love with me?'

'Because it's true,' he smiled, looking relieved to have finally unloaded his secret.

There was no denying that I'd had a crush on my boss from the day I set eyes on him, but I'd never have acted on it. 'Mr Norman, although I confess that I've struggled with my feelings for you, I'm not going to have an affair with a married man.'

'Who said anything about having an affair? I know this sounds strange, but can I drive you home tonight and explain?'

Intrigued as to why he would tell his wife he was in love with me before he had even given me any indication about the way he was feeling, I agreed to let him take me home. My immediate thought was that he wanted to save his marriage, and by telling his wife how he was feeling about another woman before he acted on it, they may still have a chance. I didn't see any harm in hearing him out.

I made it through the rest of the day and got into Mr Norman's car a second time. We pulled up at my place. He took my hand and poured his heart out, telling me how much he loved me and had tried to fight his feelings. He said that he was going to leave his wife, if I would have him. He knew nothing about me, at least nothing about the real me. Up until now my secrets had protected me, but they also stopped me getting close to people and having honest relationships.

'Mr Norman, there is so much you don't know about me,' I said, unable to look him in the eye.

'I doubt that anything you have to say will shock me,' he said, taking my hand.

At the time I was not aware how my past conditioning and experiences made me very vulnerable. Like a dog who'd suffered years of abuse I'd wag my tail at the first show of kindness, and follow anyone home. I didn't know what I wanted or needed. Mr Norman was making a huge declaration, and he didn't have the first clue about who I really was. He'd fallen in love with a woman I'd created.

Not since Jack Gazzard had I opened up to anyone. At that stage, not even Vicki knew about my past in any detail. But if he was contemplating leaving his wife for me, I had to be straight with him. If he rejected me, once he knew my story, then we could part knowing that we'd not done anything to cause either of us any shame.

'Well, for starters, I am not a widow and my son isn't dead,' I told him. For several hours I talked about my life, breaking down as I confessed to the lies I had told to keep people from discovering my shameful past. 'One day, I'll be reunited with my son and he'll be a part of my life,' I insisted, trying not to get emotional again.

'Nothing you have told me changes a thing. I have two children and they will always be a part of my life. Do you have trouble accepting that?'

'No.'

'Well, there you go then,' he said, smiling, as if that was all we needed to discuss. 'Are you going to invite me upstairs?'

After I caught the caretaker perving through my bedroom window I had vacated the flat in Bellevue Hill. Vicki was going to be out of town for a month and let me camp at her place while I found somewhere else to live. That little voice, the one we all have inside, was telling me this was not a good decision, but I invited Mr Norman up to the flat. I'd made many confessions to him that evening, but I had still kept a secret hidden. At that point I'd never had an orgasm with any man. Something blocked me, preventing me from letting go and unleashing the passion I knew I was capable of. There was no way I could contemplate the thought of Mr Norman leaving his wife if I wasn't going to be able to lose my sexual inhibitions. And there was only one way to find out.

Our intimacy that evening had none of the usual clumsiness that comes with making love with someone for the first time. Everything just seemed to flow. It would have felt clichéd to tell him how special it was, so I said nothing and pretended that having multiple orgasms was passé for me.

When we showered together before he had to go home I couldn't reach behind his large frame to get the soap. 'Please pass the soap, Mr Norman.' I giggled at the absurdity of using his formal name.

'Don't you think you should call me Darrol, when we're alone at least?'

The next day, Darrol wasn't due into the office until after lunch. It was around 10 a.m. when Jan transferred the call.

'Good morning, Mrs Norman,' I said, trying to sound normal.

'I just want to thank you for last night,' she said, without a hint of sarcasm in her voice. Unable to respond, I waited.

'When Darrol came home last night we made love like we haven't done in years, and I want to thank you for helping me save our marriage.'

She sounded genuinely relieved and grateful. I felt as if someone had just slapped both sides of my face with a hot iron. My mind went blank but I managed to mumble a reply, 'I'm very pleased for you, Mrs Norman.'

My instinct was to grab my handbag and leave. Mrs Norman's words played over and over in my head. *We made love like we haven't done in years.* I decided to confront him before I went.

Darrol came into the office about an hour later. He sounded cheerful when he asked me to come into his office. He spoke before I could tell him about the call from Mrs Norman.

'Do you have a bed for me?' he asked. 'I've left my wife. My bag's in the car.'

For the second time that morning I was speechless. What a clever manipulator Mrs Norman was; she actually had me believing that Darrol had gone home and made love to her after he left me. I was so relieved I didn't even mention her call. Darrol moved in with me that night.

'How did you explain this to your children?' I wondered aloud.

'I haven't spoken to them about it. What happens between me and their mother is none of their business.'

Before Vicki got back we found an apartment to rent in Edgecliff. I had a container of household goods stored and Darrol's brother Bob, who had a ute, drove up from Lugarno to help us collect it. I thought it was a big favour to ask of Bob, whose first child, Justin, was born that day.

'He owes me,' was Darrol's reply.

The abusive calls that Darrol's wife had started making to the office soon escalated to calls in the middle of the night.

'You'll go to hell!' she'd scream. Darrol's wife was a Jehovah's Witness and if she believed I'd lied with my hand on the Bible it would have placed me beyond redemption.

On the second payday after we started living together I didn't get my monthly commission. I was expecting a generous sum for numerous placements I had made with AGC, a large finance company in the city.

'That wasn't new business. AGC was a client before you started working here,' Darrol said.

'Mr Norman, that isn't fair and it isn't what we agreed to,' I said, upset that I had to remind him of our original deal.

'We agreed to ten per cent of all new business, and AGC is not new business,' he insisted.

'No, we agreed to ten per cent of all placement fees.'

'That's not what I recall.'

I started to doubt myself and wondered if perhaps I was mistaken. It hadn't occurred to me to put our original agreement in writing. I'd worked with men whose word had been their bond. Thinking that all men could be trusted in this way would prove to be a costly mistake.

After Darrol and I moved in together, Darrol's wife Jenny started making it difficult for him to see his children. At that stage Matt was about thirteen and Willow was twelve. One night, Darrol went over to Kirrawee, about an hour's drive from Edgecliff, and when Jenny refused to open the door he threatened to kick it in.

On one occasion, Willow had been away visiting a relative in Queensland. Darrol and I drove out to the airport to meet her. I waited in the car. Jenny pulled up in a car alongside, with Willow in the passenger seat. Jenny glared at me and mouthed, 'You filthy slut.'

A short while later my head hit the passenger's window before I was flung forwards. Jenny crunched the gears before backing up and ramming me again. Willow appeared to be screaming for her mother to stop. Darrol was coming towards us. When he saw what was happening, he started to run.

'I'm going to call the police,' I said, clamouring to get out on the driver's side.

Darrol asked me to stay in the car and let him handle it. No one was seriously hurt, and the incident wasn't reported to the police. Still, Jenny's car needed a new radiator, and both cars needed to go to the panel beater. After the incident at the airport the abusive calls from Jenny stopped. Or so I thought, until one night around 8 p.m. the phone rang. It was a male voice which, at first, sounded quite normal.

'I'm Jenny's uncle Jack, you dirty, filthy slut. I'll cut your head off.'

'Listen up, you crazy old bastard. Threaten me again and I'll call the police,' I said, more bravely than I felt, before slamming down the phone.

'They call him Jack the Axe,' Darrol said, sounding amused when I told him who was calling.

'You might find this funny, but I don't. If it doesn't stop I am going to the police.'

The threats from Jack the Axe stopped.

One night I suggested to Darrol that his children come to our place and spend some time with us. We arranged to meet in a car park at Ramsgate to discuss this with his wife. Darrol got into the back seat and I sat in the front, facing Jenny. She wasted no time launching into a finger-waving tirade that had nothing to do with us having the children come to stay. She quoted passages from the Bible, regarding adultery, and told me that I'd burn in hell for what I'd done. Darrol said nothing, seemingly quite alright with me being treated as the only wrongdoer in all of this.

'Alright, I'll agree to allow the children to visit, so long as they don't witness any sodomy,' she finally relented.

'I beg your pardon?' I said.

This wasn't the first time that Jenny had said something that left me utterly speechless. Several seconds of startled silence passed before I could collect my thoughts enough to say that should we ever engage in such activity the children wouldn't be invited to watch. I was so shocked by Jenny's remark I didn't ask Darrol for clarification on the way home, and he never offered any.

A few weeks after this meeting I got another call from Jenny. 'You'll be sorry,' she said, 'Darrol's so tight with money I had to go to charities to dress myself and the kids.'

'It'll be a cold day in hell when I'll need any man to support me,' I said, putting down the phone.

11

Weathering the storm

'I've bought a boat!' Darrol announced, bubbling with enthusiasm. A Christmas present to himself, he explained. 'It's a Hartley 21,' he gushed, expecting that I'd know it was a small wooden-hull trailer-sailor. 'It was a bargain. Jenny's uncle only wanted $1100.'

Why he thought Jack the Axe would want to do him any favours was a mystery.

The morning we picked up the boat we left the car at Rose Bay, where Darrol had arranged for a mooring, and caught a taxi to the Spit at Mosman. It was a glorious summer's day, with scattered clouds and a light breeze playing under a sapphire-blue sky; Sydney Harbour at its spectacular best. Darrol handed over the cash without even inspecting the boat.

Setting sails on a Hartley 21 is quite a production. Firstly, timber batons need to be threaded into the slots along the sail before it can be hoisted. The canvas was dry and stiff as a board. After some pushing and cursing we got the sail up and we were underway. It struck me as strange that we were the only boat heading out onto

79

the harbour, while a flotilla sailing in the opposite direction at a cracking speed tossed us about in their wake.

'We'll live on that hill one day,' I said, pointing to the palatial homes gracing the hill overlooking Clontarf Beach.

'Dream on,' Darrol scoffed.

By the time we turned into the main harbour the sky was as purple as an overripe plum. The Sydney Harbour Bridge and Fort Denison were completely obscured by the squall about to engulf us. It was eerie. We were the only fools on the water. Not even the ferries were running.

'Perhaps we better think about getting into life jackets,' I said, trying not to sound too dramatic.

'I know what I'm doing; I sailed on a boat from England.'

I was later to discover this was pure fantasy. Darrol had no sailing experience at all. He came to Australia, a Ten Pound Pom, on a passenger liner with his mother and two brothers.

I checked under the seats. There were no life jackets on board. By the time we reached Rose Bay the boat was gunnels under and taking on water. I kicked off my shoes in case we had to swim.

'Pull the sail in and I'll get the engine going!' Darrol had to raise his voice to be heard.

'Shouldn't you get the engine going before we pull in the sail?' I shouted back.

Just then a wave hit the boat sending me crashing onto the deck. 'Just pull in the fucking sail!' Darrol screamed, ignoring my predicament as I struggled to get to my feet. 'Fuck!' he yelled, shaking his hand and spraying blood all over me.

The outboard motor had kicked back, dragging Darrol's hand into the pulley and cutting his index finger to the bone. I pulled a cloth napkin from the picnic hamper we'd taken with us and tied it tightly around the wound.

'Did you check the fuel?' I asked.

His face said it all. With no engine and no sail we were at the mercy of the storm, bobbing around like a cork in a barrel. I scrambled to hoist the sail back up again. The boom swung around, smacking me in the face and almost knocking me overboard. Blood gushed from my nose.

'You'll have to pick up the mooring under sail,' he yelled.

Fortunately, I'd been sailing before and knew what this meant, but in these conditions it was going to be easier said than done. Grabbing the slippery railing in one hand and the long handled boat hook in the other, I leaned over the bow as far as I could. Through the dim light I could see the sandstone retaining wall of Rose Bay, just metres away. If we hit the wall we were goners. Hanging on for dear life and groping into the blackness below, the hook caught hold of a mooring.

'That's not our mooring!'

'It is tonight!' I screamed back. With an almighty adrenaline rush, I hauled the ball and chain out of the water and attached it to the boat. We started spinning in the turbulence, narrowly missing other boats. With nothing as practical as a torch or flare on board, I pulled off my blood-soaked top, whistling and waving frantically, hoping to catch the attention of the man locking up the Rose Bay marina.

'What are you doing out here!' He sounded angry as he tossed us a line. 'How could you have missed the storm forecast?'

We got home drenched and exhausted; both of us needed first aid.

'I think you need a few stitches in this finger,' I said, examining Darrol's wound.

'No, just put on some Savlon and wrap it up tight.'

Darrol flicked on the TV to catch the news. The storm, the worst to hit Sydney in years, was being described as a hurricane. Gale-force winds brought down trees and ripped the roof from homes and factories across the city. We watched on in alarm as boats in Rose Bay were picked up by the wind and flipped over like cardboard boxes. Miraculously, Darrol's boat survived the storm but a few days later we got a call from the Maritime Services Board to say the boat had sunk on its mooring. It was full of dry rot and not worth salvaging. I didn't know it at the time but that day would come back to haunt me as the clearest premonition I could ever have as to what my future with Darrol would hold.

'You're still friends with the mother of an old lover?' He queried when I told him that having Christmas lunch with Peggy Gazzard was somewhat of a tradition.

'Yes, and why not?' I asked, 'Peggy's a good old stick and I'm all she has. She thinks of me as a daughter.'

In spite of Peggy's stern outward appearance there was still plenty of the little girl in Peggy and she loved Christmas as much as I did. She always put up a tree and set the table with her best china and cutlery. She was a wonderful cook and regardless of the often scorching heat, she always served turkey and ham with all the trimmings. After the Christmas pudding, with hard brandy sauce, we exchanged gifts and cracked open a box of Darrell Lea chocolates to have with coffee.

'Is she always that rude?' Darrol asked on the way home.

'Rude? How was she rude?'

'Putting covers on the lounge before I sat down,' he huffed, 'I was wearing my best clothes.'

'Once she knows you aren't going to shed hair, she'll stop doing it,' I laughed.

'I'd like you to meet the Lavender Hill Mob,' I said, when I suggested that we have a New Year's Eve party, hoping to cheer Darrol up after losing his boat.

'I hate parties.'

'You'll like my friends; they're a bit quirky but that's what makes them interesting,' I enthused.

The mob was made up of Noel Christensen and his brother Phil, who published magazines connected to motorsports and greyhound racing. Myles was working as a sales manager with Kawasaki, and arrived with his wife, Gail, and her sister, Christine, who was also my old flatmate. Gabor 'Gary Sellers' Selmeczi had come to Australia from Hungary after the revolution. Gabor was working in the personnel field at the time but had aspirations of owning his own hi-fi store. Billy, the wedding singer, had a great voice but for some reason never hit the big time, and Pommie Dave, a former merchant seaman, owned VIP limousines and always shamelessly name-dropped when he recanted stories of the famous people he knew.

'Yes, I take Tina to the gym. You know she works out four hours a day. She's got great legs,' he'd insist, in case we missed the fact that he chauffeured Tina Turner when she was in town.

I'd unpacked the box that contained a pile of LP records and asked Darrol what kind of music he preferred.

'I don't like singers,' he said.

'What? You don't like vocalists? At all?'

'I can't stand singers, any singers,' he replied.

How did I get hooked up with a man who doesn't like singers? I wondered. This could be awkward.

There were three things the Lavender Hill Mob liked to do when they got together. One was to sing, and another was to eat, so I cooked up a storm. After everyone had their fill the real fun would start, because the third thing they liked to do was laugh.

'Sensational food, Princess,' Myles Stivano said, going back to the table for a second helping of Moroccan lamb.

Billy was off in the corner tuning my guitar. Gabor, who was gifted with a very fine voice, was warming up to give his rendition of 'Danny Boy'.

'Sing "Star Wars",' Phil, known for his jocular teasing, called from across the room. Gabor wasn't amused and grumbled something about 'pearls before swine'.

Pommie Dave did his tired old act of vaudevillian one-liners. We'd heard them all before but laughed anyway. Myles was making a racket in the kitchen, and before he turned it upside down I went out to help him gather appliances and gadgets he used to mimic 'Joe the Gadget Man', the spruiker for the Sydney-based hardware store Nock & Kirby. Every Saturday afternoon on TV, between the staged contests with Killer Kowalski and Brute Bernard, stars of World Championship Wrestling, Joe the Gadget Man would chop, slice and dice his way through myriad vegetables demonstrating the latest kitchen appliances. Myles had Joe's act down pat, and from the moment he tied on his apron, working through the appliances spread along my ironing board, he had us roaring with laughter, except for Darrol who remained pan-faced. Myles didn't like to lose an audience member, so he immediately launched into his impersonation of W.C. Fields. 'Ahhhh . . . never give a sucker an even break, or smarten up a chump,' he mimicked perfectly. 'Children? Yes, I like children, girl children, about eighteen or nineteen.'

That got a laugh.

Later Myles took me quietly aside. 'Ah, Princess, is it in order if we have a smoke?'

'If you want to smoke you'd better go up to the roof.'

During the night everyone kept disappearing and coming back with the giggles – looking for more food. Darrol tried to loosen up but he didn't look comfortable. He started cleaning up, a signal for everyone to go home. As Myles was leaving he checked to make sure Darrol wasn't within earshot. 'What are you doing with that fucking wood-duck?' he asked.

Darrol hadn't said a word to me after everyone left and I wanted to clear the air before we went to bed. 'What's eating you?' I asked.

'That Myles called you Princess.'

'Yes, he's always called me that.'

'So, you have some history with him?'

'Not in the way you seem to be implying.'

'What was that funny smell I could smell?'

'You've had a sheltered life,' I grinned, 'that was marijuana.'

'Lucky for those blokes you hang around with that I didn't know that. I'd have thrown them all out,' he said, indignantly.

'If you'd done that, I'd have left with them,' I said, letting him know these weren't just blokes I hung around with. They were like brothers.

On my birthday in January the girls in the office had bought me a cake and I was away from my desk washing my plate when Jan popped her head into the staff room.

'There's a man in reception to see you.'

'Did he say who he is?'

'No, but I think you should see him,' she said, rolling her eyes.

Half expecting it to be one of Mrs Norman's crazy relatives standing there with an axe, I stormed into reception.

'*Guten tag*, Katy. Happy birthday,' Karl said, handing me a bunch of long-stemmed red roses.

You could have heard a pin drop. Every female in the office had stopped what they were doing and gawked at Karl. Even the clatter of typing tests ceased.

'Thank you, Karl,' I said, taking the roses and reaching up to kiss his cheek.

Darrol was out of the office but due back anytime.

'Jan, I'll be back in an hour,' I said, grabbing my handbag and walking out the door ahead of Karl. God knows what I'd have said if we'd bumped into Darrol on the stairs. Karl and I went across the road and ordered a coffee. Robyn, the waitress, who'd seen me at the café numerous times with Darrol, raised her eyebrows when she clapped eyes on Karl.

'How did you find me?' I asked, as we took a table in the far back corner.

'Your old work told me,' he said. 'You are not happy to see me?'

Karl had gone to the last place we'd had contact. It'd been well over a year since I'd caught up with anyone there; they knew I was working at Manpower, but I hadn't had the chance to tell them about Darrol and me. Truth be known, I was ashamed to admit I was living with a married man.

Karl took my hand and the electricity between us could have sparked a bushfire.

'Karl,' I started, squeezing his hand, 'I wanted to write but I couldn't find the words.'

He took something from his pocket; a small jewellery box.

'Karl, I'm sorry, but things are very complicated.' I put my hand over his, so he wouldn't open the box.

'You have other man?'

'Yes, I do.' There was no point trying to explain.

Karl looked crushed. I felt like trash. *Would he have come back if I'd told him I had a son, and how I came to lose him?* As he walked me to the street corner my head was pounding and I wished I could turn back the clock and do things differently. But time only travels forward. We can't go back and rub out mistakes. Trembling, and still holding the roses, I closed my eyes and waited for the lights to change. For several seconds I could smell him and feel his body heat. Then he was gone.

There was a busker playing on the corner of Pitt and Hunter. As I passed, I laid the roses inside his guitar case.

12

You're a dreamer

Since coming to Australia as a teenager Darrol had lived in the southern suburbs and, from what I could tell, never ventured very far. When I suggested that we inspect a property on Sydney's north shore he raised all kinds of objections, making the need to cross the Harbour Bridge to get to work sound like some arduous process requiring a passport renewal. After I convinced him that the north shore was an area poised to see spectacular investment potential, he finally agreed to come and inspect a two-bedroom apartment on Spit Road at Mosman, with views over Quakers Hat Bay. The asking price was out of our range, but I felt it could be negotiable.

'They'll never take that,' Darrol said, when I suggested we make an offer.

'It's a deceased estate; they'll take what they can get for it.'

'You know, Kay, you can be ruthless.'

'Ruthless?'

'It's an old lady's place.'

'It *was* an old lady's place and now she's deceased, with no heirs, and the executors are turning the asset into cash.'

I was annoyed that he accused me of being ruthless. I felt that the offer was reasonable, as we would need to redecorate. The vendors weren't insulted. Darrol arranged the finance. We split the mortgage payments and all other expenses, fifty-fifty.

Before moving in we redecorated the unit, creating a cosy bolt-hole to escape to after a hard day. We bought a set of wrought iron outdoor furniture for the covered patio so we could enjoy a pre-dinner drink and watch the sun set over the water.

'To our cubby,' we said, raising our glasses to toast our new home. The next few months were total bliss. By day we worked within metres of each other and the business started really picking up pace. By night we enjoyed quiet meals at home alone and hours of sensual lovemaking.

One morning, we were enjoying a leisurely ferry ride to work. 'Take a look at this,' Darrol said, handing me the newspaper he'd been reading.

The headline story was about a man who'd killed his wife and hung himself in his cell while awaiting sentencing. I was wondering why Darrol thought I'd be interested, then I saw the name of the man – Angelo Angeledes.

'You said he'd kill himself, rather than face justice,' Darrol remarked, before turning the page.

'What's this?' I asked, bending to pick up the eye-catching package that was gathering dust on the floor of Darrol's office.

'More rubbish from America,' he said, referring to the boxes of promotional material that often arrived from Manpower's head office. I had to agree that the stuff for Valentine's Day was far too kitschy for our market, but Darrol's kids liked the heart-shaped sweets it contained. Admittedly, the promotional packs didn't usually contain much that could benefit our office, but occasionally I'd find something useful.

The intriguing catch phrase 'Predictable Performance System' that was written on the outside of this box suggested something altogether different. It took two weeks for me to read through the contents and put all of the pieces together. In its current format the program was overkill, but with some paring down and a bit of tinkering to meet our budget and the local market needs, I saw exciting potential. Convincing Darrol was going to be the biggest obstacle.

'Forget it. The American approach just doesn't work here. These programs have been tried, and failed. Our market isn't that sophisticated.'

'This is kick-arse material. You've been sitting on a goldmine, letting it gather dust for two years,' I said, unable to conceal my irritation. He continued to argue as if Australia was a backwater with entrenched parochial ideas.

'Piffle! The market is crying out for something better and no one is offering it. I believe we can create a demand for a better service that our competitors won't be able to match,' I argued.

Finally, he agreed to let me introduce components of the program, but only those that required minimal outlay. It gave me something to sell, and I was determined to keep working on him until I had the whole program operational. Meanwhile, the phones never stopped ringing.

Darrol came back from his solicitor one evening flushed with rage. 'For her share in the company, all she wants is the fucking house, the furniture and her car!' He ranted, pouring a large glass of Johnnie Walker, straight, and tossing it back in one go. 'I put my inheritance into that fucking house,' he raved, pouring another generous glass and gulping it down like it was needed for medicinal purposes.

'What's the house worth?'

'About $41,000. But there's a mortgage of $11,000 to pay out.'

'Do you have $11,000?'

'That's not the point! She never put a bloody thing into that property and I worked my arse off,' he said, pouring another drink, which almost emptied the bottle. 'That bloody bitch has gone on a disability pension so she can get Legal Aid!' he frothed. 'There's nothing wrong with her. She just needs to get a fucking job.' He smashed his fist onto the table.

'Darrol, give her the house. The company has more potential than a house in Kirrawee.'

'I built that deck using hand tools!'

'If we keep going the way we are, you'll be able to afford to pay people with power tools to build your next deck,' I said, hoping to get him to see the bigger picture.

Darrol spent the rest of the night with his head in the toilet bowl. The next day he came back from his solicitor's after signing the property settlement looking like someone who'd lost a pound and found a penny.

'Well we better make this company work now, I'm cleaned out,' he said, pouring himself a stiff drink.

'Give me the go-ahead with these systems and within five years this company will be turning over millions,' I said, trying to lift his spirits.

'You're a dreamer,' Darrol shook his head.

'Darrol, if your dreams don't scare you, they're not big enough,' I laughed, replacing the stopper in the whisky decanter and putting it back into the cupboard.

Modifying the US program for the Australian market proved a real challenge. The additional workload and pressure I was under often caused a bleeding nose to gush all over me, and whatever I happened to be doing at the time.

'Darrol this is too much. We're going to have to let the permanent placement division go,' I told him.

'No way. If you can't do both then drop this silly idea of introducing that crap from the States.'

As Darrol didn't have to pay royalties to the US for permanent placements, he was reluctant to see that revenue go. After giving the problem considerable thought I came up with an idea that would enable us to make permanent placements, while freeing me up to work on the programs from the US. I called this new program Job Prove, and the service was in the name. Instead of referring applicants for permanent placements in the usual way, and taking a commission, we made the selection and sent the best candidate to work as a temporary with the company for six weeks, to prove whether or not it was a match. If both parties were happy after the six-week period, the client took the temporary onto their permanent payroll with no placement fee.

'And you think you can sell this?' Darrol asked.

Helena Ricardo was the personnel manager of Citicorp, a multinational banking and finance company that had absorbed Australian Guarantee Finance, one of our major accounts. I set up a meeting with her to test the water. We deployed over fifty temporary workers a week to Citicorp, as well as having an endless stream of permanent placements to fill. I left Helena's office with my briefcase bulging with new job descriptions.

Now that I wasn't earning any commission, I broached the subject of a pay increase with Darrol. 'John Plummer told me you were money hungry,' he said.

That night we had our first heated argument over money. The next pay I received what I thought was a modest increase, although it fell short of what I'd been earning with commission.

*

The situation at home was becoming more complicated. Jenny had gone from not wanting the children to stay with us at all to fobbing them off on us every weekend and school holidays. Initially, Darrol had bought fold-up beds for them to sleep on, but now that they were spending more time with us I felt we needed to make their accommodation more comfortable. Setting up the second bedroom for Matt and Willow intensified the loss of not having Adam in my life.

'Matt, what are you doing here?' I asked one night when we came home to find Darrol's son sitting at our front door, looking totally dejected and clutching a couple of green garbage bags containing his clothes.

'I've had a fight with Mum and she's thrown me out.'

Darrol called his wife to find out what happened.

'He smashed all my pot plants!' she screamed, as some sort of defence for driving her fifteen-year-old son across the city and dumping him like an unwanted cat. Matt didn't go back to his mother and we enrolled him into Balgowlah Boys High.

Matt was strikingly handsome and tall like his father, but with olive skin and honey blonde hair. People stared at him when he was in public and he thought it was because there was something wrong with him.

'Oh, Matt, you're so handsome, you could be a movie star, that's why they stare.'

Matt blushed. He wasn't used to compliments.

Apart from helping with the washing-up, Darrol didn't see his role as extending to helping with the general housework, and having a teenager living with us made extra work for me. 'My mother worked and she didn't have a cleaner,' he argued.

'Yes, and she worked herself to death and was cold in her grave before her sixty-fourth birthday.'

I found Manuel in *The Manly Daily*. It was $35 well spent to come home to a pristine apartment on a Friday night and to be able to relax on Saturday morning reading the newspapers from cover to cover.

Steven Berkoff was starring in *The Fall of the House of Usher* and getting rave reviews. 'Let's get some tickets,' I enthused, handing Darrol the paper to check out the review.

'We can't go out and leave Matt at home alone. And we can't take him to the theatre, he'd be bored shitless.'

'Matt isn't a baby. He may even enjoy a night on his own, did you ever think of that?'

On Friday night we brought home a cooked chicken, some chocolates and a bottle of Coca-Cola – Matt's idea of a perfect meal. He looked as happy as a puppy with two tails at the thought of a night on his own.

Before I met Darrol I was a regular theatregoer and seeing Steven Berkoff, an artist with electrifying magnetism, live and so close I could reach out and touch him, was spine-tingling. That night broke a long drought of cultural starvation and Darrol and I found something we both enjoyed doing together, which proved to be a powerful aphrodisiac for us both.

The next morning I jumped into the shower while Darrol made us a cup of tea. I heard clanging and banging and went to see what was up.

'Bloody lazy kid,' Darrol grumbled, as he started to clean up the mess.

'No,' I said, nudging him out of the way. 'Please let me deal with this.'

I gathered the chicken bones, chocolate wrappers, crockery, cutlery and empty Coca-Cola bottle and took them to Matt's room. Darrol watched nervously as I pulled back the doona and spread everything along the full length of Matt's bed, then neatly pulled over the cover and fluffed up the pillows.

'You can't do that; he'll go off his head! We don't know what he's likely to do.'

'I know that he'll never leave the kitchen in that state again.'

Matt came home from the beach, sunburned and exhausted. We had dinner and watched *The Bill*. Matt was very fastidious with his personal hygiene and always showered before going to bed. Darrol and I were already in bed and held our breath, expecting some kind of reaction, but to his credit we didn't hear a peep out of him. The next morning he was up and gone before we got up. The dishes had been washed up and put away, the garbage was in the bin, and the sheets on his bed had been changed and placed in the washing machine. Matt never left as much as a teaspoon on the sink again.

About four months after Matt moved in I noticed that he never had any homework. I'd not even seen him with a book in his hand. He was in Year 10 and I thought he ought to have had some assignments. When I mentioned this to Darrol, he questioned Matt, who confessed he'd been wagging school every day and going surfing. Darrol exploded and had Matt cowering on the lounge protecting his head. There was no way Matt could catch up in time to sit the exams so I suggested we take him out of school.

'He's not leaving school until he gets a fucking job, I'm not keeping him,' Darrol said.

'Darrol, I think we need to get some counselling for Matt.'

'He's not crazy, he's just lazy.'

'I don't think he is crazy or lazy, but he clearly needs some help and I don't think you or I can provide it.'

Darrol knew what Haig Masters had done for me and I suggested that I contact him. Haig and I had spoken on the telephone a number of times since the confronting session at the Boulevard Hotel and I told him that I'd followed his recommendation and entered the personnel industry. He introduced a select number of his clients to Manpower and having Haig's recommendation was an automatic door-opener. After I gave Haig an outline of what was happening with Matt, he asked me to send some photographs and handwriting samples.

'I don't need to see the boy. I'll be able to give you and the father enough to help him,' Haig said, when he called back to give us an appointment time and date.

'He wants $500 an hour? He better be bloody good for that,' Darrol said, when I told him Haig's fee.

It was disturbing to hear Haig talk in some detail about the issues concerning Matt. He dictated, into a tape recorder, his recommendations as to how we could best help. 'You need to be patient with the boy. Try never to question him, let him come to you. More importantly, never cross-question him,' Haig said, handing us the cassette, along with some handwritten notes he'd made.

Haig agreed that the best thing for Matt at that time was to take him out of school. The pressure of trying to catch up on almost two terms of missed work was futile, and would cause him unreasonable distress.

Every Saturday morning Matt and I pored over the jobs vacant in the local paper. He wasn't old enough to drive so something local was going to be more practical. A job came up and he expressed enough interest for me to call and get him an appointment.

Matt hated anyone touching his head and his shoulder length hair would need a trim for a job interview. I'd been cutting Darrol's hair but Matt surprised me when he agreed to let me give him a haircut. I made him a corduroy jacket and bought him a nice pair of slacks. Although I'd given him some coaching, he looked terrified the morning he left for his first job interview.

'Call me at work afterwards and let me know how it went,' I said, giving him a hug.

All morning I was anxious, I understood how daunting interviews could be for a first-timer as shy as Matt.

'I got the job!' Matt gushed, sounding happier than I'd ever heard him, when he called to give me the good news.

The next week he started working as a trainee picture framer at an art gallery owned by Eric Phillips and his wife, actress Ruth Cracknell. Matt never had to set the alarm to get to work and he never missed a day.

Helping Matt find his first job left me with a deep sadness that I'd not made contact with Adam, who'd be turning fourteen in January. It drove home just how much I was missing, including the birthdays and Christmases that were gone forever. There had been recent changes to the Family Law Act, introducing something called 'irreconcilable differences' as grounds for divorce, attaching no fault or blame to either party. With these changes to the law I knew that if I'd tried to see Adam the McNortons may not have been able to stop me.

While part of me yearned to reach out, I was worried that crashing into Adam's life after so many years would create turmoil for him. Perhaps John McNorton had remarried and Adam thought another woman was his mother. For years I'd lived with the grief of being separated from my son, not being able to hold him and watch him grow, clinging blindly to the hope that we'd soon be together again. Now that the door was open for us to be reunited I was finding excuses. I had become paralysed by the fear of being rejected.

13

Try this for size

'This is Dad's . . . err . . .'

Slut, I was often tempted to add when Matt and Willow were unsure about how to introduce me to their friends.

Although we'd been living together for over two years, Darrol's children didn't know where I fitted into the picture.

'I don't want to get married again,' Darrol said, dismissing the idea when I suggested that we get married.

'Darrol, this is very important for the children, they need to feel that they're on solid ground,' I reasoned.

'I'm not getting married again, and that's that,' he said, without even looking at me. It annoyed me that he was so adamant about this and wasn't even prepared to discuss it.

'Alright, but if I'm not good enough to be Mrs Norman, I'm not good enough to help raise your kids and run your business,' I said, packing a bag and walking out the door.

He found me at my friend Peggy Gazzard's place and agreed to us getting married, but wanted nothing to do with the wedding plans and especially none of the cost. He didn't want anything fancy, he said. I got the feeling that Darrol was only acquiescing because he didn't want to lose the goose that was laying the golden eggs. For my part, I'd thrown everything I had into developing the business and creating a home to bring me closer to the day I could have Adam back in my life. If everything fell apart now I'd be back to square one.

Even if I wanted to I couldn't have splashed out on a big wedding. But I did want the day to be special and invited thirty guests to join us for the wedding and reception dinner at the Fisherman's Lodge in Watsons Bay. Darrol wasn't the slightest bit interested in the wedding plans, and as the big day loomed it became harder to maintain enthusiasm.

One morning, I picked up the phone to hear a familiar voice.

'Hello, Richard.' It was an old friend from Bondi and a good mate of Danny Frawley.

'G'day Kay, I'm sorry to tell you this but Danny passed away last night,' he said, breaking down.

Nothing can cushion a blow like that. It slams into the gut like a lead ball coming at speed. Danny was the first person who'd befriended me when I arrived in Bondi almost twelve years earlier. I was full of remorse. I'd known Danny had cancer, but had been so caught up in the whirlwind of everything happening in my own life, I hadn't visited him in hospital. Now it was too late.

Mourners were spilling out onto the street at the front of St Margaret Mary Catholic Church in Rose Bay when I arrived. I wasn't surprised to see such a big send-off for Danny. Not only was he a decent bloke in his own right, but he was also the only son of pioneer Rugby League player, Dan Frawley, who is named on the list of Australia's 100 greatest players. Danny's elderly mother,

Pearl, was stoic in her grief. Her composure was remarkable and I told her so. 'He's gone to our Lord,' she said, taking my hand to comfort me.

Myles spotted me and came over to offer his arm and escort me into the church.

'G'day Princess, it's a sad day eh?' he said, solemnly.

It wasn't until I saw the coffin that it really hit home and I wished I could have seen my old friend's mischievous smile one last time.

'I'm pleased there was no music,' an old girlfriend of Danny's whispered as we followed the coffin out of the church, yet it was the lack of music that made this funeral all the more tragic for me. As I drove slowly behind the hearse to Waverley Cemetery I thought about the special person Danny Frawley had been, with the chorus of Joni Mitchell's 'The Circle Game' playing over in my mind.

It was the night before the wedding and I still hadn't finished my dress. I'd set up the sewing machine on the dining table and worked furiously, with no margin for error. My head felt like a water balloon ready to burst. I stuffed some cotton balls into my nostrils and tied a scarf around my face, like a masked bandit, so if my nose exploded the blood wouldn't ruin the dress before I got the chance to wear it. Exhausted, I fell into bed around 3 am, but after a few hours sleep I was up again to add the final touches.

'Darrol, you do know that we're getting married today? Have you bought me a ring?' I asked, as I was packing a bag to go to Peggy's. I was appeasing her superstition about the groom not seeing the bride in her dress before the wedding.

He looked vacant. Then suddenly, as if he'd had a bright idea, he pulled out a drawer and produced an old trinket box.

'Here, try this for size,' he said, fishing out a plain gold ring and tossing it onto the bed.

The ring felt warm, like it had just been taken from someone's hand.

'Wasn't this your mother's wedding ring?' I asked, pressing the ring into the palm of my hand.

'Yes, but she doesn't need it anymore.'

'And you call me ruthless?' I said, handing the ring back to him without trying it on. Upon reflection, I could have spared myself a lot of heartache and disappointment if I'd just said, 'Fuck it! I don't want to marry you either.'

Pommie Dave was picking me up from Peggy's in his limousine to take us to Watsons Bay, collecting my girlfriends Vicki and Diana on the way. Noel Christensen generously offered to be the photographer as a wedding gift. He could be relied on to take good photographs even if I felt worthless.

'Your dress is unusual. Is this a curtain cord?' Peggy asked, picking up the end of the cord around my waist. After paying for the reception and estimating the cost of the alcohol, I couldn't afford a nice belt, so I had to improvise. 'Aren't you wearing anything on your head?' Peggy added when she saw I wasn't wearing a hat or carrying flowers. The orchid corsage pinned to my dress was more than enough frippery for the way I was feeling.

A marriage celebrant officiated, and I had written the wedding vows. I'd given them to Darrol well beforehand but hadn't seen him practising. He stumbled a few times but finally got through it. His mother's wedding ring fitted perfectly.

Darrol didn't have a speech ready and when it looked like getting embarrassing his brother, Bob, jumped to his feet and rescued him.

I'd hired a band and following the main course couples got up to dance. Darrol asked me to dance a slow number with him. It was the first and last time we danced together.

Kristine, my new sister in-law, told me it was the nicest wedding she'd ever been to. I was pleased that the guests didn't pick up the vibe that both Darrol and I were just going through the motions.

'I'll get that!' Darrol announced as the reception drew to a close, whipping out his chequebook to pay the drinks bill as it was brought to the table. '$90 for port? That's the last time you lot are invited,' he said, trying to sound jocular.

As the guests were leaving they thanked Darrol for the wonderful evening. Of course they presumed that he'd paid for everything, and he allowed them to think so. 'If you'd told me you were going to help out, I'd have been able to afford a decent dress,' I said, as we drove away.

For our wedding night I'd booked us into Noah's in North Sydney. It was nothing flash, just a standard hotel room, but quite fitting for a night that barely raised enough interest from me to fake an orgasm.

As their mother was a Jehovah's Witness, Matt and Willow had reached their teens without ever celebrating Christmas. The happiest memories of my childhood centred on Christmas, and even though I couldn't share it with my own son, I wanted to maintain the tradition.

Having invited all of Darrol's family to our place for dinner, I went into Mrs Santa mode, shopping and cooking for days.

'Why do you have to go overboard?' Darrol grumbled when I came through the door loaded up with more parcels.

'Bah, humbug! You bloody scrooge. Has anyone asked you to pay for this?' I asked, handing Matt the box to unpack the Christmas tree. Matt and Willow were very excited and got right into the Christmas spirit. Sitting on the floor with them wrapping the presents was a stark reminder that Adam would be having Christmas elsewhere, without a gift under the tree from his mother.

After dinner everyone sat around chatting and exchanging gifts, and I joined Darrol's cousin on the patio while she had a cigarette.

'Darrol's not the man he's cracked up to be,' she said, out of the blue. When I didn't respond she tried again. 'I've never forgiven Darrol for what he did to our Dinah.'

Darrol's mother was called Annie, but since she was a child she had been called Dinah, by certain members of her family.

'Really? What did he do to Dinah?'

'Dinah only had a few months to live. Looking after her was too much trouble. One night, he bundled her into his car and drove her up to my place and left her with me. She died broken-hearted.'

If this snippet of information was intended to deflate my Christmas spirit, it worked.

'You've fallen on your feet marrying Darrol,' she said, changing the subject.

'Being married to Darrol has nothing to do with what I achieve in life,' I said, picking up our glasses and going inside.

14

Kay handles that

'Do you think a Mercedes sports car is a practical family vehicle?' I asked, as Darrol jangled the keys to his new car in my face. The 450 SLC manual, with cramped back seating, seemed totally impractical to comfortably accommodate two tall teenagers. To top it off, Darrol had no idea whether or not I could even drive a car with gears. There'd been no prior discussion with me about getting a new car, which he'd picked up the same day he was collecting his younger brother, Peter, from the airport.

Peter, a carpenter by trade, had been in the police force in Canada for fifteen years, but hadn't risen above the rank of constable. He'd come back to Australia to see what his chances were of getting a job with the New South Wales police force. In all the excitement of seeing Peter, and taking the wheel of the new car, Darrol parked on the street and forgot about the 3 p.m. clearway on Spit Road. The motorcyclist in the transit lane wouldn't have seen Darrol's car, parked on the bend, until he hit it. Fortunately, the motorcyclist, who'd catapulted over the vehicle, survived with minor injuries.

'There isn't a scratch on the Merc,' Darrol said, sounding relieved.

'The motorcyclist is lucky to be alive,' I said.

'He shouldn't have been in the transit lane anyway,' Darrol said, trying to rationalise his error that could have killed someone.

'Neither should you,' Peter replied, sternly.

That night Darrol had a migraine and went straight to bed after we came home from dinner. Peter liked a drink and had earned the nickname 'have-a-chat'. To hear him tell it, Canada was the greatest place on earth. He drove Darrol nuts comparing every little thing – even the toilet paper was softer in Canada. Peter confided in me that he was very unhappy in his marriage and if he could get into the police force here, he was going to leave his wife and come back to Australia. Already in his late thirties, with no rank in his favour, he was very disappointed in his career.

Peter only had two weeks to get around and visit all the family, who were keen to see him. More often than not he rolled in the door after ten o'clock, still keyed up and wanting to chat and listen to music. Darrol went to bed and left us to it. I'd recently bought a Dr Hook album and when the hit song 'When You're in Love with a Beautiful Woman' started to play, Peter pulled me up out of my chair. Dancing around our small lounge room with my brother-in-law was as much fun as I'd had in years and his visit had been a welcome distraction. We'd formed a bond of friendship during his stay that I never felt with Darrol, and his time with us came to an end all too soon.

'Darrol's the luckiest man in the world,' he said, wrapping his arms around me at the airport. He seemed reluctant to let go.

I tried to lighten up the moment: 'Well, at least something in Australia was able to top Canada!'

*

My opinion was not sought regarding the decision for Willow to leave her mother's place and come to live with us full-time when she finished school at the end of the year. The sibling rivalry between Matt and Willow often reached crisis point, and Darrol's only way of dealing with it was to come down heavy on Matt. Having them both living with us and sharing a bedroom was going to be difficult. 'We are going to need a bigger property,' I told Darrol when he finally disscussed it with me.

We inspected a four-bedroom townhouse in Balgowlah. It had dreadful shag-pile carpet, but was very spacious with a large kitchen and family room, and a deck overlooking a park. It also had two toilets, separate from the bathrooms. Having sold the 'cubby' in Mosman and making a tidy profit on the purchase price in only two years, we didn't need to take out a mortgage to upgrade to this considerably larger property.

The Balgowlah house was settling just two weeks before Darrol and I were due to leave on a business trip to the US, Canada and England. I pushed myself to get unpacked so Matt would know where to find things. I cooked meals, dating and labelling them for the freezer. I went out to get a new toaster and saw a demo of the latest innovation in kitchen appliances – microwaves. They looked just the thing for defrosting and re-heating food. I bought one on the spot, showed Matt how to use it, and left him with enough meals in the freezer so that he wouldn't have to cook while we were away.

'Can I get Sammy from Mum's?' Matt asked, now that we had a place that would accommodate pets.

'Sure, it will be lovely to have a little dog around,' I said. I'd so missed not having any pets.

Manpower's Honolulu office had glorious views over Waikiki Beach and although the operation wasn't as slick and efficient as I was expecting, the management and staff were very hospitable and made us feel welcome. We took a daytrip to Maui which, after the initial shock, provided an experience of a lifetime when I realised the 'things' bumping into me in the surf were giant turtles.

The temperature dropped to 7°C in Vancouver. The chill at Peter's house was even more displeasing with two precocious children who ruled the roost and Peter's wife, Oriel, wearing a permanent scowl. We took Peter and Oriel out to dinner to the strains of his youngest daughter screaming the place down because she was being left at home.

It was a relief to be on our way to Milwaukee and Manpower's head office, which was the main purpose of our trip.

Bill 'Duke' Gallagher, picked us up from the airport. Bill was a giant of a man, bearing a strong resemblance to the actor John Wayne and sporting a smile that seemed to say, 'Howdy partner'. Bill looked after the franchise operations around the world and we'd spoken on the phone several times.

He took us straight to head office, the sprawling complex easily the size of a large shopping mall. Although this time pre-dated computer surveillance systems, head office was reminiscent of George Orwell's 'Big Brother', keeping tabs on every arm of the business. While it was exciting that we had access to the innovations that came from the multinational think-tank, I was also grateful for the distance between our small operation and the sometimes overbearing control Manpower HQ represented.

Jim Fromstein, a Vice President and brother of CEO Mitchell Fromstein, had been assigned to take care of us. On our first day we enjoyed an informal lunch before getting down to business in the boardroom. I'd never been in a room with so many tall handsome men in my life; it seemed that every executive at Manpower HQ was a Vice President. They showed a genuine curiosity about what we were doing to make the business work in Australia, given it was where they'd failed. As soon as I had started working with Darrol in 1977 I realised that the promotional material he had been using was out of sync with the Australian market.

Produced in the US in 1972 much of their publicity was dictated by Affirmative Action legislation in the US, which required they include images of black Americans. In Australia, the 'White Australia' immigration policies weren't fully dismantled until 1973 and images of black people, of any ethnicity, were not well received. In fact, any mass mail-out of the US Manpower brochures would, I imagined, have gone straight into the garbage bin. I'd refused to use this material and instead composed personalised letters of introduction to get my foot in the door. Not wanting to embarrass Darrol or the other executives present at the meeting, I accredited the introduction of the Job Prove initiative as the main component of the Australian company's sharp turnaround in recent times.

'Tell me, what's this Job Prove all about? It seems to be working, without affecting the core business,' Jim enquired. Manpower was marketed as a temporary help specialist and the US franchises had shied away from any connection to permanent placement agencies.

'In Australia, we have a much smaller market so we have to be able to offer permanent and temporary help solutions. Job Prove does this.' I went on to explain how I'd come up with the idea for structuring the program. The heads in the boardroom nodded approvingly.

'So you've modified the PPS to suit Australia?' Jim asked, using the acronym for the Predictable Performance System, developed in the US.

'Yes, it was necessary to make some modifications. The Australian market is resistant to anything that hints of being "made in the US". We are still a bit parochial in that way,' I said, being diplomatic by not mentioning that, as it was, the program was overkill.

The executives sitting around the table looked at each other in astonishment. I hadn't realised that franchisees in the US didn't have the luxury of tinkering with anything developed at Head Office.

'What are your thoughts on the PPS, Darrol?' Jim asked, realising that Darrol had been left out of the conversation.

Darrol looked awkward. He'd never shown the slightest interest in how the systems worked. Still, he seemed to be enjoying rubbing the noses of the Americans into it a bit, even if he wasn't up to speed.

'Kay handles all of that,' he said.

Thinking that I might like to go shopping, they assigned the wife of one of the senior executives to take me uptown. She thought I might be interested in clothes, but I told her I'd like to find a quality giftware store as I wanted to leave a memento of our gratitude to the people who'd made our visit so enjoyable. This left me with only half a day to go through the various departments at Manpower, ransacking the place like a pirate, filling boxes with the latest promotional material that would work for us with minimal modification, as well system updates, which I had shipped back to Australia.

Jim Fromstein was quite touched by the lovely Stuart Crystal paperweight I gave him. I also passed on a gift to his brother, Mitchell, whom it seemed was too busy to take time out of his day to even say hello to us, despite having travelled halfway around the world to meet him. It was a silver tray with a card that said, 'I hope this serves to remind you of your friends and associates at Manpower Australia.'

Nothing about Manpower UK impressed me at all, but one of our contacts in London was in-the-know and we scored two front-row tickets to the opening performance of Ronald Harwood's brilliant play *The Dresser*, starring Tom Courtenay in the role of Norman. It was breathtaking, and when the cast came out for the curtain call I was the only person in the packed house to get to my feet and give them a well-earned standing ovation. I think I even copped a wink from Tom Courtenay.

'Kay, that was so embarrassing. What you need to understand is that these are frequent theatregoers. They see this level of performance every night,' Darrol said, as we left the theatre.

'What bullshit, no one sees a performance of that calibre every night of the week. You Brits take this stiff upper lip nonsense too far.' The reviews for *The Dresser* were that it was the most outstanding production to hit the West End in years.

When we were planning our trip to the UK, we had obtained the AAA Road Map and prepared a route to follow. Although Darrol had lived in England for the first seventeen years of his life, he'd never had the opportunity to see much of it, and this was his first trip back in over twenty years. There were places of special significance to me as well. I particularly wanted to go up to the Lake District. Ever since I was at school I'd loved poetry and the way simple words could be used to express big feelings. From the opening line of William Wordsworth's 'Daffodils', 'I wandered lonely as a cloud', I was captivated. The thought of retracing the footsteps of this great thinker filled me with awe.

It was mid-summer and still twilight when we pulled up at the Old Bakehouse in Colyton, a medieval village in Devon. I wanted to look around before dark, because I knew that bright and early next morning Darrol would have the car packed ready for another mad dash along the motorway. Meandering down a cobbled lane the unmistakable fragrance of roses flooded my senses. Following my nose I stood on a ledge and peered over the hedgerow of a delightful thatched-roof cottage with blood-red blooms, as big as saucers, climbing up the whitewashed walls.

'Oh my, look at those roses,' I said to Darrol as I climbed up onto the hedgerow to get a better look.

'You're Australian,' a female voice on the other side of the hedgerow said.

'Is my accent so obvious?' I chuckled.

'Yes, I'm afraid so,' she smiled, slipping her hand out of the gardening glove. 'I'm Kay Booth, how do you do?'

Kay invited us into her cottage for some refreshments and explained that her keen ear for the Aussie accent came during World War II when her husband was sent to a makeshift military hospital at The Old Mill, a property in the Southern Highlands of New South Wales. (By a strange coincidence it had also been Jack Gazzard's family home!) As it turned out, this brief encounter with Kay was one of the few highlights of the trip. She and I communicated by snail mail for many years afterwards; when her letters stopped coming I presumed she must have passed away.

The next day we drove non-stop to Hereford, pausing briefly for a quick cup of tea at the Royal George Inn at Lyonshall where Darrol's father had his last beer. From there we called in to see Darrol's cousin, Lenny, who was still trying to scratch a living out of the rundown family farm, where Darrol's family had lived before settling in Australia.

It wasn't hard to imagine how tough things must have been for Darrol's mother, a widow left destitute with three boys, trudging around in the bog of that miserable place, which in her day wouldn't have had electricity or a proper bathroom or sanitation.

When Lenny invited us in for tea the stench almost bowled me over, reminding me of one of my grandmother's idioms that 'soap's cheap and water's free'.

Thick black soot, the residue of decades of industry in the Colne

Valley, still clung to the dwellings in the little town of Marsden, where Darrol was born. Aunty Ivy, a born-and-bred Marsden lass on his mother's side, was a natural storyteller. She had me in fits of laughter reminiscing about Darrol's childhood, which was a far cry from the tales of dire hardship he liked to tell. It was 'our Darrol' this and 'our Darrol' that; he was definitely the favoured son.

Darrol went off to get some milk and Aunty Ivy broke down as she told me that Darrol's mother, 'our Annie', didn't have a stone to mark her grave, which was a shameful neglect in a small town, akin to a potter's field burial. While Darrol may not have been in a financial position at the time of his mother's death to return her ashes to England, a duty falling to a cousin by marriage, he was able to afford a headstone to be put on her grave. The fact that he hadn't done so was made all the worse for knowing how much his mother had adored him, and the hardships she had endured.

As we drove out of Marsden, without visiting a stonemason, I told Darrol that as poor as my family were we always respected the dead.

After a brief stopover in Blackpool to visit some of Darrol's other aunts we headed off to Cumbria and the Lake District. We visited Dove Cottage in Grasmere, then Cockermouth, the birthplace of William Wordsworth, where I bought a cookbook that many years later would become my 'bible' for a restaurant I would open.

We broke the trip home with a few days in Hong Kong. On the top of my shopping list was an Oriental carpet. It took me more than an hour to haggle with the trader at the Eastern Trading Company, for what Darrol thought was an extravagant and unnecessary purchase. 'You're paying for it,' he said, leaving the shop.

Much to his father's surprise Matt had taken very good care of himself, the house and the dog while we were away, but the moment I walked through the door at Manpower the next morning I sensed something wasn't right. Moira, the service supervisor, my most trusted employee, looked agitated and asked to see me in my office. She didn't hold back when she told me how disappointed she was that some of the staff had taken advantage of our absence.

'Also, you need to speak to Bryce about playing tricks on the phone.'

'What kind of tricks?'

'He calls with a stutter and pretends to be a client with an order. He wasted ten minutes of my time with that nonsense and thought it was a great joke.'

Darrol had hired Bryce to manage the Parramatta office, which was primarily servicing industrial clients. Business had picked up, with Bryce making regular sales calls, and Darrol seemed to want to put me and Bryce in competition with each other. There was no comparison between the office servicing and industrial work, which was mostly unskilled labour, and it annoyed me having to state the obvious.

'Bryce wants to introduce the office servicing programs into Parramatta,' Darrol informed me one morning.

'Does he? That would mean I'd have to stop what I'm doing to train him, and I don't have time to do that right now.'

The truth was I felt Bryce had a hidden agenda, and until I discovered what it was, he wasn't getting his hands on anything I'd developed.

'Perhaps you're afraid that he'll outdo you.'

I laughed out loud. 'It's annoying enough that you're attempting to put the branches in competition with each other, but to attempt that between Bryce and me is a silly game; neither of you can win.'

'If I say he can have the programs, he can have them,' Darrol said, trying to pull rank on me.

Even though we'd been living together for over three years

at this stage, and I'd already been appointed a director of the company, in the office I still referred to Darrol as 'Mr Norman'. He didn't realise that I did this with a tongue-in-cheek attitude, but even so it was a mistake on my part; he really did believe I felt subordinate to him.

'Darrol, let's get something clear. I work with you, not for you. And be warned, Bryce has an agenda,' I added, walking away.

After that, I never addressed Darrol as Mr Norman again.

While I was pondering how to out-manoeuvre Bryce, I took a call from a man with a stutter.

'Bryce cut it out, this is not funny,' I snapped.

'B-B-B-Bryce?'

'Stop it, Bryce!'

The stutter was pronounced, and the tone definitely angry, but I understood well enough when the man said, 'My name is John, I'm the chief accountant with Brambles and you've just lost an account.'

'I apologise,' I started to say, but he hung up before I could finish.

Flushed with anger and embarrassment I called Bryce to have it out with him. 'You're a clown, and when I discover what your agenda is, you are gone.'

'Come on Kay, don't be like that, it was all in good fun,' he said, in a mocking tone.

'That's Mrs Norman to you. And don't push your luck. If it comes to a real contest you'll lose,' I said, hanging up the phone.

Curiosity caused me to check Bryce's employee records. What I discovered had the potential to cause a serious blowout, so I decided to wait until Darrol and I got home that night to discuss what I'd learned.

'He's a married man,' Darrol said when I asked him why he was paying Bryce a salary on par with mine and giving him full use of a company vehicle, while I was getting around on public transport.

'What's that got to do with anything? I'm a married woman

and my workload and responsibilities far exceed Bryce's,' I argued, infuriated that Darrol wouldn't acknowledge the double standard.

'You also have the privilege of being my wife.'

I burst out laughing. 'I don't want privileges, fairness will do me. I want my salary increased to match yours and I want shares in this company.'

The shouting would've been heard two streets away.

'This is my company. I lost a fucking house to keep it!'

'All the company had at that time was potential. I've had to fight you every step of the way to get us to where we are now. If I don't get the recognition I deserve, I'm going to resign and see how far you get without me!' I threatened.

With that, I packed a bag and booked myself into the Manly Pacific Hotel. The next day, Darrol came to the hotel and we thrashed it out. He agreed to increase my salary and promised to make me a shareholder. I didn't specify how many shares; I left that up to him. I suppose I wanted him to put a value on the contribution I'd been making to the success of the company, without my having to ask. Not insisting to have this documented was another bad decision and one that would cost me dearly down the track.

In the months that followed the pressures at home and work became a juggling act and I battled to keep all the balls in the air. We'd expanded to take the first floor at our Hunter Street location in the city and I'd convinced Darrol that we needed to completely refurbish both offices.

'We ought to ban smoking in the office,' I said, screwing my face in disgust as we scrubbed the brown sludge of nicotine residue from the walls before repainting.

Darrol disliked smoking as much as I did, and agreed. Jan, a chain-smoker, wasn't happy and resigned. As this ban came into effect some years before smoking bans were legislated, it had to be made very clear at the interview for permanent employees that an infringement of this policy would result in dismissal, and they had to sign an agreement to this effect. Ashtrays were removed and we had to fashion our own 'No Smoking' signs for applicants. Pretty soon absenteeism, due to illness, saw a sharp decline.

By the time I had proof of what Bryce was up to, it was too late. He'd set up his own employment agency in the Parramatta area taking our major account, which was turning over close to a million dollars, along with all the temporary employees with experience at the plant.

Giving Bryce free reign with too much emphasis on one major account was risky, but Darrol wouldn't listen. Bryce boldly reproduced timesheets and other operational material that was so similar to ours it may have breached Manpower copyright. For a moment I thought we had him.

'Why don't you contact the US and let them know what he's done? Surely they won't be passive to him stealing their intellectual property?'

'They won't do anything. The copyright doesn't extend to Australia.'

'Then why are we paying franchising fees if we're open to anyone just taking everything they want?'

Devastated by Bryce's betrayal, Darrol became so despondent he said he was going to close the Parramatta office altogether. We had two loyal employees, Jenny and Robyn, who'd been working with us since before Bryce joined the company and were quite capable of holding things together until we worked out a plan for recovery.

Darrol had become accustomed to the role of managing director, driving around in his flash car. There was no way he was going to roll up his sleeves and get out in the field trying to drum up business. However, the thought that Bryce might walk away unchallenged really enraged me. I told Darrol that there was no sense in tossing the baby out with the bath water. I could transfer Kerry Mackey and with my help we could put the Parramatta office back on the map.

'Kerry doesn't have the experience to deal with industrial clients,' Darrol argued. It was typical of Darrol to presume that a woman would be out of her depth dealing with male clients and taking on management responsibilities.

'Nonsense, Kerry deals with industrial clients every day in the city office.'

Kerry Mackey was a tiny little woman with a sweet smile and gentle nature, but she was also tough and ambitious. I knew she could handle the job. What she didn't know could be taught – and Kerry was a fast learner.

Kerry jumped at the chance to work closer to home and help me rebuild the Parramatta office. To make things even more convenient for her, I arranged for her to have the company car Bryce had been using.

At this stage I had no idea how I was going to manage my workload. In addition to being solely responsible for hiring, training and supervising the staff, and monitoring every aspect of the Office Service division, I personally supervised several major accounts, including Citicorp (formerly known as AGC) whose business I'd reactivated in the first month I joined Manpower and which by this time generated over a million dollars in revenue. Even though I was almost staggering under the weight of working ten-hour days, and still taking care of our home, I was determined that Bryce would know it was 'game on'.

*

As I still didn't have my own vehicle, the first day I went out to the Parramatta office I took the red rattler from Wynyard. I hadn't been on a train since the day I'd left the western suburbs fourteen years earlier: a teenager with a suitcase, a sewing machine and a ticket to nowhere. Now I was a woman with a new life, far from anything I'd have imagined possible. Still, I felt my teeth clench as the train rumbled over the bridge at Lidcombe, where I'd last spoken with John McNorton, pleading with him to let me see Adam. The train stopped at Granville Station, almost in front of the kiosk where I used to work and where, in the car park late one night, a really bad decision turned my whole world upside down. The closer we got to Parramatta, the more anxious I became. My pulse was racing by the time the train stopped. *What if I bump into someone who recognises me? What if I bump into Mrs McNorton and Adam, and have to walk right past them?* I took a deep breath and scurried across the road with my face tucked into my chest.

Manpower's Paramatta office, based in Argyle Street, was accessed via a filthy flight of stairs that patrons from the pub next door used as a urinal. Jenny and Robyn did their best to cheer the place up, with flowers and drawings from their children and grandchildren pinned to the walls, but it was like putting lipstick on a pig.

'Bryce managed alright,' Darrol smirked, when I returned later that evening and told him I didn't know how we kept staff nor did any business out of that office.

'We can't do what I have in mind in that rat hole, we need to relocate.'

'We're in a recession in case you haven't noticed,' Darrol said, as if he thought he was telling me something I didn't know.

'Are we? I am too busy to notice.'

The recession gave us some leverage to score a spacious office in Macquarie Street, a perfect location at a reasonable rent. We gutted the place and brought it up to a standard comparable with the city offices. Kerry exceeded all expectations and we hit the ground running. Before long we needed to hire and train more staff to cope with the new business and I was stretched, almost to breaking point, but with the enormous satisfaction of blocking Bryce's every move.

15

Seeing purple

Willow had moved in with us after she finished Year 10, and the squabbling between her and Matt started on day one and didn't let up. Around and around they went like caged cats.

As I had done with Matt, I helped Willow to get her first job as a dental receptionist in Mosman. She'd only been there a short while when she brought her new boyfriend home to meet us. He was clearly an adult and Willow was barely sixteen. I knew that he wasn't going to be content with holding her hand for too long and I broached the subject with Willow.

'We've already done it,' she told me.

Willow hadn't had any instruction about protecting herself, and it seemed pointless and perhaps hypocritical of me to preach abstinence. 'We'd better get you a prescription for the Pill,' I said. 'And don't worry, I won't tell your father.'

One Friday night, Darrol and I were going out for a casual meal and Matt, who'd overcome much of his shyness, decided to join us. Willow was going to a friend's place for a sleepover and we'd brought her home a barbecue chicken with all the trimmings to have before she left. When we got home she'd gone, leaving a mess in the kitchen. Darrol was grumbling as he started to clean up.

'Not so fast,' I said, stepping between him and the sink. 'What's good for one is good for the other,' I insisted, nudging him out of the way.

Matt smiled. 'You're gonna do it. Aren't you?'

Matt and I had never discussed the chicken bone incident at Mosman but he would have realised it was my doing. He started jumping around like Rumpelstiltskin, picking up all the rubbish and crockery. He fussed about like a stage manager in Willow's room, trying to gauge where her bum would land for optimum impact.

'What's the matter with you?' Willow asked when she heard Matt chuckling to himself at dinner the next evening.

'Nothing, I just thought of something funny,' he said, tongue in cheek.

That night Willow was the last to go to bed. Unlike Matt, she made a terrible racket as she cleaned up the mess. She turned the washing machine on after midnight to make her point. To make mine, I got out of bed and turned it off.

Not long after this incident Willow started to run a bit wild and do things that were not age-appropriate. Although she trusted me enough to confide in me, she was behaving recklessly, putting her health and safety at risk. I put my foot down and told her if she didn't smarten up I'd tell her father. Then, without discussing it with me, Darrol told me that Willow was going back to live with her mother. I had no idea what was said between them, but Darrol's increasing hostility towards me was evident. Not wanting to betray Willow's confidence I didn't try to explain myself to Darrol.

Peace returned to the house but my inner turmoil was becoming much harder to ignore. The nose bleeds were frequent, the ugly weeping herpes on my chin had become a permanent fixture and my fingernails looked like gnawed bones. Materially I had everything I could have wished for but none of it brought me any joy. It was like climbing a mountain, one treacherous cliff face at a time, without ever reaching the summit or enjoying the view. For almost fifteen years I'd worked myself to breaking point, clinging to the slimmest thread of hope that I'd ever see the day when I could go back and be someone my son might be proud of. Even though I'd achieved that goal in a material sense I still felt insecure; after all, I had no idea what my son had been told to explain my absence.

Unexpectedly I reached a turning point one night when I invited our next door neighbours for dinner. John had an intelligent and enquiring mind and Cynthia was a hilarious snob. It would be a few years before Roy Clarke's highly amusing, fictitious character, Hyacinth Bucket, pronounced 'bouquet', would entertain us in the long running series *Keeping Up Appearances*, and when it did I almost fell over laughing. Cynthia was a dead ringer for Patricia Routledge, and I wondered if Roy Clarke and Cynthia had ever met.

'What do you think about karma?' John asked.

John looked surprised when I told him that I thought karma was the direct consequence of making good or bad decisions, even having good or bad thoughts. This led to a discussion about meditation. When I mentioned that I was having trouble managing stress, John recommended a hypnotherapist in the city. The session with the hypnotherapist was useful insofar as I came away with some relaxation exercises. Practising meditation every day helped, but seemed to cause another problem. During each session it felt like I had someone with me but I couldn't see them. It wasn't the first time in my life that I'd experienced this. When I was a child, no matter how grim things became, I never felt completely alone and used to talk to my guardian angel as if she were real, because to me, she was. I'd make deals and promise to do certain things if she helped me. Miraculously it seemed, more often than not, help came. But by the time I was eighteen I'd stopped praying to ethereal beings with gossamer wings.

The next time we met I asked John if he'd ever felt that he was being followed by something or someone he couldn't see. He gave me a book called *Reaching for the Other Side* by Australian author Dawn Hill. Once I started reading it I simply couldn't put it down. At the back of the book was a recommended reading list and the address of the Society for Psychical Research, which was close to our office at Wynyard. One lunch hour I decided to check it out.

'Hello,' I said, introducing myself and trying not to react to the receptionist's arresting appearance. Everything she was wearing was purple. Her glasses were purple, she was knitting a purple jumper, the pens and accessories on her desk were purple, and her hair was dyed purple. Even her lipstick and nail polish were purple, and I almost laughed out loud when she introduced herself as Violet. From my reading I'd learned that purple was the highest vibratory colour associated with spiritual attainment. Perhaps by drenching herself in varying shades of purple, Violet was hoping to fast-track her journey to divine enlightenment.

'Oh, you have someone with you,' Violet said, wistfully. 'She's trying to get in touch with you.'

'So it's a woman? Can you see her?'

'No, I'm not clairvoyant, but I can sense that you have someone with you.'

Violet gave me the address of the Spiritualist Church in Chatswood, and told me to pick a flower for the reading.

'I'd like to come with you,' Darrol said, when I told him that I was going to check it out. This didn't surprise me. His aunts in Blackpool and also a cousin in Australia were Spiritualists.

We arrived early at a small, nondescript building in a suburban street in Chatswood. It was going to be a 'flower reading', so I placed my flower onto the stage for the psychic medium. The service started with some Christian hymns and prayers and I was losing interest fast. Then the medium, a man dressed in black and wearing a massive cross on the end of a chain around his neck, started to read the flowers. He picked up my flower.

'You have someone with you. She is trying to reach you.' He looked around the room for a taker. 'This person was very close to you, she wants to get in touch with you.'

Trying to maintain a poker face I didn't respond. For all I knew, Violet could have clued the medium up to keep an eye out for me. Darrol and I stayed behind for a cup of tea and a biscuit after the service. A diminutive woman, dressed in various shades of pink and purple, approached me. There was a strange beauty about her that reminded me of Bette Davis in *What Ever Happened to Baby Jane*.

'Hello, I'm Patricia; I have a closed healing circle in Manly, would you like to join us?' she smiled, cocking her head to one side, like an inquisitive puppy.

Mindful that we looked affluent and had arrived in a gold Mercedes, I was wary of a scam, but prepared to stay receptive and follow this adventure to see where it took me.

We arrived at Patricia's flat a few minutes early. She giggled and flirted with Darrol and showed us through her photo album. She'd been quite a stunner in her day, a crowned beauty queen in the UK, but that had been some time ago. As the evening progressed I decided that the whole scene was too theatrical for me to take seriously.

'Wait!' Patricia said, as she was about to close the circle. 'There's someone here for Kay. She's been trying to reach her.'

I shot a look at Darrol. *This will be interesting.*

Patricia started giving me symbols.

'She says she's in a beautiful garden and that you will know what that means.' I shook my head. 'Sorry, that means nothing to me.'

'She's handing you lavender.'

I was losing patience. 'Unless she can give you a name, I am afraid I have no idea who this spirit is.'

Patricia's head started to gyrate. *Here we go.* I was expecting her to fake an out-of-body, head-spinning performance that would put Linda Blair of the *Exorcist* to shame.

'Her name is Daphne,' Patricia said, her chin falling sharply forward onto her chest, as though someone had cuffed the back of her head.

'Did I hear her say Daphne?' I asked, shocked. I looked across to Darrol, who'd turned quite pale. He nodded.

'She's been trying to reach you,' Patricia repeated. 'She said that you will be able to connect with her now.'

The first thing I did when I got home was go to the telephone book. Aunty Daphne and Uncle Jack's phone number was no longer listed. Uncle Stan was still listed in Wentworthville and Uncle Les was still at Cabramatta. By this time it was after midnight. I'd have to wait until I could make some phone calls.

The next day I locked my office door so I wouldn't be disturbed. After several false starts I lunged at the phone and dialled Uncle Stan's number. It rang out. I dialled Uncle Les's number and his wife, Shirl, picked up almost immediately.

'Hello, Shirl. This is Katie'

'Katie who?'

'Phyllis's daughter.'

'Oh my God! We thought you were dead. How've you been, dear?' she asked.

How have you been, dear? Sixteen years had passed since we had last spoken and on that occasion she told me I'd only be welcome in their home if I gave up my son for adoption.

'Shirl, I'm trying to reach Aunty Daphne but they're not in the phone book.'

'Oh dear, Daphne died.'

I've no idea if I was even polite to Shirl before hanging up the phone. Stunned by this revelation, I went into Darrol's office.

'Aunty Daphne is dead.'

All we could do was stare at each other.

We had a quiet room at home with a leafy outlook across the park where I used to meditate. It was still light outside when I lay back in the recliner. I was drifting into a void that gradually grew darker, when suddenly a burst of bright light seemed to explode in my head, jarring me into an upright position. I opened my eyes, expecting to find Matt looking startled that he had disturbed me by turning the light on. The room was dark. Then I felt a definite presence and I didn't dare move. My heart was thumping as my eyes adjusted to the dim light. I was alone. Or at least there was no other person in the room.

'It's me Katie,' I heard Daphne's voice as clearly as if she was standing right next to me. In my mind's eye I could see her lovely face, just as I'd remembered her before the beatings got worse. Cradled in her arms was a huge bunch of lavender, her signature fragrance that I'd forgotten with the passing of time.

The next day I called Uncle Stan's place and Aunty Shirley answered.

'Hello, Aunty Shirley, this is Katie. How are you?'

'We're well, love,' she said, as if we had only spoken yesterday.

Aunty Shirley passed the phone to Uncle Stan. 'Hello, love, we thought you were dead,' he said.

'Hello, Uncle Stan, it's good to hear your voice again. I'm very sorry to hear that Aunty Daphne has gone.'

'Yes, she went a week before my birthday; knocked down by a car, she was. Lucky Mamma was already gone; I don't think she could've taken Daphne going so soon after Phyllis. Jack McCarthy's gone, too.'

In a few short sentences I learned that as well as Aunty Daphne having passed, my mother, grandmother and Uncle Jack, Aunty Daphne's husband who'd been a key figure in my childhood, were also gone. This would deny me the chance to sit with them as adults and try to get some answers to questions, like who was my father? Even though I hadn't spoken to anyone in my family for a long time I still harboured the idea that one day we would be reconciled. As I tried to digest the enormity of this news I wasn't paying full attention to what Uncle Stan was saying, until I heard him mention Adam.

'I've kept all the newspaper clippings of Adam's football,' Uncle Stan went on. 'I used to send cards for his birthday, but I never got any reply, so I stopped.' Uncle Stan had adored Adam. It was so typical of him to clip the articles from the paper and save them. After filling Uncle Stan in on aspects of my life, I gave him my phone number and thanked him for all he had done for me.

During the call I managed to hold my composure, but afterwards I was reeling to hear news of my son. Uncle Stan had assumed that I knew something of Adam's life, and of his football career, but I knew nothing. All I had was the bond we shared from the moment I knew he'd been conceived, a few photographs, and an unshake- able belief that we would one day be reunited. I went over and over the conversation in my mind, recalling the warmth in Uncle Stan's voice, especially when he spoke of Adam. For all these years I hadn't contacted Uncle Stan, because John McNorton told me he wanted nothing to do with me. To learn that Uncle Stan had tried to maintain contact with Adam, but was shut out, filled me with sadness. It also came as quite a surprise to hear that Mamma, my grandmother, had passed very recently. The last time I'd seen Mamma she was in Dubbo Base Hospital with kidney failure and wasn't expected to live. Adam was about two months old and John McNorton had driven us out to see her. I wanted to make peace with her before it was too late and show her Adam, her first great-grandchild. She looked frail, straining her neck to see him. 'He's a beautiful boy,' she said, and then lay back and closed her eyes. It hurt to learn that she lived for another sixteen years and never even tried to contact me, or Adam.

'It's time, dear.'

This was the next message from Aunty Daphne. I knew what she meant. We went to Patricia's circle one last time and I told her about my visits from Aunty Daphne, and thanked her for her guidance. Mediums like feedback.

'You'll have a child. She'll be a Gemini with raven hair, blue eyes and skin like Snow White,' Patricia told me as we were leaving.

'What a lovely prediction. I hope you really are psychic, Patricia,' I teased.

16

'Hello, Mum'

'Hello, Mrs McNorton, this is Kay.'

'We were wondering when we'd hear from you,' she said, not sounding the least bit surprised.

When I was married to her son, John, I had called Mrs McNorton 'Mum', but now I wanted to keep things formal and polite.

'Mrs McNorton, I'm calling to see whether or not Adam is ready for me to make contact with him.'

'I suppose so, if he wants to,' she said.

She told me that John had never remarried and that he and Adam were living with her.

'I'll send Adam a letter to start with, and see how he feels,' I told her.

My Darling Adam, my trembling hand hovered over the blank page as I tried to find the right words.

Over the years I'd written hundreds of business letters to introduce myself and get a foot in the door. This letter to Adam represented the biggest challenge of my life. For hours I sat at my desk with Adam's photographs propped up in front of me, as page after page was scrunched up and tossed into the bin.

Then I heard Aunty Daphne's voice in my head: *Speak from your heart Katie, your boy will remember the love you have for him.* From that point I was able to find the words to convey how much he meant to me and how I hoped that we could be reunited. I closed the letter by telling Adam I'd call him at 4 p.m. on a certain day and if he wished to speak to me I would like that very much. When the day and hour arrived when I was to make the call, I was terrified, not knowing if my son would pick up the phone or even want to talk to me. The phone rang and was picked up on the first ring.

'Hello, Mum,' he said, before he'd even heard my voice.

'Hello, Adam,' I said, hoping he could feel my smile and sense how overjoyed I was to be talking with him. 'I have missed you, my darling. Have you been happy?'

'I've missed you. Yeah, I've been alright.'

My heart was beating out of my chest. He couldn't see the tears streaming down my face but I didn't want to completely break down and embarrass him. I paused and took several deep breaths before I tried to speak again.

'Would you like to see me?'

'Yes, I would.'

Adam had been just under two years old, with few words in his vocabulary, the last time I had seen him. Now, it was almost impossible to take in that we were having a conversation. He told me that he was finishing school in a couple of weeks and we arranged for me to go to his place on the day school broke up.

After we hung up, I couldn't stop crying. They weren't tears of sorrow, as they had been for so many years, but rather pure joy, the kind that fall in torrents when you hold your newborn for the first time.

It was disappointing, although I really ought not to have been surprised, that Darrol wasn't the least bit interested in any of this. In the five years we'd been together, during which I'd helped to raise his children, Darrol had never asked if I wanted to make contact with Adam, or any other member of my family for that matter. There were times when it was difficult not to feel resentment. I told him that I was going to need to borrow his car.

'What do you need the car for?' he asked, irritably, as if he hadn't heard a word I'd said about going to see Adam.

'I'm not catching two buses and a train to Parramatta and back, that's why I need the car.'

That night I fell asleep to the sound of Adam's sweet voice saying, 'Hello, Mum,' over and over, like a soft and soothing lullaby.

Finally, the day arrived and I was careful not to overdress. Darrol's car would make all the statement I needed to show the McNortons how much things had changed for me. I'd planned to arrive early to allow for a private chat with Adam's grandmother. On the way I stopped to get her and John a small gift. She liked flowers, and as I recalled, John liked a drink.

'Hello, Mrs McNorton.'

'Hello, Kay. It's lovely,' she said, taking the potted cyclamen. Coming face to face after fourteen years was awkward for us both. When I enquired after Harry, her husband, she told me he'd passed away when Adam was very young.

'What a pity, Harry adored Adam. How's life been for Adam?' I asked.

'He likes the girls, but he doesn't like school,' she said. 'He's an angry boy. He almost ripped the back door off its hinges one day.'

'I guess he had a lot to be angry about, not having his mother.'

This made her bridle. 'I was only fifty-four when you deserted Adam; you have no idea what it was like.'

We stared each other down while I collected my thoughts. 'Please don't try to rewrite history to suit. I never deserted Adam,' I said.

Just then, Adam came crashing through the door, as boys do. He dropped his bag. I stood up and opened my arms wide. He was almost running as he came straight over to where I was standing and put his arms around me.

'Hello, Mum,' he said, kissing me and holding me tight.

'Hello, my darling,' I said, pressing my face against his.

For several moments we just held onto each other, trembling slightly, our hearts beating against each other. The sheer relief of holding my son again and breathing in his unique scent, washed away years of pain and anguish. I knew that Adam was feeling it, too. He turned to his grandmother and said, 'My mother thinks I am the most beautiful boy in the whole wide world.'

Those were the last words I had said to him on the night I left, when he was only twenty months old. I was reminded of Haig Masters' comment about Adam and I having a special bond and how everything that happens to us remains stored in our body.

Not long after, John arrived home from work.

'Hello, Kay. Nice car,' he said.

'Thank you, but it's my husband's,' I said, holding out the bottle of vintage port.

'I don't drink or smoke these days,' he said, declining to take the bottle.

'Take it anyway. It's coming up to Christmas. I'm sure someone will enjoy it.'

John and his mother were both looking very uncomfortable and from that point it wasn't possible to have the kind of conversation with Adam I so longed for. As Adam walked me to the car he told me that he was going to try out for the New South Wales Rugby team. He asked if I would come to some of the matches.

'I wouldn't miss them.'

I told him that Matt and Willow were both looking forward to meeting him.

'You are the most beautiful boy in the whole wide world,' I said, hugging him one more time before I got into the car.

'I love you, Mum,' he said, leaning through the window to give me a kiss.

'I love you too, my darling,' I said, before driving away.

I looked through the rear-view mirror. He was still waving when I turned the corner. I was on autopilot, which was just as well, because I could hardly see the road ahead for the tears that kept flowing. My mind flashed back to the months before he was born. He'd kick to make his presence felt, and I'd rub my tummy reassuringly. When he was a toddler, in winter we'd snuggle up together under blankets to keep warm in a house that had no heating. Taking baths together, massaging his head, singing him to sleep – so many precious memories that for fourteen years had preserved my sanity until Adam and I could see this day.

That night, Darrol was more interested in what was for dinner than anything that had happened for me on one of the most momentous days of my life.

Not wanting to give the impression that I was attempting to buy Adam's affection, I held back on lavishing him with presents at Christmas and suggested that we meet in the New Year. We could celebrate his sixteenth birthday together, and I planned to do it in style.

To mark the occasion of us coming back together, I'd taken the engagement and wedding rings John had given me to a jeweller and had them refashioned into a dress ring made for Adam's little finger.

We met at the Summit Restaurant in the city, a few weeks after Christmas. Adam was impressed with the view. A photographer came to the table and I asked Adam if we could have a photo taken together. His tentative smile and clenched fists indicated that he wasn't comfortable.

'What's wrong?' I asked, reaching across the table to take his hand after several long silences.

He pulled back. 'How could you just go away and have two children and leave me behind?' he choked, as if this question was stuck in his craw and he needed to spit it out.

'I don't have any other children,' I said. 'Where did you get such an idea?'

'Gran told me that you had run away with a man and had more kids.'

'Adam, that isn't true. I don't have any other children. I never wanted any children until I got you back.'

My heart was breaking to learn that history was repeating itself and Adam had grown up believing that his mother didn't want him. When I was five years old my grandmother had told me that my mother had threatened to kill me by throwing me over a balcony. Throughout my childhood the horror of this played over in my mind. *What was so awful about me that my mother wanted me dead?* I had eventually asked Aunty Daphne, who was there the night my mother left. According to her, my grandmother was trying to stop Phyllis from taking me and standing guard over the cot. Phyllis pushed her aside and said, 'I'd throw her over the balcony before I'd let you have her.' Aunty Daphne stepped in and carried me from the room. The next day my mother was gone.

Biting my lip and fighting back tears I listened as Adam continued. He'd been told that his father had come home from work to find him alone in the house, hungry, crying and covered in his own excrement, and that I'd run away to Queensland and had two children by another man.

'How old were you when Gran told you that?' I queried, in disbelief.

'About eight. I found a picture of you and kept it under my pillow every night.'

It was several moments before I could even speak. Remembering what it had been like for me as a child to be told my mother didn't want me, I told Adam the truth about the night I left him, and how I had put him to bed and tucked him in with his panda bear. Although he was clearly conflicted by the variance in the stories, I could see that he wanted to believe me.

'This isn't a Christmas gift, it's a welcome back, my darling. It's made with the diamond and gold from the rings your father gave me. I hope you like it,' I said, handing him the box.

It was a perfect fit.

'It's really nice, thank you,' he said, fiddling with the ring on his finger before leaning across the table to kiss me.

The next day I called Mrs McNorton to arrange a time to see her when neither John nor Adam would be at home. 'I need to see you as soon as possible,' I said.

Mindful that Mrs McNorton was an elderly lady I was nevertheless determined to get to the bottom of why she had told Adam such a terrible lie. I declined the offer of tea and got straight to the point. I told her exactly what Adam had told me.

'Did you tell Adam that story?'

'Yes, I did,' she said, bursting into tears.

'So you just made it up?'

'No, Sandy Andersen told me.'

That didn't make sense. When I was married to John, Mrs McNorton didn't even know my friend Sandy. That's when it dawned on me that Michael, Sandy's husband, must have made good on his threat. Michael had forced himself on me when I was barely fourteen and was living on the charity of my neighbours, the Andersens. When Michael got what he wanted from me he turned his attention to Sandy. Sandy soon fell pregnant and she and Michael were married. A couple of years later, after I had given birth to Adam, Michael discovered where I was living and working. He was waiting for me after work late one night and I foolishly got into his car, 'just to talk'. He forced himself on me again. About a week later he had called at the house during the day and threatened me – if I didn't run away with him to Queensland he'd tell my husband that he 'fucked me'. Not expecting anyone to believe me, the shame that this would bring upon me was terrifying, causing me to panic. Perhaps when Michael discovered I'd gone, he had tried to make sure the McNortons would never take me back, and told Sandy what he'd been planning. She in turn must have told the McNortons Michael's distorted version of events.

The mention of Sandy's name made sense of something else Adam had said. When I was still married to John, I had no clue about post-natal depression, and had to get through it on my own. I'd told Sandy about the dreadful day when I just couldn't get out of bed, and when I finally did, I had gone to Adam's room to find he was covered in his own shit. I could see how the stories of what Michael had been planning and something I had told Sandy might get mixed up in the mind of an eight year old. But where this story was completely wrong was that Adam had been told I'd abandoned him, and that I'd left him alone in the house.

'Why would you tell Adam such a dreadful story, when you must have known the truth?' I asked, ignoring her tears.

'Adam was a difficult child and he was playing up one day and I was angry.'

'He was eight years old. Surely John told you what happened the night I left?'

She told me that John told her nothing.

It was time to put an end to this charade. I reminded Mrs McNorton about the police officers who had come to the Lidcombe flat two weeks after I left John. She knew I'd left Adam with his father; she also knew the game was up and broke down.

'You don't know what it was like living with Adam. He's violent and difficult to handle. He breaks things,' she said, as if any of that could justify poisoning the mind of an eight year old against his mother.

At this point I reminded Mrs McNorton of what my situation was at the time. I had been a completely traumatised sixteen year old, with a newborn, isolated in a place not fit for a dog, unable to even put decent clothes on our backs. In desperation, I got a job working from 10 p.m. until 2 a.m., serving coffee and tea on Granville Station.

'I was a child with a child, for pity's sake. Would you have allowed that to happen to your own daughter?'

'I'm sorry,' she said, breaking down again.

'It's Adam you need to apologise to.'

'What about what you did to Sandy Andersen?' she asked, appearing to regain her composure and insinuating that I had tried to break up Sandy's marriage to Michael.

'I didn't do anything to Sandy, but I could have run away with her husband and taken Adam with me if I'd wanted to live with a rapist.'

'Rapist?' she scoffed.

'Yes, I knew at the time that's what you'd say.'

Mrs McNorton went to her grave without apologising to Adam or admitting the truth to him. The effect of her lies would be revisited upon my son and me for decades to come.

17

Family reunion

'We haven't had sex for weeks,' Darrol protested when I showed no interest in getting amorous on a wooden slat-bed with a paper-thin mattress in a room reeking of stale tobacco in the hotel we were staying in. The decision to take the trip to Queensland had been arranged at short notice. I was almost dead on my feet and Darrol hadn't needed much convincing that we both could do with a week away. At the time, Noosa had seemed like the perfect place to recharge.

'It was cheap,' he protested, when I asked him what possessed him to book us into such a dive. I reluctantly agreed to have sex, but made no effort to pretend I was enjoying it. The next morning, I realised I'd forgotten to take the Pill for three days.

It wasn't unusual for my period to be late, but when I still hadn't had a show for six weeks I made an appointment to see my doctor.

After the examination, he smiled. 'Your baby is due on or around 23 May.'

'I'm pregnant?' I asked, to make sure I wasn't imagining things. For several moments I was totally speechless.

'I trust this is good news?' the doctor asked, gently.

'Yes, it is the most wonderful news,' I replied, feeling the smile stretching across my face as the news sunk in.

The circumstances were vastly different from the first time I had heard similar words but the effect was the same. I felt an instant connection between me and my child. I couldn't wait to tell someone.

On my way back to the office I stopped for a coffee in Australia Square. Robyn, the regular waitress, sensed my jubilant mood.

'I'm pregnant,' I whispered. Robyn's eyes filled with tears and she wrapped her arms around me. This was a very generous gesture from Robyn, who'd told me she and her husband had been trying unsuccessfully for years to have a child. Thoughts of Adam came to mind and I tried to imagine his reaction when he heard he was going to have a little brother or sister.

During the previous year Adam had become Captain of the New South Wales Junior Rugby Team and had been selected to play for Australia against New Zealand. It was a proud moment when we had a photograph taken at the airport, with Adam wearing his green and gold blazer.

'You're Adam's mother?' his team manager had asked, surprised that someone my age could have such a big strapping lad as my son. Now I wondered how my pregnancy would be perceived – at thirty-four years of age I might look a bit old to be having a child.

I was feeling apprehensive about telling Darrol. We'd never discussed having children and to dump this on him without warning might be a shock. When I knocked on the glass partition to get his attention back at the office, he could see that I was excited and motioned for me to come in.

'You're looking pleased with yourself. What's happened?' he asked, putting aside his newspaper.

'I'm pregnant.'

At first he smiled, and I went to go into his arms, but the smile vanished before I took a step.

'I don't want any more children,' he said, stopping me short.

I backed away feeling like I'd been hit in the guts with a wet bag of sand.

'Do you understand what I just said? I am pregnant.'

'Well I don't want any more children and that's that,' he said, as though we were in a business meeting and he had the first and last word on the matter. 'And besides, you said that you didn't want any more children.'

I remembered the conversation we'd had in the car at Paddington when we'd first started to get to know one another. I had told him that I didn't want any more children until I'd been reunited with Adam. He had the chance then to tell me he didn't want any more, and if he had done so, that would have been the end to any relationship between us. I was twenty-seven at that time, and while having a child was far from my thinking I had never discounted the prospect of having more children and surrounding myself with a loving family.

'You've tricked me into this,' he said, defensively.

It was like a red rag to a bull. 'Tricked you? If I'd wanted to trick you into getting me pregnant I would've picked somewhere more comfortable than a flea-bitten dive in Noosa.'

'We can discuss this at home,' he said, returning his attention to the article he'd been reading.

As far as I was concerned there was nothing to discuss. I was going to have the baby, whether he liked it or not.

Darrol's reaction re-opened some deep wounds concerning my first pregnancy, when no one but me had wanted my baby to be born.

All kinds of obstacles had been placed in my way as people tried to convince me that I was too young and could never raise a child. At fifteen years old, and unmarried, they probably had a reason to be concerned, but I never expected this reaction from the father of my second child, whom I'd been living with for seven years. We were in a very sound financial position, and there was no reason, that I could see, for Darrol's objection. Except perhaps a fear that I'd stop working and he'd have to run the company without me.

I returned to my office, packed up my desk and headed for home.

As I waited for a taxi on Hunter Street, Guido, who worked the fruit barrow at the front of our office, called the daily specials to the passers-by as he bagged fruit and rummaged around for change in the pocket of his worn leather apron.

'*Buongiorno signora! Come sta?*' Guido greeted me, polishing a red apple before handing it over.

'*Grazie*, Guido. I'm going to have a baby,' I said. I wasn't expecting this to be of any interest him, I just needed to hear myself say it.

His face lit up. '*Fantastico! Bella donna!*' he said, throwing his arms around me.

'Thank you, Guido,' I said, hugging him and fighting back the tears. This was the reaction I'd wanted, but didn't get, from my husband.

I'm having a baby! I wanted to scream it from the taxi window.

Patricia, the medium from Manly, had said I would have another child. So far at least one part of the prediction was correct; my baby would be a Gemini.

That night when I told Matt the good news he threw his arms around me. 'That's cool!' he said with genuine enthusiasm. I called Adam and got the same reaction. I'd have to wait to tell Willow, as she was still with her mother and I didn't like to call her there.

Joan McCaffrey, a neighbour and devout Catholic, was surprised when I told her I was pregnant. She knew how hard I worked and the long hours I'd been putting in to build up the business. 'God will bless you,' she said, giving me a hug. 'Most women in your position would consider having a baby an inconvenience and get rid of it.'

Peggy Gazzard broke down when I called to give her the good news. She'd been disappointed when Jack and I broke up and would have liked to have seen us marry and have a child together. 'Nanna Peg has a nice ring to it, don't you think?' I said. She brightened and asked me when the baby was due.

By five months I was looking like I might be having twins and driving Darrol's car became impossible. I couldn't get close enough to the steering wheel to reach the clutch. We had a row about the need for me to have my own vehicle, but when I told Darrol he'd have to take over the running of the Parramatta office because I wasn't travelling out there on public transport twice a week, he had a change of heart.

'Oh what a lovely car,' Peggy Gazzard said, when I took her for a ride in my new Volvo.

'Yes, it has a cassette player,' I said, opening the sunroof and turning on Nina Simone's 'Here Comes the Sun'.

'It was so good of Darrol to get this for you,' she said, running her hands over the soft leather interior.

'Darrol didn't get this for me, it's a company car.'

'Well, he owns the company, doesn't he?' Peggy asked, pouting.

'No, we both own the company,' I corrected her.

Somewhere in Peggy's mind I still lived above a shop in Bondi and worked in a bar in Kings Cross.

Matt was the glue holding me together at that time. He used to call me at work to ask if the baby was moving yet. This was something I would have expected Darrol to do, and his total indifference triggered old memories of when the nuns at St Margaret's had treated me like I was the devil's spawn and resorted to all manner of ill-treatment to pressure me into giving up Adam for adoption. After four months of this stonewalling from Darrol by day, and by night still expecting me to satisfy his sexual needs, I'd reached breaking point.

My friend Vicki recommended a solicitor in Pitt Street, not far from our office. He'd handled Vicki's boyfriend's divorce and she said he wasn't greedy.

After listening to my situation he told me that he was obliged to recommend that Darrol and I seek marriage guidance counselling.

'I'm not going to see a shrink. You're the one with the problems,' Darrol said when I suggested that we make an appointment as advised. 'You have no idea about family. Look at your role models,' he scoffed.

Darrol had never met any of my family so I took this to be a racist dig at Aboriginal people in general. 'You're not fit to clean my Uncle Stan's boots,' I said, walking away.

The next day I called Maurice, the solicitor, and he cautioned that this was probably not a good time to be making big decisions. 'A divorce will almost certainly involve the break-up of your business.' It was a sobering conversation.

When I got home that night, Matt told me that he'd moved his things into another room so that I could set up the nursery in the sunnier room overlooking the park.

Adam was turning eighteen on 29 January and called to say that his grandmother was throwing a party for him and apologised that she didn't want me to be invited. He told me he was inviting his Uncle Stan and Aunty Shirley, as he wanted someone representing me to be there, and although I understood why Mrs McNorton would not want me at the party, it still hurt to be sidelined on such a special occasion. When we celebrated his milestone birthday on a dinner cruise on Sydney Harbour the following week, it was the first time Adam had seen me since the pregnancy was beginning to show.

'This is definitely a boy,' I chuckled, patting my bump, 'he kicks as hard as you did!' Adam looked pleased. As we hadn't seen each other for my birthday a few weeks earlier, he handed me a gift. It was a framed photograph of himself, flanked by a beaming Uncle Stan and Aunty Shirley, taken at his party. They hadn't been in a photograph together since his christening and I was proud that he had insisted on them being there to celebrate his coming of age. As well as giving Adam a gold neck chain for his birthday, I shouted him and his girlfriend to a night in the Executive Suite at the Wentworth Hotel, with a late check-out, and told them to order whatever they wanted from room service.

One morning I was having a shower when I noticed clumps of my hair were falling out and clogging the drain. I'd already lost so much hair due to the stress of my first pregnancy; my hairline had noticeably receded and there was a thinning on the top of my crown. At this rate I was going to need a wig, but there was no time for self-pity. We were expecting a visit from the franchise owners of the Manpower office in Calgary, Canada. I met Karen and her partner, Brian, at the airport. After I'd given them a tour of our offices, Karen asked if I could show her around Kings Cross. As we drove along Darlinghurst Road even I was shocked at the apparent age of the child prostitutes. My stomach turned revolutions as I imagined old creeps, like Uncle George from my childhood, slobbering all over them.

'Have you seen enough?'

'Yes, indeed!' Karen said.

I suggested that we go to the Sebel Townhouse for a meal before I took them back to their hotel. We walked into the restaurant and Haydon, the manager, came over to greet me. I apologised for not having made a booking, but as it was only six o'clock I was hoping we could have a quick bite. Haydon showed us to my favourite table next to the windows and, handing us the menus, advised that they were having a private function that evening and the restaurant had to be cleared by nine.

Karen and Brian were bubbling after visiting our offices and they wanted to discuss the ins and outs of the business. I lost track of the time and noticed that we were the only table still seated, all the other tables in the restaurant had been removed. Among the crowd that had started to fill the room were many famous faces, but that wasn't unusual for the Sebel Townhouse. Then I saw Elton John talking to a British rock star, whose name I couldn't put my finger on. I caught Haydon's attention and he came to our table.

'What's going on?'

'It's Elton John's wedding reception,' he whispered.

After paying the bill I slipped Haydon a handsome tip for not tossing us out and embarrassing me. My associates from Canada were delighted to have inadvertently ended up at Elton John's reception, when he married Renate Blauel in Sydney.

It wasn't until I was driving home that it occurred to me that it was Valentine's Day. I couldn't remember the last time Darrol and I were romantic on Valentine's Day, or if in fact we ever had been. I felt the baby kick.

'Happy Valentine's Day, my darling,' I said, gently stroking my bump.

*

As the baby started to grow and make its presence known, I felt the isolation from my family more and more. Since I'd been with Darrol my entire focus had been on making a home for him and his children. Now that I was reunited with Adam and having another child, I wanted my children to be connected to my family and also our culture. I'd arranged for Uncle Stan, Aunty Shirley and my brother Robbie and his family to come to Balgowlah for lunch. I'd lost contact with my brother Dan, but Robbie was looking forward to meeting my son for the first time. I was disappointed when Adam didn't show.

Darrol was confused as to why I called Robbie and Dan brothers, when they were actually my mother's brothers, making them my uncles. I explained that Mamma, my grandmother, had seven children by two husbands. Uncle Les, Uncle Stan, my mother Phyllis and Aunty Daphne were born to her first husband. Then to her second husband she had Kevin, who died young, Robbie and Dan, who were closer in age to me. When my mother left me with Mamma, her youngest sons and I were raised as brothers and sister.

'So they're really half uncles?' Darrol asked, trying to piece it all together in his mind.

'No, we don't talk in halves, they're my brothers,' I said.

To my delight, Aunty Lorna came with the rest of the family. I adored Aunty Lorna, Mamma's sister, who had often stood between us when Mamma was about to give me a belting. 'Leave the kid alone, she's only a baby,' Aunty Lorna would say, pushing Mamma out of the way. Aunty Lorna was the only person in our family who wasn't intimidated by Mamma, and Mamma knew that Aunty Lorna would drop her where she stood if she pushed it too far.

'You're havin' a girl!' Aunty Lorna said, throwing her arms around me. Being with my family again was like reconnecting with the missing link to my whole existence. Looking into their faces I could see traces of myself, my mother, Aunty Daphne, Mamma and Granny, through whom we could trace our lineage back to a time before the 1788 invasion. We had a history that connected us to this land and each other in a way that nothing else could. They were my mob and being back in their company made me realise how deeply I had missed them.

'G'day, Katie,' Robbie smiled, and put his arms around me.

Growing up, Robbie and I were the black sheep of the family. Mamma hated Robbie's father and Robbie paid for that every day of his life, being told he was just like his 'fucking no-good father'. Robbie's daughter, Lisa, was now nine or ten and bore a strong likeness to our side of the family. Uncle Stan and Aunty Shirley were constants – a pair of bookends, always kind and caring to each other and everyone around them.

For Darrol, this family gathering was probably the first time he realised he had married into an Aboriginal family. He was polite, but stayed in the background.

Aunty Lorna finished her tea and handed me the cup. 'Whadaya see, Katie?' she asked, reminding me of our favourite game when I was a child.

Feigning a look of deep concentration, I peered into the cup, turning it around in my hands for dramatic effect.

'You're going to die with a broom in your hand, Aunty,' I laughed, handing her back the cup.

'Jesus! Not yet I hope,' she said, with that big laugh of hers I'd missed so much.

'Here love, I've been looking after this for you,' Uncle Stan said, pressing something metal into my hand. It was my Bronze Medallion from the Lake Parramatta Life Saving Club. At the time I was the youngest person to obtain a Bronze Medallion and that was because I'd lied about my age and told the examiners

I was twelve years old, the minimum age, when in fact I'd only just turned ten. I'd left the medallion behind when Mamma sent me to Bidura Children's Home; trust Uncle Stan to know what a treasure it was.

Before they left Aunty Lorna took me aside. With tears welling in her eyes she said, 'I'm sorry, love.' She was referring to a time when I was unceremoniously banished from Nudgawalla, an outback sheep station where Mamma had worked as the house-keeper and cook to a wealthy family. The station-owner's wife had accused me of touching and taking her things, and Aunty Lorna knew it wasn't me and said nothing. I'd been banished from the property as a result and had returned to the city, only to be buffeted between a children's home, then across the road to Sandy Andersen's place, and then to Aunty Daphne's, where Uncle Jack held such tight control over his family they were afraid to speak.

'Aunty, there's no need to apologise. I've worked out why that happened,' I said, acknowledging the guilt she must have been feeling over the years. We hugged, both crying, then she pulled back and looking me straight in the eye she asked: 'Whadaya doin' married to him?'

About two weeks later I got a call from Uncle Stan.

'Aunty Lorna's gone, love,' he said, gravely. 'She was vacuuming the lounge and poof! Off she went, just like that.'

18

The Junior Princess

Seven months into my pregnancy, exhaustion took on a new meaning. I was still working full-time, cooking meals, making clothes for the family and taking care of most of the domestic duties. By the time I finally got into bed each night, the last thing I wanted was sex. Darrol became increasingly frustrated and impatient, turning our bedroom into a battleground. When I reached my last trimester, he made a suggestion that caused me to flare, reminding me of his ex-wife's comments about sodomy, and I opted to sleep in the spare room.

My labour started around 4 a.m. on 23 May. I got up, showered and started timing the contractions. Around six I called the hospital to tell them I was coming in.

As Darrol and I drove to the hospital in silence I recalled the night I went into labour with Adam. Then, as now, my emotions were running high. We stopped at a set of lights and, without even looking at me, Darrol announced that he wanted to 'witness the birth'. When I told him that I was going to have a natural childbirth he laughed and said that he'd lived on a farm and had seen cows giving birth.

As we pulled up in front of St Margaret's Hospital in Darlinghurst my pulse was racing. I hadn't been near this place since Adam was born; it was ironic that I could now afford one of Sydney's best obstetricians, but he only delivered at St Margaret's Private Hospital. At least this time, there'd be no fierce old nun standing over me, telling me I was going to burn in hell for my sin.

After introducing the doctor to Darrol I mentioned that my husband wanted to be present at the birth. The doctor looked surprised. During the pregnancy he'd asked if my husband was attending and I'd said no. I repeated what Darrol had said about living on a farm and his eyebrows arched.

'You'll be a while yet. I'll pop in from time to time to see how things are progressing,' the doctor said, before going on his rounds.

As the contractions intensified I leaned forward with my arms on the bed, head down, knees bent, panting and counting.

'Shouldn't you get onto the bed?'

Shaking my head, I tried to control my breathing until the contraction subsided. 'Please don't talk to me when I'm having a contraction, I need to focus.'

Then, midway through a very strong contraction Darrol panicked and started rubbing my back. I lost my concentration, and struggled to hold it together until the pain subsided.

'If you can't handle this, please leave. But if you stay, don't talk to me and don't touch me again!' I snapped, wiping the perspiration from my face and regaining my composure, just in time for the next contraction. This continued throughout the day with midwives monitoring the labour.

'You're doing nicely. It won't be long now,' a midwife said, after taking my temperature. 'Would you like some more ice?'

How different this birthing experience was from the first, when I had been left unattended for hours. There had been no ice to quench my thirst and when I had cried out in pain I was told, 'Be quiet, there are other women on the ward.'

Just when I was starting to think I couldn't take any more and was going to ask for some pain relief, the doctor examined me. Slipping his hands into surgical gloves, he smiled. 'Okay, on the next contraction, let's get to work.'

At this stage I had no idea if Darrol was still in the room. He certainly wasn't holding my hand. I could feel the baby's head at my opening.

'Don't push. I'm going to have to give you an episiotomy. You have a great deal of scar tissue from your first birth.' The doctor gave me an injection and waited for it to take effect. As he started to cut, I shivered and sucked in a deep breath.

'Geez!' I said, clamping my eyes closed. When I had been giving birth to Adam nobody was concerned with my suffering – I'd been a wicked girl and God was punishing me for my sins – they'd just cut me, without anything to dull the pain.

'My goodness, can you feel that?' the doctor looked alarmed.

'No, I'm just remembering the last time it was done without any anaesthetic.'

A sudden whoosh, followed by a loud wail, and I collapsed on the pillow, relieved that my baby had been safely delivered.

'What a set of lungs,' I laughed, and cried with joy. It has to be a boy, I thought, turning my head to check the exact time of the birth.

'It's a girl,' Darrol said, smiling. The sister handed me our daughter and Darrol cut the umbilical cord. As I put her to my breast, tears poured out of me, dripping onto her beautiful face.

'Hello Savannah Harriet,' I said, kissing the top of her bloodied head.

Meanwhile, the doctor looked worried. 'The placenta is lodged. I'm going to have to give you a general anaesthetic,' he said.

'Can't you pull it out? I'm pretty tough, I've just had a baby,' I laughed.

Several minutes passed and the doctor started to look more anxious. I tried pleading. 'Please, I can take it,' I begged.

Ignoring my pleas he got on the phone to the anaesthetist. 'Get down here, immediately!'

Having just delivered, without drugs, I was looking forward to giving my baby her first bath. I didn't trust hospitals and was starting to fret at the thought of us being separated. I handed her to Darrol and told him not to let anyone take her. 'We'll bathe her when I come around,' I said, before they put the mask over my face.

When I came to, Darrol was sitting in the chair in the corner, looking besotted with the little bundle in his arms.

Too wobbly to walk, I was lifted into a wheelchair. A nurse showed Darrol how to cradle the baby, while I reached over, gently sponging her with warm soapy water.

This was a powerful moment. For the first time, we shared the joy of this divine creation with the most perfect porcelain skin and a mop of jet-black hair, just like Snow White. We'd have to wait to see if her eyes would remain blue.

When I called Peggy Gazzard from my private room and told her the name I had chosen, she burst into tears. 'A little girl? How lovely, and a Gemini too,' she added, very pleased that she and Savannah shared a sign of the zodiac.

'Savannah Harriet?' Darrol asked, after I hung up. 'So, I don't get a say in the name?'

For nine months Darrol hadn't even acknowledged the pregnancy, and I didn't think he cared about a name. But he was Savannah's father, and it was never my wish to exclude him.

'Alright, you can choose Savannah's middle name,' I said, by way of compromise. He chose Jane. Perhaps he'd forgotten that was also the middle name of his first daughter, named after his paternal grandmother, whom he hardly knew.

Myles Stivano was the first person to arrive the day after the birth; carrying a bunch of long-stemmed red roses and a bottle of Moët et Chandon. He leaned down and gave me a kiss before he went to give Savannah an inspection.

'The Junior Princess,' he said, smiling and nodding his approval.

By 7 pm the whole Lavender Hill Mob had arrived, after word had gone out that 'Flo's had a sprog'. Phil looked so sweet with the pink teddy bear he had brought as a gift and tucked into Savannah's cot.

'Do they serve tea?' Pommie Dave asked before disappearing out the door to go rustle something up.

A short while later the sister in charge wheeled in a trolley with several silver teapots and a stack of white bone china cups and plates of biscuits, enough for the fifteen people crammed into my private room.

After everyone had gone and Sister was wheeling out the trolley, she turned and said, 'Mrs Norman, please inform the rotund gentleman that we are not running a hotel.'

The next day, flowers and gifts from family, friends, staff and a few clients filled my room. Darrol came to the hospital after work and only left when he had to, around 10 p.m. He sat in the chair and held Savannah the whole time.

'She'll get pretty used to that,' I laughed.

*

Savannah had been born on a Wednesday, and as my wounds were considerable, I had to stay in hospital until the doctor cleared me to go home. To ensure that we wouldn't spend a day more in this place than necessary, I took a warm bath twice a day and tossed in a kilo of salt. It stung like a thousand hornets, causing my teeth to chatter, but I was ready to be discharged first thing Monday morning.

'This is a beautiful little beastie,' the paediatrician said, after examining Savannah.

'I bet you say that to all the mothers,' I laughed, but secretly agreeing with him and feeling very proud.

'No, I don't. Some babies are so ugly they need to go back into the oven until they're cooked,' he said. 'This one's really special.' With twenty stitches in my crotch it really hurt to laugh.

Matt and Willow hadn't been brought to the hospital to see the baby. Matt, who must have been out of his skin with anticipation, was out the door when he heard the car. He'd taken a sickie and was disappointed that the baby was asleep when we arrived. 'What time does she wake up?' he asked, hovering over her, ready to pounce the minute her eyes opened. 'Oh, the little Widgie!' he cooed, taking her into his arms and giving her the nickname that he would often use.

Willow was having issues at her mother's and didn't come to see Savannah for a few weeks. Her reaction, although not as responsive as Matt's, was warm – she clearly liked having a little sister.

At eighteen, Adam had an active sporting and social life. Getting him to stick to a plan, even to see his little baby sister, was difficult. I was worried that he may have had some misgivings about me having another child; after all, we'd only been reunited for two and a half years, but when he finally did meet her, his heart melted.

My life felt almost complete. The only thing that would have made it better would have been a loving husband to share it with. It seemed that once we got home with our baby, and Darrol no longer had an audience to play the doting father in front of, he had very little hands-on involvement.

He wasn't happy about my decision to breastfeed. 'Women aren't interested in sex while they're breastfeeding,' he complained.

Two weeks after I came out of hospital I took Savannah into the office to meet the staff, who showered us with gifts and lined up to hold her.

While I'd been away Darrol had organised the relocation of the company to bigger premises on Pitt Street. Although considerably larger than the previous offices in Hunter Street, I thought it was still too small for the future expansion I had in mind.

Darrol had given himself a large office with big windows, lashing out on a new timber desk, a smart leather executive chair and a bookcase that was stacked with tattered old training manuals going back to the 1970s. In one corner were two tan leather lounges and a coffee table with a pile of *Business Review Weekly* magazines.

My office appeared to have been an afterthought. Darrol's old desk and chair had been squeezed in for me to use, but they took up too much room, and when I wheeled in Savannah's pram it was a snug fit.

This proved difficult when, three weeks later I went back to work part-time, taking Savannah with me. She was still on four-hourly breastfeeds around the clock. Instead of savouring all the joys of motherhood that I'd previously been denied, I maintained a ridiculous schedule, trying to prove to Darrol that having a baby wouldn't change anything between us. In reality, it changed everything and with the wisdom of hindsight I realise I was trying to be Wonder Woman in a nursing bra.

It was a Saturday, a freezing cold, miserable day in June. Even though it was only mid-afternoon the day was as black as night. Rain pelted against the windows and the wind was stripping the trees in the park.

Darrol and Matt had gone to help Willow, who'd moved to a flat in Mosman. They got back around 3 p.m. I'd just finished giving the baby a feed and had collapsed in the recliner chair in the nursery.

Darrol barged into the room without knocking. 'What's for lunch?' he demanded, holding the door open and ignoring the fact that I was naked with our one-month-old baby sleeping in my arms.

'Whatever you can find,' I said, 'and please close the door.'

'Have you done the shopping?' he pressed.

'Does it look like I've done the shopping?' I replied, putting the baby down and slipping on my robe.

He stormed off, ranting about how he'd worked all morning and I couldn't even do the shopping. The commotion woke up the baby.

'Did you seriously expect me to go out in this weather, so you'd have the makings of a sandwich for lunch?' I asked, packing an overnight bag.

Having been raised around domestic violence, I was determined that no child of mine would have to experience it. When issues between Darrol and me reached a flash point, I simply packed a bag and booked myself into the Manly Pacific Hotel.

The concierge reached for his phone when he saw me getting out of the lift, carrying a bag and pushing the pram. 'An executive suite, with a view, for Mrs Norman,' he said, without me having to say a word.

It took a few days for the flowers to arrive. In the meantime, I relaxed with the luxury of room service and gourmet meals, with disposable nappies delivered to my room.

When we were leaving I left Darrol to settle the account.

Two months after I'd returned to work full-time I noticed an unopened box from Manpower's head office, sitting in a corner of Darrol's office. This time I didn't ask if I could take a look at the contents. It contained a program called 'Skillware' a user-friendly system for training and testing word processor and computer operators.

My pulse raced with excitement as I worked my way through the new material and realised its potential, but when I showed it to Darrol he was less than enthusiastic. 'Don't get big ideas about that stuff from the US, we can't afford it,' he said.

I told him that if we didn't get ourselves up to speed and invest in computers we would become dinosaurs in the industry within five years.

One morning Darrol asked me to join him in his office for coffee, which was a rare moment. There simply wasn't enough time in the day for me to enjoy coffee breaks, but he said he needed to discuss something.

'I'm bored,' he said, running his hand over the soft leather lounge.

'Bored? How can you be bored?' I was astounded.

'I don't have enough to do.'

After the incident with Bryce, Darrol lost confidence and retreated into the ivory tower he'd created for himself. Since we'd introduced a new program for industrial services, hiring and training the personnel in that division had also fallen to me. I told him that if he needed more to do, he could take this off my hands. I went to my office to get all the material he'd need and dumped it onto his desk.

More information arrived concerning the IBM/Manpower partnership agreement recently signed in the US. This came about after IBM had conceded that Manpower's Skillware programs exceeded anything IBM could produce. IBM sold the hardware and Manpower provided the training. In addition, Manpower also received a commission from IBM for any computer hardware that was sold. It was a perfect partnering of two specialist companies to meet the demands of a rapidly changing workplace. It was impossible to forecast what this meant in real dollar terms, but I expected it could produce revenue of around one hundred million a year. When I told Darrol he said that I read too much science fiction.

After months of badgering he finally agreed to make a modest investment and purchase two word processors to use as a trial. Within months we were making plans to open the first word-processing training centre in Australia, with two additional offices, one in North Sydney and another in Bankstown.

We were a few years away from being able to take on something like the IBM/Manpower partnership, but my plans with regard to recruiting and training staff were to achieve that end.

At seven months Savannah was very active and taking her to work was no longer possible. With no confidence in the unregulated child care centres, I told Darrol that I wanted a nanny to look after Savannah at home.

'That'll cost a fortune,' he protested.

This wasn't negotiable as far as I was concerned and I suggested that we could put the nanny on Manpower's payroll.

After all, she would have the most important job of anyone in the company.

Jillian was a trained mothercraft nurse who was hired after I'd seen a dozen applicants I wouldn't have left alone with my cat. I stayed with Jillian for a week to observe her and try to get Savannah adjusted to a new routine. The night before I was going back to work, I was filled with trepidation.

'You'll never be happy with anyone,' Darrol snapped.

The next morning Savannah could sense something was different and started to get agitated. She reached out to grab my hair and clothes as I was leaving the house to go to work. 'You have to stay home today my darling,' I said, gently prising her fingers away and kissing her. The piercing screams and images of her contorted little face haunted me as I drove away.

Around 10 am I was having a quiet moment in my office, trying to contain the emotion of having to leave Savannah so distressed, when Kerry Mackey from the Parramatta office arrived for our appointment. She'd called to say she had something important to tell me, and wanted to do it in person.

Hoping that Kerry was going to tell me she was pregnant, I was dumbfounded when she told me she was resigning. Worse still, I was hearing for the first time that the recently hired male at Parramatta had been promoted over her head, with an increase in salary, and he had been given the vehicle she'd been using.

Naturally, Kerry had assumed that I knew about this and her disappointment was apparent. I assured her that it was news to me.

'Is there anything I can do to get you to reconsider?' I asked her.

She told me she'd found another job already and would start in two weeks. I was devastated to lose her and promised her that I would never let this happen to another woman in the company again. By this time we were both in tears.

'He's a man,' was all Darrol could say about a decision that cost us one of our best employees. He was adamant that men should earn more than women. I told him that I didn't agree and neither did Kerry, and that she'd taken a position as the senior personnel officer with Arnott's Biscuits. It took a few moments for this to sink in. Arnott's was one of Parramatta's major industrial clients.

'Let's hope that Kerry isn't vindictive,' I said, leaving his office in disgust.

19

Putting runs on the board

'I was just curious,' Darrol said, before waxing lyrical about the spectacular water views from the property he'd inspected in Gordon Street, Clontarf. 'They're asking $555,000, it's way out of our range.'

Over the previous few years Darrol and I had purchased a number of properties that included the townhouse in Balgowlah, units in Fairlight and Neutral Bay, and a block of flats in Chiswick. It was obvious to me what we ought to do and I suggested that we sell those investments and put the money into our private residence, which was exempt from capital gains tax.

'Who's the agent?' I asked.

'It's being sold privately. He's a solicitor, settling a divorce.'

I suggested that we make an offer of $400,000 on the Clontarf property to get the ball rolling.

'He'll never accept that; this is a stunning home,' Darrol said.

The vendor was an arrogant man who didn't like dealing with a woman. When I called to make the offer he laughed and told me that my offer was insulting. I told him to think about it and get back to me if he wanted to make a counter offer. He called back a few days later and it was my turn to laugh. My advantage was I hadn't seen the property and had no emotion tied up in the negotiations. I let it rest for a week and went back with our increased offer of $440,000. 'Take it or leave it,' I said. 'There are plenty of properties available in that bracket.'

Grudgingly, he accepted the offer, and after that I left all of the financial arrangements to Darrol and our accountant, William.

The first time I saw the property was after we'd exchanged contracts. I hated it. It was a complete mystery how Darrol thought I'd find a three-storey, lolly-pink and white monstrosity with an excess of Corinthian columns and pot-belly balustrades anything but grotesque.

The entrance to the property was down a steep set of cracked concrete stairs, with no handrail. There were no fences or gates, and the shared driveway with the next door neighbour meant Savannah would have to be watched very closely. The house was in no way child-friendly and I was gob-smacked that this hadn't been taken into account.

'Oh God, no!' I said, when I saw the ugly shag-pile carpet. It looked like dead grass, flattened by a steamroller, had spread through the house like out-of-control kikuyu. Darrol, Matt and Savannah all had severe allergies to dust mites. The Balgowlah property had shag-pile carpet and we had argued constantly about having it removed.

'There's still plenty of wear,' Darrol said. Meanwhile they would all suffer, especially Savannah, who was too young for antihistamines.

'Mercy,' I gasped, as we entered the kitchen.

'It won an award,' Darrol said, not understanding my objection to the black wallpaper with white daisies pasted over the walls and ceiling. Sliding doors off the kitchen led to a narrow landing dropping away suddenly down yet more steep stairs to an L-shaped swimming pool.

'Wow!' was all I could manage as I drew back the curtains around three massive glass walls in the main lounge. Even on a cloudy day the 180 degree view of Middle Harbour was breathtaking.

'Wait until you see the master bedroom,' Darrol said excitedly, leading us up the spiral staircase, covered with kitschy foil wallpaper, all the rage in the 1970s. The top floor had sky-blue shag-pile, acres of it, in a room easily as big as the main lounge, with a more spectacular view. A pebble-crete patio off the bedroom would have accommodated ten people sprawled on sun lounges, with enough room for a barbecue and jacuzzi. The balustrade provided no barrier for a child, who could easily tumble into the pool two floors below. The walk-in robe was more spacious than my office. The mosaic-tiled ensuite included a sunken bath with gold taps and gilded cupids shooting arrows in every direction.

Darrol took us back downstairs. The double garage on the bottom level had a door leading to the pool. There was no safety fence.

The only saving grace of this property was the address and the spectacular water views. It could never be over capitalised, which was just as well, because I could see where $100,000 needed to be spent before this house could become a home.

Darrol looked quite crestfallen that I wasn't as taken with our new home as he was, so I thought I'd better lighten up. 'I told you we'd live on this hill one day,' I smiled, trying to sound enthusiastic and reminding him of the prediction I'd made when we'd sailed past Clontarf several years earlier.

As we drove away I mentioned that we needed to install a pool fence.

'We don't need a pool fence, we can watch the baby.'

'We're going to need a pool fence,' I repeated, firmly.

We moved into the new house in March 1985. Savannah was crawling and walking around furniture. The dusty carpet played havoc with her sinuses. Fed up with arguing about replacing the shag-pile I went and bought several large Oriental carpets. Before long, Savannah came a cropper on the hard surface of the patio. Matt rushed to pick her up. 'Ouchy bonk!' he said, kissing her tears. He couldn't stand to see his little Widgie cry.

After that I had the surface of the patio off the main lounge covered with green outdoor carpet. It looked a bit ordinary, but it would only be needed until Savannah was steady on her feet.

Watching Matt with his little sister warmed my heart. Looking out for her when I had something to do was never a problem. He'd resigned from the gallery in Crows Nest, after working with them for five years. He tried hairdressing for a while, but what he secretly wanted was to work with animals, particularly exotic animals, like crocodiles. In the meantime, he was working with us at Manpower, taking care of what little industrial work we handled through the city office.

One year after relocating our offices to Pitt Street, we were bursting at the seams and had to break our lease to secure the top floor of the Dymocks Building on the corner of Hunter and Pitt streets in Sydney's CBD. I'd personally designed every aspect of the new office, installing the latest in ergonomic equipment and an office for myself that was large enough to sit two extra people. Darrol's office was next to mine with an adjoining door. We installed a fully-equipped kitchen, a staff room and a conference room for training and conducting demonstrations of our operating systems to clients. The new location included a word-processing training centre, the first of its kind to be introduced in Australia.

We had a grand opening, inviting established clients and those we were still hoping to impress. Manpower Australia had a state-of-the-art service unlike anything else that was available, placing us light years ahead of the competition.

'This is truly impressive,' Helena Ricardo of Citicorp said after we'd given her a guided tour.

My schedule over the previous five years had been too hectic to attend meetings with Darrol and our accountant, William.

'Do you want to know the bottom line?' William asked one day, popping his head into my office on the way to speak with Darrol about the year-end reports.

'Only if we didn't crack $6 million,' I smiled.

'You did that and some.'

It was my responsibility to forecast the revenues each year and this wasn't a hit-and-miss figure. I put the runs on the board and I trusted William and Darrol, without question, to keep a tally of the score.

As they were leaving to go to lunch, they stopped by my office. William congratulated me on the results; it had been another great year of growth.

'I don't know how you do it. This office is so quiet, yet I look at the balance sheets and the results are there.'

'It's the old duck-on-the-pond story,' I said. 'Everything looks calm on the surface.'

'The results you achieve for a relatively small marketing and advertising expenditure are quite remarkable,' William said.

'The results come through the people,' I replied, looking at Darrol, who was forever moaning about how much time I spent on staff training and development.

*

On Savannah's first birthday Matt was still working at Manpower and I invited him to join us for lunch. Jillian had been instructed to bring Savannah to the city by midday so we could celebrate together.

'How did Savannah get that bruise on her face?' I asked, when I saw the mark the size of a thumb print that hadn't been there when I had left that morning.

'She bumped into the door in the kitchen,' Jillian replied, unconvincingly.

After lunch, when Savannah realised that she was going to leave without me, her screams stopped pedestrians on the street. It was her birthday, and this was too much. I told Jillian she could have the rest of the day off.

Savannah cheered up as soon as she walked through the door into Manpower, running straight to Moira, who always made a fuss over her. I tidied up my desk and took her home.

The next morning Savannah's screams intensified as I left the house. By this age she had a few words to express her feelings. 'Mum, Mum, no, no,' she wailed.

Around 11 am I got an urge to go home that I couldn't ignore. As I pulled up at the front of the house I could hear Savannah even with the windows closed. Without stopping to grab my bag or lock the car I raced for the house, just in time to catch Jillian with Savannah in a headlock, trying to force-feed her. So preoccupied with tormenting my baby Jillian didn't hear me come into the house. 'Eat this you spoiled little bitch!' she said.

Savannah's mouth was clamped shut as she tossed her head from side to side. 'Get away from her!' I yelled, rushing to Savannah and taking her out of the highchair. Jillian grabbed her bag and bolted.

'Ouchy, Mum,' Savannah sobbed, burying her face into my neck.

*

After weeks of advertising without success, a cousin of Darrol's who lived at Palm Beach mentioned that the daughter of a friend was looking for work. I'd met Simone when she was about eighteen but I couldn't say I knew her well, so I arranged for her to come and see me and Savannah. Ten minutes into our conversation my instinct was to ask when she could start. I knew I'd found the angel I'd been looking for.

Simone was able to start immediately, and on her first day we went over the death-trap we called home. 'As you can see this is a very unsafe house for a toddler. Every external door must be kept closed and locked,' I said.

While Simone might have looked like a 'flower child' with daisies in her hair, she was a triple-certificate nursing sister and very practical.

Simone had been working for us for a few weeks when her little boy, Dylan, who was about three years old, had a terrible experience in a day care centre. 'Bring your son to work with you,' I suggested.

Darrol wasn't keen on the idea but I saw no reason why Simone couldn't bring her son with her; he was only eighteen months older than Savannah and taking care of two children wouldn't stretch Simone. Besides, I thought it would be good for Savannah to have another child to interact with, remembering my son's isolation when he was a baby.

When Savannah started kicking up a fuss to see them leave in the evenings, I knew she was in good hands.

Usually I tried not to bring work home on the weekends, but as I'd made so many adjustments to the original operating systems from the US I needed to put together a training manual for our operation. I'd asked Darrol to take care of Savannah while I got it done. He grumbled something about needing to wash his car.

After an uninterrupted hour I was making good headway when Sammy, Matt's dog, started barking. When the barking continued with no one attempting to quieten him down, I went downstairs to see what was happening.

The garage door was open and Matt and Darrol were engrossed in something. It was a rarity to see them doing anything together that didn't lock them into a fierce battle.

'Where's the baby?' I asked.

They both looked at me blankly.

Sammy started barking again. It came from the backyard.

'The pool!' I pushed past, nearly knocking them both over.

Sammy was standing between Savannah and the pool, barking frantically. Savannah thought it was a game and started to run towards him.

'No!' I screamed, scaring the wits out of her. She flopped on the ground and started crying. My heart was pounding with relief as I drew her into my arms. Sammy came over for a cuddle as well. Sammy adored Savannah and shadowed her everywhere she went. I was so glad he was with her that day.

'Darrol, get a pool fence!' I said, shaking with rage.

'A pool fence will spoil the aesthetic of the yard.'

'A dead baby at the bottom of a swimming pool is a bloody awful aesthetic. We'll be at the Manly Pacific, call me when the pool fence has been erected.'

Ever since Sammy came to live with us Matt and Darrol had fought over him getting a bath. He was a small cross-breed long-haired dog with an adorable personality, but he really got on the nose if he didn't get a bath every week. To make things worse we didn't have a side gate to keep him in the yard, so he'd go on the road and roll in dead birds. The final straw came when Sammy was found curled up on a neighbour's bed and she presented us with a bill for $1500 to replace the king-size silk bed cover, which had to be tailor-made to match the expensive drapes.

'Get the dog,' Darrol ordered Matt, as he grabbed his car keys.

Matt put Sammy on his lead and took him to the car. Sammy's tail was wagging; he was excited about going out in the car. I thought they may have taken him to the dog wash but when they came back Matt was holding Sammy's collar and lead and his face was flushed red from crying. I asked what had happened.

'I had the dog put down,' Darrol said.

'*What?*'

Matt, who was in shock and inconsolable, went to his room.

'All he needed was a bath and a side gate to keep him in the yard,' I said, distraught. Not only had Sammy been killed, but Darrol had made Matt go with him and didn't even bring the dear little dog home to be buried. Sammy had saved our daughter's life and was tossed unceremoniously into landfill.

'Matt will never forget this and neither will I,' I yelled.

When Savannah started calling for her little mate Darrol said, 'Sammy's gone to heaven. He was on the road and got run over by a car.'

20

I prefer red

Life around me was becoming harder to manage. I wasn't seeing Adam as much as I would have liked, but that wasn't always due to things happening at my end. Adam was an adult now and living independently. I knew he had a new lady in his life and I really didn't expect him to be on my doorstep every week.

It was coming up to Christmas and my mob had arranged to visit us at Clontarf. This was the third time I'd invited Adam to come and meet my brother, Robbie, who'd been disappointed on the other occasions when Adam hadn't shown.

'This is for you, Savannah,' Robbie said, scooping her up into his arms when he came through the door.

'Thank you, Uncle Robbie,' she said, hugging the Cabbage Patch doll.

Robbie wasn't to know that I despised those butt-ugly dolls with forlorn faces. They were a total aberration. Mass-produced and marketed as unwanted and abandoned by their mother, they even came with birth certificates and papers to send back to register the adoption. Today those dolls would cause an outcry. Back then the treatment of unmarried girls and their babies lost to adoption still hadn't become public knowledge. Savannah named her doll Ursula, a rather sophisticated name for a two and a half year old to come up with, but Savannah was an unusual child. We didn't send away for the adoption certificate.

'You know, Katie, I was there when Phyllis, Mamma and Jack died, and they all asked after you. They'd be so proud of ya darlin',' Robbie said, putting his arm around me and marvelling at the view. Robbie knew I didn't get here because I'd married into money.

We held back lunch, but it was clear that Adam wasn't coming. This time he didn't even call. I felt hurt and 'shamed' but I also sensed that Adam was still conflicted over things his grandmother had told him, so I didn't put pressure on him to spend time with me and my family. I'd done all I could do to get him to understand my side of the story, but I also didn't want him to think ill of his grandmother. We both loved Adam and we had both made mistakes. Hopefully, with time and maturity, Adam would be able to forgive us both.

In the New Year I got a call from Robbie.

'I've got the big C. It's in my lungs.'

Robbie had been eighteen when he was conscripted in the first ballot for National Service in 1965. Prime Minister Robert Menzies was going 'All the way with LBJ', and Robbie was among the first contingent of Nashos shipped off to Vietnam. He was wounded in action in 1966. He became the fifth solider in his regiment to be diagnosed with lung cancer, and yet the government continued to downplay the effects of Agent Orange.

There was a chance that they could operate and Robbie sounded optimistic. 'I'm gonna fight this,' he told me, bravely.

I wasn't as confident and told him to let me know if he needed anything. It was probably an old wives' tale but Mamma always said, 'Once they open you up, the big C spreads like wildfire.'

Robbie's cancer had spread too far to operate and when he needed to be heavily sedated he was sent to Concord Repatriation Hospital. Robbie was lying, uncovered, on a bed in the middle of a long row of beds, with other sick and dying men who were given no privacy. Some of the men nodded and attempted to smile, while others rolled onto their side with their backs to me as I walked past. Robbie's lips trembled as he tried to speak and seeing him in so much pain shook me to my core. Even dosed up on morphine he had to pause between sentences to catch his breath.

'Katie, until my life insurance is paid, Sharon won't have enough money to give me a decent funeral,' he gasped, with tears rolling down his face. 'I need to ask you for a loan?'

The last time I'd seen Robbie cry he was only fourteen. It was on the night our brother, Kev, had died. Kev had been thrown from a mate's car that took a bend too fast. Robbie was unhurt in the back seat. Kev was still alive when Robbie got to him but he died in Robbie's arms, waiting for the ambulance. I'll never forget the sight of Robbie, flanked by two policemen, distraught and covered in blood, with Mamma pulling her hair out and wailing to the heavens, 'Oh Jesus! Why did he take Kev? Why wasn't it you.'

'Now this is only a loan,' Robbie repeated. 'As soon as Sharon gets the money, she'll pay you back,' he said, when I handed him a cheque that I knew would more than cover the funeral costs.

Robbie was in too much pain to be touched. I stood beside his bed and hugged myself, hoping he could feel it. 'I love you Robbie, you were always my favourite brother,' I told him.

'I love you too, darlin',' he said, puckering his lips.

Gently, trying not to lean on him, I reached over to give him a kiss. As I left the hospital that day I didn't expect to see him alive again so it was a profound relief to get a call from him a few weeks later to say that he was at home and 'on the mend'.

By 1987 the company was turning over millions, and producing an after-tax profit in excess of one million dollars a year and growing. It wasn't unusual for me to be handed a pile of documents to sign, with no explanation of what they were for. My general attitude was if I couldn't trust my husband and my accountant who could I trust? One morning, I was taking a break in my office and took the time to scan the pile awaiting my signature. I noticed that my tax return for that year was included. I hadn't looked at my tax return in any detail for years. Making money for its own sake had never been my motivation for doing anything. For three years I'd believed that I'd been made a shareholder in the company so I was shocked to see there was no provision for unpaid dividends on my tax return, and there ought to have been.

When I confronted Darrol about this he just stared at me, as if he was trying to think of something to say.

'You haven't given me the shares you promised, have you?' I questioned.

'Oh, that's William's oversight,' Darrol mumbled.

'Really?' I said, in a tone that conveyed I wasn't buying it.

'I'll ask him to get it organised.'

At the time, if I'd let Darrol know how I felt about this everything would have blown up and I just didn't have the strength to cope with any more drama. A few days later he handed me a document to sign and, unlike many he had given me previously, he told me what this was for.

'This is for the allocation of one-third of the shares in the company to your name,' he said with a big smile, as if he was giving me a gift I wasn't earning. 'And I've put your salary on par with mine.'

My salary was increased to $150,000, which was a staggering $40,000 pay rise.

'And you told me that you didn't pay yourself a decent salary,' I said, signing the bank deposit authority.

'Have you backdated this to when the shares were promised?' I ventured to ask, as I put pen to paper on the shares allocation agreement.

'You're never satisfied are you?'

Although we'd been living together for ten years, Darrol and I had never had joint finances, so I only had his word regarding his income. Given his attitude that men should earn more than women, I ought to have asked more questions. It was disappointing that he saw my input into the company to be one-third compared to his two-thirds, and I'd live to regret accepting this offer.

As Darrol was getting more involved in the operations in western Sydney, he was finding it a strain driving a manual car in heavy traffic. One morning he said that he was going to trade in the Mercedes and get an automatic. It was coming up to the end of the financial year, and it was a good time to consider upgrading. I told him that I'd go with him and we arranged to meet at the Mercedes dealer on Parramatta Road.

When I arrived he was already talking to a salesman and inspecting a 450 SLC automatic; dark blue with cream leather upholstery.

'This is a nice car,' I said, opening the door of a red 280 CE coupe.

Darrol came over to take a look at the coupe, with the salesman trying to drag him back to the more expensive vehicle they'd been discussing.

We hadn't talked about me getting a new car, but I thought if it was good enough for him then it should be good enough for me.

'I'd like to take this for a test drive,' I said to the salesman.

'Your husband is very keen on the 450 SLC,' the salesman said, with irritation in his voice.

'We'll be buying two vehicles – one for me and one for my husband,' I told him. 'I prefer red.'

Darrol was caught by surprise, but said nothing.

After taking the coupe for a test drive we haggled over the trade-in. The salesman asked how we were intending to finance the vehicles. I turned to Darrol and asked if he had the company cheque book. He wrote out a cheque for the total amount.

The salesman looked astounded: 'Do you mind if I call your bank?'

While the salesman completed the paperwork I emptied the glove box in my car.

Darrol would take longer to make up his mind and I had to get to an appointment. 'I'll see you back at the office,' I said, kissing Darrol on the cheek, before driving away in my new car.

This was when I discovered that appealing to Darrol's ego was the way to get him to agree to something without an argument. Paying cash for two luxury motor vehicles certainly appealed to his ego.

21

A day of healing

Robbie called to say he'd gone into remission, and was arranging for a family reunion at his place, inviting members of our mob from near and far. A 'day of healing' he called it. There'd been bad blood in our family going back decades. Most of the people who'd fired these divisions were cold in their graves and I agreed it was time to let the past go.

When we arrived Uncle Les and Aunty Shirl made a bee line to talk to me. 'Please forgive us, Katie,' Uncle Les said, his eyes welling with emotion. Shirl too, was biting her lip. They'd carried the guilt for a very long time for shutting the door on me and Adam when I needed a place to take him home from the hospital, but time, and being reunited with Adam, had healed those wounds.

'Times were different back then. Let's just go forward,' I said, giving them both a hug.

Trudy, one of Aunty Daphne's daughters, was a married woman now with three children of her own. She still had a mass of flaxen curls and walked on tippy-toes like her mother. Seeing Roberta,

Aunty Daphne's youngest daughter, who was now all grown up, made me realise just how much time had passed. It became even more obvious as we watched Savannah splashing around in the pool with Trudy's children. *How very different their childhood is from ours*, I thought, as they flicked water into each other faces, squealing with delight.

'G'day, Uncle Ringer,' I said leaning down to kiss the soft brown face of Granny's only surviving child, which made him my great-uncle. I hadn't seen him or my Aunty Merl since I lived with Aunty Lorna at Lansdowne Street, thirty-two years earlier, and yet he didn't even question how I could remember him after all that time.

Uncle Ringer, whose real name was Vincent, had travelled from Tuncurry for this reunion. Aunty Merl was a Beetson, and her nephew, Arthur 'Big Artie' Beetson, the first Aboriginal person to captain Australia in any sport, was my cousin.

Robbie had the Weber going and someone made a crack about blackfellas and our passion for cooking and eating outdoors, and how easy it was now that we didn't have to rub two sticks together.

'So we're not good enough for the McNortons?' Robbie jibed, recognising that this wasn't the first time Adam hadn't shown for a family gathering. I felt shamed by this and didn't try to make any excuses.

After lunch I took Shirl, Uncle Les's wife, aside. There was something I needed to know and I knew that Shirl had been my mother's best friend, which was how she met Uncle Les, whom she later married. Uncle Stan would know the answer to my question, but it would be almost impossible to get him to talk about the dead.

'Shirl, I need to ask you a question that's been bugging me all my life and I don't want any bullshit. I just want a yes or no,' I said, backing her into a corner. 'Uncle Jack was my father, yes or no?'

My mother had been eighteen when I was conceived. She'd already been married and would have needed to get a divorce to marry my father – a messy business back then, and my family were Catholic. Even then, she still would have needed parental consent to remarry, since she'd not come of age.

My hunch was that Jack McCarthy was my father, who for some reason, Mamma hated with a passion. She had refused to allow Jack and my mother to marry. I was nine months old when my mother disappeared, leaving me with Mamma. Two years later, Jack married Daphne, my mother's younger sister.

Some of this was merely speculation, and I wanted to know the truth.

'Please don't ask me to answer that,' Shirl's voice was fearful, as if I'd asked her to reveal the darkest family secret.

'Yes or no, Shirl? I know you know the answer,' I persisted.

'Yes,' she said, breaking down.

For the first time in my life I had a confirmation of the identity of my father that made sense, particularly given the way Uncle Jack was always there for me when I was a child. He even wanted to adopt me at one stage, but Mamma wouldn't have a bar of it.

This was interesting but I'd need more than Shirl's say-so before I could be sure. Uncle Stan had seen me talking with Shirl, and would have been able to tell by her reaction that I was digging into the past. As I approached him he started rubbing his hands together – a sign that he was nervous about something. I chose my words very carefully, but still he tried to dodge the question.

'He could have been,' he said, and wouldn't be pressured to say more.

Trudy and Roberta, Aunty Daphne's daughters, had been sitting at the table watching all this unfold. I motioned for them to follow me to a bedroom where we could talk in private.

'I've unearthed a big family secret here today,' I said, and they got excited thinking I was going to reveal a great scandal.

'We knew that,' they said in unison, when I told them that we were not cousins, but sisters.

Trudy told me that after Aunty Daphne died they'd found a letter from my mother to their mother. 'You know, Trudy,' I said, sitting next to her and taking her hand, 'Mamma used to try to turn me against Uncle Jack. She told me once that he only wanted me for my cherry and that when I was old enough he'd take it.'

Trudy stared at me. 'Nanna must have known things she never told anyone, because he took mine when I was eight,' she said, matter-of-factly.

If I hadn't been sitting down, I'd have fallen down. Trudy went on to tell me about the horrific abuse she experienced. 'One time he held a gun at my head, while he made me blow him,' she said, with almost total detachment, as though it had happened to someone else and she was merely conveying the story.

'Where did he do these things? Did he take you away some-where?' I asked, knowing that their house was small and there were few places, except perhaps his beloved pigeon coop, where he could do this.

'No, he did it in the bathroom.'

My head fell into my hands as I recalled the night when Trudy was whimpering in the bathroom and I went to check on her. The door had been locked, but she said she was alright and I went back to bed. Trudy told me that the sexual abuse, and the beatings that came with it, continued until she was fifteen years old, when a school counsellor got involved and Trudy was removed from the home. With nowhere to go she ended up in Bidura Children's Home. I felt sickened hearing these stories, but what I couldn't get past was how Aunty Daphne allowed this to happen – I couldn't accept that she didn't know. If Mamma knew Uncle Jack was capable of this, why wasn't something done to protect her other granddaughters. These were questions that would never be answered.

'No wonder Aunty Daphne stepped in front of a car,' I said.

'You know Katie, I've wondered about that too,' Trudy said.

After years of constant abuse at the hands of Uncle Jack, and witnessing the horrors Trudy endured, it wasn't hard to imagine that Aunty Daphne had committed suicide.

Stevie, Trudy's older brother, hadn't come to the reunion, so I couldn't ask him why, as he got older, he didn't step in and help. When I asked Trudy, she said, 'Stevie still calls me and tells me how much I must have enjoyed it.'

When we returned to the rest of the party and made an announcement about Uncle Jack being my father, all hell broke loose. Les and Shirl left without saying another word.

'There's no way McCarthy was your old man, Ray Burgess was your father,' Robbie insisted.

After what I'd just heard I was hoping Uncle Stan was right and 'he could have been my father' was more of a possibility.

Darrol had been keeping an eye on Savannah while all of this was going on, but it was time to go. She was starting to act up and Uncle Robbie was threatening to give her a 'paddy-whack'.

Robbie and Sharon took me aside and handed me a cheque, a repayment of the loan. I told them to keep it, that money was a gift, but they insisted that I take it.

When I got home that night I took a shower and ran the water hard, from hot to freezing cold. Holding my head under the blast until my teeth chattered, I was trying to erase the images of the flaxen-haired little doll that Trudy had been as a child, being brutalised at the hands of her own father. Even knowing Uncle Jack was a violent man I still had trouble getting my head around what he'd done. I'd like to think that even with everything going on around me I could have helped Trudy had I known what was happening, but Aunty Daphne, who'd obviously been talking to Mrs McNorton, told Trudy not to try looking for me: 'She's gone to Germany to become a prostitute.'

Mrs McNorton had told me that my grandmother had gone to see her when I was in St Margaret's Hospital and, for reasons I've never been able to fathom, Mamma told Mrs McNorton that my mother had been a prostitute. Mrs McNorton knew I had been intending to go to Germany at one stage, because I had to obtain her son's permission to get a passport and contacted them. Somehow, this all got twisted around and had prevented Trudy from trying to find me.

This murky family history wasn't something I wanted to share with Darrol. I was having enough trouble digesting it myself. As ugly as these revelations were they couldn't overshadow the joy of seeing Robbie fighting back, and winning.

Savannah was fast approaching her third birthday. More often than not I wasn't making it home before 7 p.m. each evening and Darrol insisted that Simone hang around until I got home. This put a lot of pressure on Simone, whose husband waited in the car each night for her to finish. In the end, and understandably, she resigned. I was shattered and didn't know how I was going to explain to Savannah, who adored Simone and Dylan, that she wouldn't see them anymore. Simone said she wouldn't disappear from our lives entirely and that she was always available for back-up.

After streams of interviews I was starting to despair that I'd ever find a suitable replacement. Darrol was getting edgy and told me I was being too picky.

Finally, I interviewed Nicola, a trained kindergarten teacher who had been a nanny to a family with four kids and came with excellent references. Savannah took an instant liking to her and that was good enough for me.

Robbie's remission was short-lived. Two weeks before Savannah's party, in May, Uncle Stan called to say that Robbie 'was going' and wanted to see me.

Nicola hadn't started with us yet and Darrol wasn't too pleased about having to take care of Savannah while I went to see Robbie for the last time.

'I'm not taking a baby to my brother's death bed,' I said, grabbing my car keys.

Robbie was in a private room. Dan was there, sitting by himself, chewing the inside of his mouth. Uncle Les and Shirl looked like statues, not speaking or blinking. Uncle Stan and Aunty Shirley smiled when they saw me walk in. Robbie's wife and daughter sat beside his bed holding his hand. I gave everyone a kiss and sat on the opposite side of the bed holding Robbie's other hand. Robbie was a shadow of his former self, but his eyes were as bright and alert as ever. As we reminisced about our childhood it occurred to me that I was the one person in the family with whom Robbie had any fond memories. His brothers sat against the wall like strangers waiting for a bus.

'I'm sorry, darlin', please forgive me. I always loved you, you know?' Robbie said with tears in his eyes. I knew he was apologising for the time he had slapped me to the ground, a punishment for having lost my virginity when I was only fourteen. I didn't tell him that it wasn't something I'd done willingly – he might have killed Michael if he'd known that. He'd already put three blokes in hospital who'd tried to gang rape me when I was thirteen.

A nurse attending to Robbie told me that they were putting him on a drip, and that I needed to say goodbye. I sat quietly beside

Robbie until his eyes closed. Then I reached down and kissed him one last time and left the hospital.

The next morning, Uncle Stan called to say that Robbie slipped away during the night. It was some comfort to know that in the end he passed peacefully, but after I put the phone down I started to shake and clasped my hands in a prayer-like gesture.

'Please, please help me,' I begged, smacking my hands against my forehead, feeling that I needed an injection of strength, from somewhere, to keep going.

'Robbie's gone,' I said, when Darrol entered the room.

I don't recall if he replied, but he made no move to physically comfort me. Savannah came into the room and saw that I was crying. 'Mum, Mum,' she said, her little lip curled up as she ran towards me protectively.

'Uncle Robbie has gone to heaven,' I said, hugging her for comfort.

'Like Sammy?' she asked.

'Yes, darling,' I said, and she snuggled into me. She knew that meant he wasn't coming back.

On the morning of Robbie's funeral I was feeling emotionally and physically spent. Darrol wouldn't take the day off to look after Savannah, and Simone wasn't available. I had no choice but to put her into a day care centre at Balgowlah for the day. I could still hear her screaming as I drove away. Somewhere en route I went into autopilot and ended up at Lake Parramatta, where Robbie and I had spent a large part of our childhoods.

The month of May is too cold for swimming and being there midweek I had the lake to myself. Sitting at the spot where Robbie had tried to comfort me when our dog had been skittled on the road, it felt like my chest cavity was being hacked open from the inside to allow for the enormous emotion to push its way out. My sobs echoed across the lake as I recalled the happier times in my childhood, most of which had involved Robbie in some way. We'd been separated when I was only fourteen, and had not been reunited until we were both middle-aged. We only had three short years to share the joy of our children and the satisfaction that we'd both succeeded when others had said we'd amount to nothing. Robbie was only forty-two when he died. It was hard not to feel that life had robbed us both.

22

Fifty-fifty

Nicola started working for us a few days after Robbie's funeral. Two weeks later I announced that we would be taking her with us on a business trip to the US. After we'd completed our business in Milwaukee, we'd give her a ticket to go and visit her mother in England while we took Savannah to Disneyland and drove down the Californian coast to spend time with friends in Santa Barbara.

'We'll be home a day or so behind you,' I said.

'Seriously?' she asked.

'Yes seriously, and pack your cossie, we're having a stopover in Hawaii to break the trip to the mainland.'

Our second visit to Manpower US followed much the same routine as the first. Except this time the executives knew not to fob me off and send me shopping.

For some time I'd been trying to get Darrol to invest in the software programs integral to the IBM/Manpower partnership agreement, that were seeing revenues in the States increase at a phenomenal rate. While office automation was in its infancy in Australia, things would change very quickly. I set up a meeting with the various department heads responsible for overseeing the IBM /Manpower partnership, hoping that their enthusiasm would rub off on Darrol. The meeting was successful, and for the first time in our working lives we seemed to be on the same page. By the time we left Milwaukee and put Nicola on a plane to the UK, I was totally hyped and couldn't wait to get back to Australia to get cracking. But we were committed to visiting Jim and Cathy Scheinfeld in Santa Barbara.

Jim was the son of Aaron Scheinfeld, one of the founders of Manpower Inc., and had been Darrol's immediate superior when he worked for the company in the 1970s. I'd met Jim and Cathy briefly when they visited Australia, when I had been pregnant with Savannah. They were warm, funny and hospitable people and I was looking forward to spending more time with them.

It was a beautiful day when we picked up the car to take the drive down the Big Sur. We stopped at the Hearst Castle and Savannah gave the marble piazza a good work over with the tap-shoes I'd bought her at Disneyland.

Jim and Cathy had only recently retired to Santa Barbara and were doing major renovations to their home and garden that required three full-time gardeners. Cathy and Savannah hit it off from the start, and Savannah liked nothing more than a captive audience.

'She'll talk the leg off an iron pot,' I said, taking a photograph of them sitting in the garden with Savannah holding court.

'Only three years old. She's amazing!' Cathy said. 'I hope she continues with the storytelling. She has a gift.'

Even at this age Savannah was narrating short stories, while Nicola dutifully took dictation.

Jim was genuinely interested to learn about our success. After I outlined the new developments he leaned back in his leather recliner, taking a deep drag on an unlit cigar. Jim had recently had major heart surgery, but said he still liked the smell and taste of Havana cigars.

'She's a genius,' he said, looking at Darrol, who agreed, completely catching me by surprise.

We'd been back from the US about a week when I got a distressed call from my old friend Vicki.

'I'm in trouble, Katie,' she sobbed.

'Don't even try to explain on the phone, Vicki,' I said, before suggesting that she come and stay for the weekend.

When I opened the door I tried not to react; she was emaciated. Her once vibrant and sparkling eyes were dull and sad. We both broke down as she told me about the rare condition she had been diagnosed with, where the base of her skull was pressing on her spine. The only treatment was an expensive, and risky, operation.

'They're only giving me a fifty-fifty chance of survival,' she wept in my arms. Vicki was only thirty-five years old.

'Darling, you aren't going to get off the operating table unless you gain some strength,' I said, bluntly. 'Can you get time off work before the operation?'

Hamilton Island's resort complex, in Queensland's Whitsunday Passage, had recently opened. I booked a ticket for Vicki, Savannah and me, and told Nicola she could take leave while we were away. A break without Darrol was going to do me the world of good, I thought. For over ten years we'd lived and worked together twenty-four hours a day. Lately we had been arguing constantly, in and out of the bedroom. His nitpicking over money was really wearing me down. It got so bad that if we needed anything for the house, I just went out and bought it rather than get into a battle with him over something as mundane as towels and bed linen.

My wardrobe was made up almost entirely of business clothes, so I went shopping for casual resort wear, a new swimming costume, plus a few nice things in Vicki's size that I knew she'd love.

We had a few weeks before I could get away and I was pleased. Working at an erratic pace, without any regular exercise, and having a taste for chocolate, I'd put on some weight. It was an off-hand remark from a woman who worked for us that got me motivated to lose the extra kilos.

Fay was a supervisor at the Bankstown office. She would often flirt with Darrol but I paid no mind to it. One night at a function she sidled up to me when I was chatting with another staff member from the Parramatta office. We'd been discussing diets, of all things.

'Doesn't it make you feel inferior to have so many slim women working with you?' Fay had asked, interrupting our conversation.

Shocked by her audacity I shot back, 'When I signed your pay cheque I didn't feel inferior to anyone.'

The next day I bought the Richard Simmons workout LPs and went to my first Weight Watchers meeting. I stuck to the program and was delighted to be able to get back into a bikini before our trip away. I put it on to show Darrol.

'You're only going to Queensland to play up with other men,' he accused.

'Don't be ridiculous,' I snapped.

'I'll pay half the accommodation,' he said, trying another approach.

In the end I gave in, with a warning that we were travelling first class. I also made him promise not to moan about the cost of anything, especially anything I paid for.

Hamilton Island lived up to all the promotional brochures. Darrol was really trying to woo me, and we were enjoying each other's company for the first time in a very long time. I was hoping we'd turned a corner.

'You know, I'd really like to own a resort like this in Queensland, but we'd have to sell the company first,' Darrol said one evening when we were sipping champagne and watching the sun set.

It was the first time I'd ever heard him project an idea into the future. 'You're a dreamer,' I said, teasing him for all the times he'd said the same thing to me.

Vicki survived the operation, but her speech and motor skills were seriously impaired and she would need time to rehabilitate. Her mother lived in Wollongong and wasn't in a position to quit work to take care of her, so Vicki moved in with us. As Nicola occupied the room downstairs, we had to put a single bed in Savannah's room for Vicki.

'I am not going to ask my best friend to pay for the food she eats in our home!' I said, when Darrol suggested that we ask Vicki to pay board.

I was still reeling from the fight we had over this when he called me to his office one morning. 'The account from American Express has arrived; we need to have a settling day for Hamilton Island.'

Settling day was what Darrol referred to when we'd settle the housekeeping each month. I kept a ledger of all household expenses, which I'd pay and we'd split the costs fifty-fifty. But before giving me his share he'd go through his cheque book for any miscellaneous items.

'I paid the milkman this month,' he'd say, deducting $41.42 from his total. I often wondered if he thought all the Stuart crystal, Wedgwood and Sheridan towels and bed linen just materialised.

When Darrol handed me the account from Hamilton Island he'd halved the accommodation and deducted an amount of $18.60 from his total, which was for souvenir spoons I had bought for Peggy Gazzard. I'd charged them to the room when I didn't have my purse with me.

'Are you telling me that after a holiday of the kind we just had, I owe you $18.60? Would you like to see the balance on my Bank card?' I asked, handing him a personal cheque for my share of the accommodation, plus $18.60. This rattled me so much I wasn't thinking straight. The American Express card was paid through the company, after all, which put him way ahead on the deal when he pocketed the cheque from me.

Vicki made slow yet steady progress and six months after her operation she was ready to go back to work part-time and live independently. While she lived with us I was able to help her organise a house and land package in Campbelltown. As a house-warming gift I gave her a charcoal sketch I'd done of 'Benny', a cat I'd once owned. Benny was the only cat Vicki had ever warmed to and when he was tortured and left on our doorstep to die, by someone who loved his birds more than cats, we were both devastated.

'Thank you, I'll never be able to repay you,' Vicki said, wrapping her arms around me for one final hug before she got into her car to go to her new home.

'We're going to grow old together and be elegant ladies doing lunch, that's all the reward I need.'

Savannah and I stood on the nature strip and waved her off. As Vicki turned the corner I felt saddened. I'd grown accustomed to having her around and I'd miss her terribly.

The reconnection Darrol and I had made on Hamilton Island proved short-lived and we grew ever more distant. I felt like the proverbial bird in the gilded cage, not even encouraged to sing. My only joy was the time I could spend with Savannah and Adam.

One morning we were travelling to work in Darrol's car. From the passenger seat I strained my neck to catch a glimpse of the trees at Kirribilli, which had already turned to autumn gold. The sails of the Opera House gleamed like mother of pearl against a deep blue sky. We lived in one of the most beautiful cities in the world but I only got to see it for a few fleeting moments each day, through the window of a moving vehicle. The pointlessness of everything I had been striving to achieve was starting to dawn on me.

Nicola was a clever calligrapher, and that year she surprised me with a Christmas gift she'd made herself. It was a pen and ink drawing of a woman being put through a mangle, having the life squeezed out of her, with the caption: *'Go ahead, you son of a bitch! Give it another turn, I work better under pressure.'* I took it to work and hung it on the wall behind my desk.

Christmas that year was a sombre affair. It took all my strength just to get lunch for Darrol and his brother, Bob, who'd recently separated from his wife.

Darrol drank a whole bottle of wine at lunch and without warning, took a running jump from the first-floor balcony into the pool below.

'There goes the Rolex,' Bob laughed, as we heard the big splash.

On 26 January 1988, the nation was all set to celebrate the 200th anniversary of the arrival of the First Fleet into Port Jackson. Darrol grumbled when I told him I wasn't going out on our boat to celebrate Australia Day.

'If we must have a frenzied day of overt nationalism, we ought to have it on a more appropriate day. Australia didn't become a nation until 1901, so why glorify a day that marks a brutal British invasion?' I told him.

'That's nonsense, Aboriginal people need to forget the past and move on. This is 1988,' he replied.

His flippancy that day annoyed me. He'd come to Australia as an immigrant in the 1950s, and was given concessions that Aboriginal people had no entitlement to, because we were not classed as citizens. His mother worked hard and managed to leave Darrol and his brothers a tidy piece of property to divvy up. No matter how hard Aboriginal people worked we had not been allowed to own property until a referendum in 1967 gave us full citizenship rights.

Starting on this day in 1788, I gave Darrol a history lesson. 'And you say we should get over it!' I was almost shouting when I finished. 'And besides, you still haven't put life jackets on board,' I reminded him.

It had been Darrol's decision to purchase 'Adjar' a forty-four-foot motor launch. The first time we went out on the water I discovered there were no life jackets on board and I'd spent the entire day on edge, never taking my eyes off Savannah. She even came to the toilet with me. After that I told Darrol we were not going onto the boat until it was properly equipped.

23

Pulling the plug

It started as a kind of mind-numbing tiredness. Then it escalated to include backaches and tummy cramps, which I put down to premenstrual pain. I kept on working through it until one day I simply couldn't get out of bed.

'I can't go to work with you today. Could you please ask Nicola if she'd make me a cup of tea,' I asked Darrol, who was about to leave for work.

Later in the day I felt strong enough to inch my way downstairs. Savannah and Nicola were in the television room. When I sat down Savannah sprang onto my lap.

'I love you, Mummo.'

'I love you too, my Possum,' I said, trying not to wince as Savannah planted what she called 'daisy kisses' all over my face.

The next morning when I was no better Nicola helped me dress and drove me to the doctor, who diagnosed my condition as 'over-worked' and recommended bed rest for a few days. It wasn't difficult to comply; I couldn't get out of bed.

Things didn't improve over the next few months and by June I needed to crawl on all fours to get to the bathroom.

'Can't you see how sick I am? Do you think I'm faking this?' I said to Darrol, when he started complaining about not getting enough sex.

'This is just an excuse, you've never enjoyed sex,' he said, angrily.

'If you can't abstain, or sort yourself out until I'm better, go to a prostitute!' I snapped. 'And make sure you wear a condom.' Darrol looked like I'd just slapped his face with a smelly rag. Even I was shocked to hear myself say such a thing.

A few weeks later, when I was feeling up to it, I made an appointment to see Maurice, the solicitor I'd spoken with a few years before about the possibility of getting a divorce. After a long and emotional outpouring about the difficulties in our marriage, I gave Maurice the journals I'd kept throughout the relationship so he'd know I wasn't making things up.

Although Darrol never physically hurt me, I felt emotionally abused. No matter how hard I worked he always found something to criticise, reminding me of the times I watched Aunty Daphne cook a nice meal for Uncle Jack, only to have it thrown against a wall.

After speaking with Maurice, it all seemed too hard. Sorting out the financial matters, which would almost certainly involve breaking up the company, was daunting. Then there was Savannah and the family to consider. As difficult as I was finding life with Darrol, it still gave me a family and a feeling of belonging. After weighing all of the pros and cons, the thought of initiating a divorce was shelved, but I felt I had to make some changes or I'd go insane.

'What for?' Darrol asked, when I told him I wanted to buy another house.

'I think it might save our marriage if we live separately for part of the week,' I explained.

'That's nonsense.'

By my calculations the director's loan account ought to be sufficiently in credit for me to purchase a new house, without needing a mortgage, but I needed Darrol's agreement, as managing director, to draw down such a large dividend.

Darrol came with me to inspect a property in Avalon.

The moment I stepped inside and saw the high vaulted ceilings and massive glass walls that brought in the view across Careel Bay and out to Lion Island, I was sold. Darrol agreed to release the deposit and to make the rest of the funds available for settlement.

As I was still dragging my feet around, I'd asked for an extension to move the settling day of the new property to early December. I was hoping an extra three months would give me time to recuperate so I'd have the stamina for the move. But, almost as soon as I realised the change was imminent I felt like a great weight had been lifted from my shoulders. I set about buying new things for the Avalon house and planning a complete refurbishment.

A few weeks later we were standing in the kitchen after work when Darrol handed me a letter from a family law firm. Attached to this letter was an evaluation of our home in Clontarf, which Darrol had completed without my knowledge. It was valued at just over one million dollars. He was making me an offer of $350,000. I was confused. At that stage we weren't intending to terminate the marriage and if we had been I couldn't understand why he'd deducted $150,000 from my share of the marital home.

'Why are you making me this offer? How did you arrive at these figures?' I asked.

Ignoring the first part of my question, he handed me a sheet of paper that listed all of the properties we'd purchased over the years. I noted the cubby in Mosman, the first home we'd bought together, wasn't on the list. I asked him to explain. 'You had no equity in that property. Your name wasn't on the deed,' he said, cracking two eggs into a pan for his dinner.

This remark hit me as hard as if he'd just punched me in the stomach. We'd been living together for six months when we purchased the Mosman property. It was his practice to shove documents under my nose, which I signed on trust, so I had no recollection of seeing any documents about the Mosman property specifically. But given that I'd negotiated the property price and paid half of all the costs it would never have dawned on me that my name was not included on the mortgage or deed to purchase.

'So why was I paying half the mortgage?' I asked.

Without looking at me he said, 'You didn't think you could live in my home and not pay rent, did you?'

In the time it took Darrol to knock up two eggs on toast, our marriage had reached a place of irreconcilable differences.

'I'm not accepting that, until I get some legal advice,' I said.

Nicola didn't work in the evening and was playing tennis that night, so I went upstairs to attend to Savannah who'd been disturbed by our raised voices. I got into her bed and sang her to sleep.

The next morning I called my solicitor and told him what had gone down the night before. I asked him if Darrol could deduct $150,000 from the equity in our home because my name wasn't on the deed of a property we bought before we got married.

'Yes, he can,' Maurice said.

Suddenly, things that had previously puzzled me made sense. Over the years any attempt on my part to enquire about our personal finances had caused Darrol to flare, blowing everything out of proportion. These conversations had often ended with him accusing me of being mercenary for having asked. It was a diversionary tactic that worked – I tended to avoid these discussions as much as possible. It came as a hard realisation that my relationship and marriage to Darrol had been built on lies from the outset. If I'd been feeling emotionally and physically stronger when I discovered what he'd done regarding the Mosman property, I'd have pulled the plug, wound the business up and made a clean break. But I didn't. Just like Peggy Levy, the woman I once worked for at Formal Wear Hire Service, I let emotion rule my head by putting the people who worked for me first. They were relying on me to continue what I was doing. I asked my solicitor to assess what my assets in the marriage were and make Darrol an appropriate counter offer.

Fortunately, Matt was already moving out. He'd resigned from Manpower and was heading to Queensland. After Matt had gone, I moved all of my personal possessions into his room. Our marriage was officially over. Although I hadn't pre-empted it, I was relieved.

While all of this was happening I made an appointment with my doctor for a routine check-up. He was very excited about a new piece of equipment he'd brought back from the US called a Colposcope, and explained the procedure saying that it could detect abnormalities with the cervix long before they appeared using a standard Pap smear. I agreed to be a guinea pig.

The doctor had said he'd only call me if there was a problem, so when he called and said he needed to see me urgently, I started to worry.

When I heard the words 'cervical cancer' I felt like I'd been hit in the neck with a poisoned dart, leaving me paralysed but fully cognisant. I listened in horror as he explained that it had all started with a viral wart infection, which had been passed on to me through sexual intercourse. It was a long time before I could respond.

'You mean a type of STD?'

'Yes,' he said.

I explained that I'd not been with a man other than my husband for twelve years. He told me this infection can lay dormant for longer than that and can be activated by stress. He told me I had to reduce my workload to alleviate the stress and have treatment as soon as possible. When I told him that I thought I was about to go through a divorce, he said, 'I'm your doctor, not your legal advisor.'

The doctor told me that Darrol needed to be treated and gave me a referral for him to see a specialist. That night Darrol was completely dispassionate when I told him about the diagnosis.

'You didn't get it from me and you weren't a virgin when we met,' he said defensively.

'I don't know if you were the carrier, but unless you want to pass it on to every woman you sleep with in the future, you need to be treated. It's highly infectious and potentially lethal for the woman,' I said, leaving the referral on the breakfast bar.

My solicitor wrote to Darrol's solicitor advising that I was medically unfit to properly instruct him. They responded by saying that they didn't accept that I could not properly advise my solicitor.

Maurice set up a meeting with Darrol and his solicitor. I was asked to wait in another office and wasn't privy to this discussion. Afterwards, Maurice said he was amused when Darrol claimed I hadn't cooked him a meal for two years. 'If my wife was capable of producing those results I'd be happy if she didn't cook for me,' Maurice had responded, suggesting that Darrol take another look at the company balance sheets, which indicated that the revenues for the company had jumped from $8 million in 1987 to over $9 million as at June 1988.

'You had a company tax bill of $500,000 and just wrote out a cheque, and he's complaining that you didn't cook for him.' I detected a tone of resentment in Maurice's voice.

Darrol also told Maurice that unless I signed the consent orders for the property settlement, he wouldn't release the funds I needed to settle the Avalon property in December, which was now only a few weeks away.

Maurice showed me the draft of the consent orders he'd prepared after the meeting. My share in our matrimonial home stayed the same, and my shares in the company remained at one-third.

'Surely, as Darrol's wife, I'm entitled to fifty per cent of the value of the company?' I queried.

'You got what you settled for,' Maurice said, reminding me that I'd agreed to accept a one-third share.

'What about the contents of the home?' Maurice asked. 'You need to provide an estimate of the value of the contents.'

The contents of the property were worth roughly $100,000. I knew this because I'd bought most of the furniture and objets d'art.

'I have no intention of fighting over goods and chattels,' I said, wanting to get this over with so I could start focusing on my health.

'Goods and chattels?' He sounded annoyed that I seemed to be flippant over a substantial amount of possessions.

We were running a company making millions with the potential for further growth. I had just been told I had a life-threatening condition that demanded I have immediate treatment and reduce stress. If I haggled over who got the Chesterfield and who got the French clock, I might be dead before we signed the agreement.

'Let him have it.'

'That's a very generous gift.'

The gift wasn't to Darrol but to Savannah. My priority was getting well and staying alive.

As I was about to put pen to paper on the consent orders I saw mention of a private company, one that I thought had ceased to exist after his first divorce. It listed Darrol as the sole owner. I refused to sign the document.

That night I asked Darrol about this company. 'You have no interest in that company and it has no assets,' he said, dismissively. 'It's just a vehicle for paying our salaries.'

I wasn't prepared to take him at his word, and I instructed my solicitor to make appropriate enquiries.

Darrol started to rant, just as he'd done whenever we tried to discuss our finances over the years. This time I wasn't running to the Manly Pacific.

Sitting on the lounge, reading Savannah a story, it struck me that I hadn't seen mention of the boat on the consent orders. I did recall signing for the boat, which we'd purchased for $150,000.

The door to the lounge was open and I could hear Darrol in the kitchen.

'What about the boat?' I called.

Something crashed into the kitchen sink and he came into the lounge room screaming abuse. 'You had fucking nothing when I met you!'

I stood up to face him.

'You on the other hand had a debt for $35,000 to Manpower US that I helped you pay off in two years!' I said, just in case he'd forgotten that he'd told me he'd borrowed the money from Manpower US to purchase the franchise in 1975.

By this time Savannah was very distressed, we'd never fought like this in front of her. I took her up to her room to get out of his way. He followed us.

As I tried to close the door he pushed it so hard I nearly fell over backwards. He was snarling through clenched teeth, waving his fist in my face. He threw a punch that veered to the side, before becoming embedded in the wardrobe door.

'I hope you've broken your hand, now get out! Or I'll call the police!' I screamed.

He went raging down the stairs and I could hear him in the kitchen. With superhuman strength I managed to push the cupboard up against the door. For what seemed an eternity I heard glass smashing and loud cracking noises, like explosions shaking the house. There was no phone in the bedroom and this time pre-dated mobile phones. Savannah dived under her bed cover and started screaming. I got into the bed with her and held her tight. I started to sing her favourite bedtime song, 'Bright Eyes' from the animated film *Watership Down*. We sang the chorus together as the racket downstairs continued. That night I didn't sleep for fear that Darrol might completely lose it and set fire to the place.

Afraid of what I would find, the next morning I slowly descended the stairs. The devastation left me speechless. Three massive glass walls in the lounge room were completely shattered. Large shards of glass pierced the lounge suites. Outdoor furniture and assorted pot plants were strewn around the room and I realised that the damage had been caused by Darrol hurling this stuff through the windows. It looked like a bomb had exploded in David Jones' house and garden emporium.

Nicola was having a few days off and Simone was coming to take care of Savannah. Simone's eyes were as big as saucers when she saw the carnage.

'O'Brien Glass is coming at ten o'clock; you may need to take Savannah out for the day,' I said, without further explanation, before picking up my briefcase, kissing Savannah, and walking out the door.

As I was backing my car out of the garage the next door neighbour stopped me. 'Is everything alright?' she asked.

'We're getting a divorce,' I said, expecting that would be enough to explain the noise from the night before.

'I was worried last night, I was going to call the police,' she seemed genuinely concerned.

'I wish you had done, I was in fear for our lives.'

Darrol came into the office after lunch and we worked together as if nothing was happening at home, but that night it was on again.

'I am not giving you another fucking cent!' he screamed, when I told him that I'd refused to sign the consent orders.

'Let's get something straight here; you're not giving me anything and until I determine what this other company is about, I'm not signing anything.'

He started swearing and cursing. Savannah was screaming for us to stop. I warned him to back off or I'd call the police.

By early December the consent orders still hadn't been signed. I contacted the vendor, hoping that a woman-to-woman discussion might get a better result than having Maurice call her to ask for another extension on the settlement. I only needed a few more days. She was totally inflexible and told me that if I didn't settle on 10 December, I'd forfeit the deposit and pay the penalty.

On 9 December I received a letter confirming that Darrol's private company had no assets. The next day I scrambled frantically to get all the documents signed, arrange bank cheques and get the money to the vendor's solicitor by 3 p.m. At approximately 2:30 p.m. I signed the deed for the Avalon property. I went home and got ready for the move the next day. Any chance of reducing stress at this point seemed unlikely.

As I was about to close the door on this chapter of my life, I paused, remembering a time many years before, when I had revisited the empty house of my childhood, the last place I had lived with my family. Nostalgically, I walked from room to room that day, my nostrils flaring at the familiar smells and faint aroma of Mamma's kitchen still clinging to the empty space. At that time I was left with nothing, not even a photograph. Now, I was leaving behind tens of thousands of dollars of accumulated possessions, but as far as I was concerned I was taking with me the most precious asset of our marriage, my daughter, and I didn't have to haggle over her.

I called Darrol to give him our new phone number.

'I'd like Mum's wedding ring back,' he said.

'It's not your mother's wedding ring, it's mine, and no you can't have it back, it's a family heirloom. It'll never get tossed haphazardly onto a bed for someone to try for size.'

It wasn't until the stamped consent orders were returned by the court that I noted my director's loan account held considerably less in credit than I was expecting. I called Maurice to query this.

'That can't be right; I've never been paid a dividend,' I argued.

'Well you ought to have checked the summary of the loan account before you signed the consent orders,' he said, defensively.

During the negotiations for the property settlement I did recall seeing a summary for the director's loan account that our accountant had provided but in all the pressure and stress I hadn't bothered to examine the details. Naively, I had believed that if William had done the calculations I wouldn't be required to check them for accuracy.

'Anyway, it's too late. The court has stamped the consent orders and you got what you settled for,' Maurice said.

At the time it didn't occur to me to seek a second legal opinion, and I rationalised this loss as trivial in comparison to the income that would still be generated from the business if things kept going the way they were.

Despite the financial and emotional hit I had taken, I felt an indescribable relief not to wake up each morning feeling trapped and suffocated. It was as if someone had turned off the jack hammers that had been drilling in my head since I ascended the stairs in Hunter Street all those years ago for my interview with Mr Norman.

24

What's happy got to do with anything?

Although we'd spoken on the phone, Adam and I hadn't seen each other for months and I hadn't involved him in my problems at home. It was probably going to come as a shock to him that Darrol and I had separated, although I didn't expect him to be particularly unhappy about it. Darrol had never done anything to make Adam feel welcome.

When I called to let him know he said, 'Mum, you deserve to be happy.'

After calling Vicki, whose reaction to my separation from Darrol was much the same as Adam's had been, I called Peggy Gazzard.

'Why Avalon?' she asked, before I'd even told her where I'd moved. Darrol had clearly been in her ear already.

'I have friends here, and I like the area,' I said.

'So there's no other man involved?'

'No, and if there was it'd be no one's business but mine,' I said, resenting this interrogation. There was a bit of heavy breathing into the phone before I broke the impasse. 'Peggy, we were not happy.'

'Happy? What's happy got to do with anything? You had everything anyone could ever want,' she retorted sharply. To women of Peggy's era, leaving an unhappy marriage wasn't an option. I didn't bother explaining that I'd been trying to work it out, and it was Darrol who'd tipped the balance when he tabled the property settlement. She didn't even ask how Savannah was coping.

Anticipating that Darrol would come and see Savannah for Christmas, or perhaps invite her to his home to have Christmas with Willow and Matt, we went shopping and bought gifts for everyone. Darrol and Matt came over on Christmas Eve morning but didn't stay long enough for the lavish morning tea we'd prepared for them. Matt looked embarrassed because he could see we'd gone to a lot of trouble to make it special and Savannah loved tea parties.

Adam and I had spent so many Christmases apart it wasn't important to either of us if we saw each other on the actual day. We agreed to catch up before New Year.

By Christmas morning Peggy hadn't touched base to see what we were doing, so I called to wish her a merry Christmas, and was very hurt to learn that she'd invited Vicki for lunch and not me and Savannah. I unwrapped the gifts we'd bought for her. Later, Vicki told me it'd ruined her day when she'd realised we'd been excluded. Peggy was upset about an earlier incident I'd been drawn into between her and her husband, Rex, who she'd reunited with when Savannah was a toddler. His father had died, leaving him a considerable estate, and he'd returned to buy Peggy the house of her dreams in Bronte. With my help, he also tracked down his son, Jack, who was living on Dangar Island on the Hawkesbury River with his partner and three young children. 'They're living like pigs,' Peggy had claimed.

Rex was keen to help Jack by buying him a property in Nimbin, but Peggy was against the idea. I told Rex I thought he should do what he thought was right. Peggy was furious. Punishing me was one thing but cutting Savannah off from her 'Poppy Rex' was unforgivable in my mind. I never saw Rex Gazzard again, and it would be many years before I would speak with Peggy.

When I called my friend Phil Christensen and he realised that Savannah and I were home alone on Christmas Day he invited us for lunch. 'Gabor's cooking Hungarian goulash,' he said.

'That'll be interesting,' I chuckled, thanking him for the invite.

My old friends, Noel and Myles, were at Phil's and it felt good to be in their company again. Myles, who was divorced by this time, wasted no time putting the moves on me and inviting me for dinner on New Year's Eve. I couldn't find a suitable babysitter for Savannah, so Myles came to our place instead. We had a romantic dinner for three and after Savannah had gone to bed, he and I moved outside to enjoy a drink under the huge summer moon. Myles asked if it wasn't 'too presumptuous' of him to have his overnight bag in the car. I shared my health concerns with Myles and he was very compassionate.

I'd never been really sick before. Mostly, I'd relied on ti-tree oil and Vicks VapoRub to cure all ills. I dreaded the thought of going to hospital, but the sooner I got treatment the better the outcome, so I waited anxiously for my surgery early in the new year. Darrol said he was too busy to take care of Savannah while I had my operation so once again Simone helped out.

The fog started to lift and after the general anaesthetic wore off the doctor told me I had a visitor. I looked up to see Myles standing beside my bed. He took my hand. He was trembling slightly; he hated hospitals as much as I did. Myles drove me to the Sebel Townhouse where I had organised to spend the night before driving home the next day.

Before Myles and I could be intimate he needed to go to see a doctor to make sure he wasn't carrying the virus. When he told me about the indignity of having a purple dye applied to his penis, exposing tiny warts that were invisible to the naked eye, he shuddered with revulsion. 'Millions of them, all over my dick!' he said. After taking the antibiotics he went back to the doctor to ensure he was clean.

Towards the end of January, Darrol called. He sounded drunk. 'This is your friendly neighbourhood rapist,' he said. When I asked him what he meant and if he was seriously suggesting we have sex, he said, 'Would that be such a bad thing?'

I told him that frankly I'd rather masturbate.

'I'll have you know I am seeing some beautiful women. All of them millionaires in their own right.'

'Well give one of them a call,' I said, hanging up the phone.

A few nights later I got another call. He'd been drinking again and asked me how long I'd been fucking Myles Stivano. I told him that it was none of his business and slammed down the phone.

'Did you tell him how often I tried in the past?' Myles chuckled, when I told him that Darrol had accused us of having an affair.

A few nights later Darrol called again. This time he was sober and asked if we could have lunch. We met in a café in North Sydney Plaza.

'When did you stop loving me?' he asked, as he surveyed the menu.

'That day is indelibly imprinted on my mind. It was 4 August 1979.'

He looked surprised; because that was the day we got married. It was also the day that I realised that whatever it was Darrol and I had together it was not, and probably never would be, a loving

relationship. At best, it would only ever be a marriage of convenience for us both.

'If you were to ask me when I began to dislike you, I could tell
you that date also. It was 20 November 1983.'

He asked what was so special about that day. I reminded him
that it was the day I told him I was pregnant. This seemed like a
good opportunity to air something that had bothered me for many
years. The question caught him off guard.

'Yes, I did,' he said, when I asked if he'd gone home after our
first night together and made love to his wife. He said she was
hurting and needed comfort.

'And you thought that making love to her and leaving her the
very next day would be comforting?' I said, folding my napkin.
The heartlessness of such an act was beyond my comprehension; I
left before my meal arrived.

Savannah was starting school in February and Darrol refused to
continue to pay Nicola through the company payroll or assist
me with after-school care. I told him I was going to reduce my
hours to accommodate Savannah's needs. Meanwhile, I'd concen-
trate on my health. Our place soon became a tea house, playhouse
and artists' workshop, and when we weren't enjoying picnics at
Clareville Beach, we'd turn the lounge room into a music hall,
where Savannah and Simone's son, Dylan, created and performed
magic shows. It was bittersweet to see Savannah enjoying all the
things that Adam and I had been denied when he was growing up.

Although Savannah was very bright, and already reading above
the average level for her age, her social skills needed development.
She was only four and a half years old when she started school,
and looking back I can see that she wasn't quite ready. Every day
that I dropped her off at school she started screaming and had to

be pulled from the car. To reduce this trauma I tried staying in the classroom until she settled, but that didn't work. She clung to me like a limpet and screamed if I left the room. I told Darrol I was going to take more leave until I could get Savannah settled.

With the reporting systems I'd set up at Manpower, I could be absent and still keep my finger on the pulse. I met with my staff once a week and was happy with how things were progressing. We were breaking all records, with over 3500 temps in the field each week.

With the time to be able to do so, I got involved with the parent body at Savannah's school. Although I didn't put my hand up for tuckshop duty, I never missed an excursion where parents were invited. When it became known that I could sew, I got roped into making outfits for the school concerts. Gradually, I was able to ease Savannah into school and by April I was ready to go back to work.

'Things have changed while you've been away,' Susie, who had been my right-hand assistant after Moira left the company, informed me when I told her I was coming back to work after Anzac Day. 'Mr Norman has created a new role for me.'

'Really?' I said. I then advised Susie that one thing hadn't changed, and for the moment she still reported to me.

Myles came to stay over the Anzac weekend. We were watching the news and cringed at a horrific road accident that had claimed the lives of a newlywed couple. A car and an ice-cream van had collided head-on, on Epping Road. The driver and the female passenger had been trapped in the car and were incinerated before they could be rescued.

The phone rang early on Tuesday morning as I was getting ready for work. It was Darrol, calling to tell me that Susie and her husband of six months had been killed in the accident on Epping Road. This took the wind out of me and I was glad Myles was there to hold me. Losing Susie in such tragic circumstances, with our last words being hostile, devastated me. I managed to pull myself together and went to the office. Given the situation, I thought we should close for the day. Everyone was walking around zombie-like, but trying to carry on as if everything was normal, when it clearly wasn't.

Something snapped that day and I felt my heart had gone out of the company. I had a strong gut feeling that I would not be coming back to the office. I cleaned out my desk and took down the plaque Nicola had given me for Christmas the previous year. I left without saying goodbye to anyone.

That night I broke down. Susie had been only nineteen when she came to work for me. I had watched her grow into a beautiful woman. She had been madly in love and had her whole life ahead of her. My grief made me do a complete stock-take of my own situation. All my adult life I'd been a workaholic, pushing myself beyond the brink and triggering a cancer, which my doctor had said was stress related. Although the recent medical treatment had been successful, I was not out of the woods regarding my health. I'd been warned to slow down and take things easy as it could flare up again. To continue working with Darrol, in what was now an openly hostile environment, was not good for me and certainly not good for the business. At this stage I'd not even told staff that Darrol and I had separated, but I got the feeling that Susie knew, which may have accounted for her attitude when we last spoke.

The next morning I called William, our business accountant, to discuss what my financial position would be if I resigned. He told me that the infrastructure of the company was solid and that I could still earn a six-figure income from my dividends, without getting out of bed. I had other concerns. I asked William what the effect would be on the business if I wasn't there – what would stop Darrol doing what he liked, to my disadvantage? William gave me an undertaking that he wouldn't see me denied any of the rewards I was entitled to, but that if Darrol changed his accountant I should call my lawyer.

Just three days after my talk with William I received a letter from Darrol, on company letterhead, setting out my entitlements. It seemed he was making me redundant, effective immediately. I called my solicitor.

'It's in your best interest to get him to buy you out,' Maurice advised.

I instructed Maurice to obtain an evaluation of my shares in the company.

When I called Darrol to offer him my shares he declined, saying that he couldn't afford to buy me out at the book value, plus the goodwill that would be applied. After the financial losses I'd already sustained in dealings with Darrol I wasn't prepared to negotiate for less.

All things considered, I decided to accept Darrol's offer for me to resign, but that I would remain a director and shareholder in the company.

The first thing that jumped out at me on the paperwork outlining the termination payout was that the calculations didn't include my long service leave. Darrol got angry when I mentioned this, claiming I'd been on holiday for six months, on full pay. I reminded him that I was taking care of our daughter, and to take another look at the balance sheets, which showed the company's revenue had jumped from $9 million in 1988 to over $15 million as at June 1989. Perhaps he really was arrogant enough to think he'd achieved that on his own. The argument became heated and I told him that if he didn't pay me what I was entitled to I'd seek a redundancy payout.

It was possible that the discussion I'd had with William and the subsequent offer from Darrol for me to resign was coincidental. At least, that's what I chose to believe. After the matter was settled I called William to thank him for his support over the years, and advised that I still wished to retain him as my accountant and executor of my Will. I expressed disappointment that the IBM/

Manpower partnership agreement I'd been working on would probably go by the wayside, unless Darrol was prepared to bring in someone from the US. 'Darrol doesn't have your vision or drive,' William remarked candidly.

When I received my Group Tax Certificate, with the super-annuation entitlement attached, I called Maurice. His only comment about the super was that it was a 'handsome sum'.

It's hard to express the intense emotions swirling around as I looked back on my marriage and business partnership with Darrol which, in spite of many difficulties, created a beautiful child and developed a company that grew from virtually nothing into a leader in the field in the space of twelve years. I left Manpower without any fanfare, and also with a deep sense of loss. I wondered if the sacrifices I'd made were really worth it. Especially in regard to the years I had lost with Adam.

25

Goodbye my friend

'Simply Stunning?' I suggested when we were tossing around names for the new bridal wear boutique we were contemplating setting up in Mona Vale.

'Yes, I like it,' Lynne agreed.

Lynne was the wife of a business associate of Myles, whom I'd met a few months after leaving Manpower. She lived close by at Terrey Hills and was looking to create a job for herself. We both agreed that there was an unmet need in our area for an upmarket bridal wear and lingerie shop. Neither of us was interested in getting involved in a business that would require taking huge risks. Having learned a lesson from my association with Darrol, I had my solicitor draw up a partnership agreement that clearly stated the conditions if either of us wanted to opt out.

On our way home from a trip to the city I stopped at Darrol's place to pick up something that Savannah had left behind. As it was a Saturday, I called to make sure he was home and that it was alright for Lynne and me to call in.

The first thing that struck me when we stepped inside the house was the new carpet. Within a year of our separation he'd had the whole house recarpeted in a cream plush-pile. His new girlfriend was an interior decorator, which may have had a lot to do with it.

As we walked past the leather-topped desk, I picked up a large framed photograph of Darrol standing with two women, taken at Randwick Racecourse for the running of the Manpower Handicap. It was a recent photograph, prompting me to ask if racing was a new interest. In my experience Darrol hated horse racing. Hanging off his arm was a striking redhead, wearing a full-length fur coat. She bore an uncanny likeness to a woman who used to work for us.

'It takes fifty dumb animals to make a coat like that,' I said, replacing the photograph.

Darrol looked like a kid with his hand caught in the cookie jar. 'By the way, Peter's coming to Australia next month,' he said, ignoring my remark.

As we drove back to Mona Vale I asked Lynne if she had noticed anything odd.

'I was too dazzled to notice anything odd,' she said.

'There's a photograph of Darrol with two women on his desk and not a single one of any of his children.'

'Things must've been pretty bad to leave such a good-looking man and that spectacular home,' she observed.

'If I hadn't been such a bloody fool I'd have left years earlier.'

The intimacy between Myles and I didn't last long. Our friendship survived intact but he didn't understand monogamy, believing that a man wasn't meant to be with only one woman, a concept that I struggled with. I laughed and said that proved he was a blackfella, because traditional culture allowed a man to have four wives.

Peter and I hadn't had any contact since our trip to Canada a few years earlier, so it came as a surprise when he called the night he arrived and wanted to come and visit me and Savannah. Darrol came with him and got annoyed when I suggested that I kidnap Peter and take him to Hamilton Island.

'She isn't your wife anymore, buddy,' Peter said, winking at me.

I'd only been joking. Peter's arrival coincided with the opening of the bridal wear shop, and I couldn't possibly go anywhere. But his comment and wink were rather suggestive, making me think that perhaps his trip to Australia had more to do with me no longer being married to his brother than anything else.

'Yes, I'm not your wife anymore, buddy,' I said, returning the wink.

Darrol got up and left in a huff.

Later that week Peter and I arranged to have lunch. Lunch turned into dinner and dinner turned into breakfast. Not surprisingly, Peter soon had an argument with Darrol. He called to say he was leaving Darrol's place and checking in to a hotel.

'You'll do no such thing. I'll come and get you,' I told him.

I wasn't afraid to confront Darrol, I'd done nothing wrong and Peter had already said that his marriage was over. Darrol was standing in the kitchen; he had just come home from work and was wearing a smart suit.

'Nice suit,' I said, casually.

'Yes. It's Armani,' he boasted.

'Oh, really,' I said. 'Turn around.'

'Why? What's wrong?'

'I just wanted to see if you had the price tag hanging out the back.'

Peter was standing at the door with his bags, ready to go. He extended his hand. Darrol made no move to shake his brother's hand or say goodbye.

After we left I gave Peter a clear warning with regard to the interference we could expect. I told him that if Darrol ever placed him in a position where he had to choose between me and him, and he chose Darrol, we'd be finished. Peter told me not to worry; that was never going to happen.

For the next six weeks Peter and I had a whirlwind courtship. I had to put in a few hours at the shop, but the business had not developed to the point where two people were needed, so we had a good deal of time together to do as we pleased. Peter loved music, singers especially, and we danced and then made love to all of our favourites. Making love with Peter after so many years of not wanting Darrol to touch me was like opening the flood gates. But lust aside, there were a lot of practical considerations that we needed to thrash out before we'd be able to think about making a life together. Peter soon returned to Canada. We'd decided that I'd follow him a month later and we'd spend Christmas together and see how things went after that.

Darrol came to Savannah's school concert, and I told him about our plans and gave him her passport application to sign. He was still hostile about my relationship with Peter and when I asked him what it had to do with him, he said he still loved me. This caused me to laugh.

'You don't have a bloody clue, do you? Love isn't about what you say; it's about what you do.'

Adam came to Avalon the week before we were due to leave. I was leaving him with the car and keys to the house, both of which were at his disposal.

We arrived in Vancouver on 22 December. Peter had found us a nice furnished house to rent in North Vancouver.

'It's snowing!' Savannah squealed excitedly on Christmas morning, pulling on her boots to go outside and make a snowman in the deep white powder blanketing the front yard.

Sitting down to turkey, ham and all the trimmings with a crackling fire and snow falling outside made a wonderful change from
the sweltering heat of an Australian summer. On New Year's Eve,
Peter and I were in the hot-tub, drinking champagne and watching
the night skiers set off coloured flares on top of Grouse Mountain,
when the phone rang right on midnight.

'We're engaged!' Vicki's and Bill's voices cried, in unison.

Bill was a business associate of Myles and a very decent man,
whom I'd rather fancied myself. My problem was I could never
make the first move, and when Bill showed no interest in me, I
thought I'd do a little matchmaking by introducing him to Vicki.
They had set the wedding date for the following year and I was
honoured when Vicki asked me to be her matron of honour.

After much discussion Peter and I worked out an arrangement
that we thought would satisfy everyone. We'd maintain two houses.
Savannah would go to school in Canada, but we'd come back to
Australia every year for the three-month vacation from June to
September. I called Darrol to advise him of this plan. He exploded,
demanding that I bring Savannah back to Australia immediately.

'Go to hell! We'll be back in June and if you don't like that too
bloody bad!' I slammed the phone in his ear.

A letter soon arrived from the Canadian Attorney General's
Office. Darrol had taken action to have Savannah returned under
The Hague Child Abduction Convention. It sounded intimidating
on paper. A representative from the Attorney General's Office
came to our home to interview us. She showed me the statement
from Darrol. I laughed out loud.

'This is a vicious and vindictive action taken by Mr Norman
because I'm living with his brother. Mr Norman is a multi-
millionaire and he doesn't pay one dollar by way of child support.
And I could count on one hand the days he has seen Savannah
since our separation over a year ago.'

'Your former husband doesn't give you any financial support for the child?' the representative asked, incredulous.

'No, not a cent,' I confirmed. 'He never has.'

She let me know that she was satisfied and I would not be compelled to return Savannah to Australia. 'If your former husband wishes to pursue this, he'll have to come to Canada,' she said.

The next day I called Darrol to tell him what the Attorney General's Office had to say. If we'd been in the same room I'm sure we would've come to blows.

A few weeks later I received a letter from Darrol with a dissolution of marriage papers attached. Although we'd done a property settlement, we'd not discussed getting a divorce. I wondered how he could have done this with me out of the country. I called my solicitor in Australia and he advised that Darrol must have lodged the application for divorce pretty soon after we separated as it took twelve months before a decree nisi would become absolute.

What a low mongrel, I thought, when I recalled how he'd since tried to weasel his way into my bed, telling me he loved me, when he'd already filed for divorce. I asked Maurice how this was possible with no provision being made for financial support for Savannah. Maurice explained that child maintenance required a separate court order if the partners did not agree on the amount involved. As it was, I was relieved to think I was finally shot of Darrol and I had no interest in haggling over child support. In my mind I had full custody of Savannah and I was quite happy to pay for that privilege. Under the arrangement Peter and I had made, Darrol would have three months a year to see her, which was more time than he'd spent with her since our separation.

To ensure Peter's two children, the eldest being eighteen and the youngest almost sixteen, knew that their father wasn't going to disappear from their lives we decided to buy a property in West Vancouver. With my superannuation, which took a hit on tax and then again on the exchange rate, I put over $150,000 cash into a property, while Peter contributed the $40,000 he got from his matrimonial property settlement. We'd needed to take a mortgage for the home but as I was still drawing a six-figure income from Manpower, coupled with a substantial deposit; the bank was satisfied with our ability to service the loan.

It was the first week in March and there was still snow on the ground, when we moved into our new home. Not long after, Adam called to say that his grandmother had passed away. Adam loved his Gran and I knew he'd take her death very hard. I wanted so much to go to him, but recognised that under the circumstances it probably wasn't appropriate, and offered what comfort I could from a distance.

Savannah was soon enrolled into West Bay School, and I tried to find things to keep me busy. On Peter's days off he sat in a recliner with the remote in one hand and a can of beer in the other, watching sport on television.

'I'm in a very stressful job,' he would say, 'the squad always go for a few drinks at the end of the shift.' This was Peter's explanation for regularly rolling in the door, totally trashed, at 3 a.m.

Just before Easter I got a call from Vicki in Australia. 'I have some bad news,' she said, breaking down. I braced for the worst, thinking Bill may have died. 'I have a brain tumour,' she sobbed. 'They've given me six months to live.'

'Darling, I'll be home as soon as I can,' I said, trying to be strong. After I hung up the phone I howled like a wounded animal. I was so angry I wanted to pick things up and throw them at the wall. Years of useless tests and unnecessary operations and Vicki had a brain tumour that wasn't discovered until it was too late. Vicki wasn't just my friend, she was like a sister. There was no way I could be so far away from her while she faced, what I imagined would be, an agonising end. There wouldn't be much that I could do, but I wanted to be available to help in any way I could.

Peter decided he would resign from his job and come with us. I called Darrol but didn't mention the call from Vicki. 'I'll bring Savannah back to Australia on two conditions. One, you make time to have regular contact with her. And two, you start making a financial contribution towards her maintenance.'

He agreed.

We couldn't leave immediately. Peter had to resign and we needed to rent the house. As I didn't want Savannah to miss any more school I told Darrol that I wanted him to come to Canada and take her back in time to start second term. Perhaps he could even take her to Disneyland on the way home.

Again he agreed. I was stunned at his total compliance.

I also told him that I wanted Savannah enrolled in Queenwood School for Girls at Mosman, as I was planning on relocating back to Clontarf when we returned so he couldn't cite the distance as a reason for not seeing her.

'Why Queenwood? Why not a public school?' he asked.

'Because Savannah will do better at a girls' school.'

He attempted to argue and I told him the conditions for her return were not negotiable.

Darrol called me from his hotel when he arrived in Canada. He didn't want to see Peter.

Savannah was happy to see her father, but I was fretting to be leaving her. Except for a handful of days since the separation, Savannah had never been out of my sight, unless it was to attend school. I gave her a big hug and promised that we'd be back for her birthday and that we'd have a party. I kept telling myself it was only going to be a few weeks, but I knew I wouldn't relax until I had my baby back. As I left the hotel that day I choked back the memory of having to leave Adam.

We got back to Australia a week before Savannah's sixth birthday. I put the Avalon house on the market straightaway. The house was immaculate when we got back and Adam was reluctant to hand back the keys to the Mercedes.

Peter didn't care to see Darrol, so I drove to Clontarf to collect Savannah, who was packed and ready to come home. She ran at me and nearly bowled me over. I picked her up and she planted daisy kisses all over my face. 'I missed you, my Mamma,' she said.

'I missed you too, my Possum.'

Vicki was undergoing chemo and being unashamedly vain about her appearance, she didn't want anyone to see her without hair. We spoke on the phone when she felt up to it.

'Oh, they're fabulous,' she said, when she received the turbans I designed and made to make her feel better about her hair loss.

It was difficult being held back when Vicki was living out the last of her days, but Bill and Vicki were madly in love and their time together was so precious. I respected their wishes and did what I could at arm's length. Some days were worse than others. She told me the pain was often unbearable and she wished it would end. Then she'd break down, saying that was a terrible thing to say because of poor Bill. Then we'd both break down and have a good cry together. I can't begin to comprehend the horror, for both of them, knowing that nothing was going to save her. I know how I felt and it tore me to pieces.

The distance between Avalon and Mosman for an 8.15 a.m. start in her new school proved taxing on Savannah. I didn't want her to have to change schools again, so I spoke with Darrol about her spending part of the week with him until the house in Avalon sold. Savannah resisted this idea when I told her, but I worked out something that meant we were apart for the most minimal time each week. It was decided that she'd stay with her father on Monday, Tuesday, Wednesday and Thursday nights. To break up the week, I'd pick her up from school on Wednesdays and stay with her until her father came home.

Darrol hired a woman called Diane to give Savannah after-school care and cook his evening meal. I wasn't given any information about Diane and I let Darrol know I was less than happy about it.

'I don't need to tell you everything,' he said.

'Where Savannah's welfare is concerned, you better believe that you do.'

On the first Wednesday that I picked Savannah up from school, a stern-faced woman answered the door.

'Hello, Diane, I am Kay Norman,' I said as we came through the door.

Savannah seemed quite indifferent to Diane and I don't recall them even speaking to each other.

Savannah and I were sitting in the television room watching *The Wizard of Oz* when Diane interrupted to announce that it was time for Savannah's bath. I told her not to bother, that I would bathe Savannah.

'Mr Norman likes her to have had her bath before he gets home,' she said, with the officious manner of a Victorian nanny.

'And Mrs Norman is advising you that she will take care of Savannah tonight, thank you.'

This arrangement wasn't going to work so I decided to put Avalon to auction to speed up the selling process.

*

By August, Peter was homesick and missing his kids. Nothing I suggested could pull him out of it. He thought Savannah was too spoilt and had too much to say altogether.

'Kids should be seen and not heard,' he said.

'Savannah will be heard,' I replied, remembering how Uncle Jack had been protected because Trudy had been too afraid to speak up. There was no way in my mind that Savannah would ever need to be protected from any member of her immediate family, but I wanted to make sure she was confident to speak up for herself in any event. If that made her appear a little precocious, so be it.

Peter became more morose and after a heated discussion, where all kinds of pent-up frustrations came to the fore, things that had nothing to do with our relationship, I suggested that he go back to Canada and sort it out.

Darrol came to visit Savannah on a Saturday when I was setting the table for a dinner party. He handed me an envelope containing a cheque for $216.66.

'What's this for?'

'That's a month's maintenance for Savannah.'

'You've got to be bloody joking?' I replied.

'You asked for a financial contribution and fifty dollars a week is a contribution,' he said, smirking at his own cunning.

The Avalon property sold at auction and I bought a house in Clontarf, a stone's throw from Darrol's place. When Savannah was older she could walk to her father's house – that was the plan. We moved in just before Christmas and I got busy with the necessary refurbishments, starting with ripping up the shag-pile carpet. For Christmas lunch that year, the Lavender Hill Mob was meeting at the Sebel Townhouse. Noel and Phil's mother, Margaret, whom I was very fond of, as well as Myles and his mother were joining us. It was a wonderful day and in meeting Myles's mother for the first time I couldn't imagine who Myles thought he was fooling by denying his Aboriginal heritage.

On 30 December I had to scramble to find someone to take care of Savannah while I visited Vicki for the last time. Myles drove me to the Campbelltown Hospital.

Vicki looked so tiny in the big hospital bed. Bill was sitting beside her and got up to greet us. Vicki smiled a big shy smile, conscious that she was still bald.

'My darling, you are so brave,' I said, reaching down to kiss her.

'No, I'm not,' she said, squeezing my hand. 'I'm so scared Katie.'

'Vicki this wasn't the deal. We were supposed to grow old together and be elegant ladies doing lunch,' I said, trying to keep some humour in the heartbreak of knowing my best friend would soon be gone forever.

'I learned so much from you Katie,' she said, smiling.

'Vicki, what could I possibly have taught you?' I laughed through the tears, kissing the prickly stubble on her head, all that was left of the blonde curls after months of chemotherapy.

'Apart from the efficiency of colour coding my wardrobe?' she giggled, 'lots!'

Even on her death bed Vicki was thinking about how to make me feel good about myself. She was the one person who never let me down. She loved me despite all my faults.

The next day, New Year's Eve, Bill called around 4 p.m.

'She's gone Kate,' he sobbed into the phone.

Even though I was able to rationalise that Vicki was no longer suffering it didn't lessen the loss or grief to know I'd never see her or hear that sweet laugh again. I felt so guilty that with only hours of her life left, I hadn't stayed right to the end. I'd been anxious to get back to Savannah. There was nothing to celebrate that New Year's Eve, which was a year to the day that Vicki and Bill had called me in Canada to announce their engagement.

Darrol said he was thinking of attending the funeral himself when I asked if he'd take care of Savannah. My emotions were already stirred up and I exploded. 'You rotten bastard! You never cared for Vicki when she was alive.'

Myles took me to the funeral. With our arms around each other Bill and I sobbed as we watched our beloved Vicki being lowered into the ground. She was buried in the wedding dress I never got to see her wear. A sleeping bride in a tiny white box, no bigger than a child would need, covered with red roses, her favourite flower.

'A lot of secrets are being buried today, Bill,' I said, gripping his arm.

Bill squeezed my hand, he knew what I meant. You could tell Vicki your darkest secrets and she would never divulge them. Years before the rest of my friends knew about Adam, I'd told Vicki, and she never said a word to anyone.

For weeks after she'd gone I'd think of her and burst into tears. Savannah would put her arms around me and say, 'Don't cry, my Mamma.'

On 25 February, Vicki's birthday, I took Savannah to visit her grave that was marked with a simple brass plaque: *Vicki Moore – Bestest friend of Bill.* It should also have said: *Bestest friend to Kate.*

26

You little ripper!

Savannah had announced that Darrol had a new girlfriend who was 'nice' and had two children. I was pleased by this news. When Darrol was chasing everything in a skirt, he never had Savannah stay overnight, which meant that unless I was prepared to get babysitters, I didn't have much of a social life.

Savannah had been to stay with her father and his new girl-friend for the weekend and he seemed to be in a great hurry when he dropped her home. As he turned to leave I burst out laughing.

'What's so funny?'

'Your jacket.' I could hardly speak for laughing.

'What's wrong with my jacket? It's a Versace.'

'Clearly you haven't seen Dudley Moore's latest movie *Crazy People?*'

'No, I haven't.'

'When you do, you'll get the joke,' I said, dabbing my eyes with a tissue.

Darrol had sold his Mercedes and bought a convertible XJ6

Jaguar. His sporty leather jacket had 'Jaguar' emblazoned across the back. There's a scene in the movie where the ad-man, played by Moore, is responsible for a huge billboard advertising Jaguar cars. The slogan was: *Jaguar – for men who like hand jobs from beautiful women they hardly know.*

Darrol left, but was back knocking on the door a few minutes later. His car had broken down and it was raining. He didn't have a mobile phone and asked to use my phone to call the NRMA. Although analogue mobile phones were available in 1991, they were very clunky and expensive, which is probably why Darrol didn't have one.

'Do you mind if my friend comes in out of the rain?' he asked. 'The vinyl roof leaks.'

When the vision with bright orange hair and skin-tight satin slacks wiggled down the hallway I had trouble keeping a straight face.

'Kay, this is Hania.'

'You have a lovely home,' she said, looking around.

I offered them a drink and we made small talk by the cosy log fire. Hania was playful and affectionate with Savannah as we waited for the NRMA to arrive and get the car going.

'This was very civilised,' Darrol said, putting down his empty glass.

'I'm a very civilised person, or hadn't you noticed?' I replied, smiling. It was the last time Hania and I would ever speak a civil word to each other.

A school report for Savannah identified she was having a difficult time keeping up at school. I spoke with the school counsellor and was alarmed to learn that Savannah was at least six months behind the reading expectation for her age. It really shouldn't have surprised me that she'd gotten behind, with the disruption to her schooling when she was dragged from one country to another and back again. I had been making hasty decisions of the heart without too much regard for anything else, but I was determined to fix it and hired a remedial teacher to work with Savannah at home as well as in the classroom. Savannah applied herself and when she was re-tested a few months later, she was at least a year ahead of the reading expectation for a seven year old.

Peter had been in Canada for the better part of a year but we had continued to maintain contact, with frequent letters going back and forth. He was planning to return to Australia in November. By this time, I would have filled all the pending orders from the shop. After Lynne had discovered I had dressmaking skills, she started taking orders for made-to-measure bridal gowns and school formal dresses. Pretty soon, my lounge room resembled a Kowloon sweat shop, and I often worked late into the night to meet the demand.

Hania moved in with Darrol and they were agreeable to having Savannah stay with them while Peter and I had some time together at the Fairmont Resort at Leura in the Blue Mountains. But when Peter got back he was distant. The person I'd been speaking to on the phone for months was now withdrawn and sullen. I wondered why he'd come back at all.

Sometime in early December, Darrol called me to say that he and Hania were engaged to be married. 'The diamond ring set me back a pretty penny, I can tell you,' he couldn't resist bragging.

It didn't bother me that Darrol was getting married again, but I was curious as to how Hania had managed to get a diamond engagement ring out of him.

In an attempt to cheer Peter up I planned a pre-Christmas get together and invited Darrol, Hania and other members of his family. Peter's brother, Bob, and his new partner, Karen, showed up, but Darrol declined, saying that he didn't think it was his social milieu.

On Christmas morning Darrol came around with an adorable Shih Tzu puppy, about six weeks old. Savannah squealed with delight and named him Chow-Chow.

'This one will have a side gate and get a bath,' I assured him.

My dear friends Phil and Noel Christensen were coming for Christmas lunch and on Boxing Day we were expecting my sister-in-law Kristine and her two children, as well as Adam and some friends from Avalon. Savannah had a sixth sense when it came to Adam. She always seemed to know if he was coming or not, and this day she was sure he was.

'Adam!' she called, bolting for the door. Adam picked her up and carried her down the stairs, with her arms wrapped around his neck. I couldn't hold back the tears of joy just looking at them. It was a stinking hot day and Adam was pleased to see our new place had a sparkling blue pool. 'Oh, yes!' he whooped, stripping down to his swimmers and diving in. Savannah jumped in behind him.

Sitting on the patio looking across Middle Harbour to Balmoral, watching the most precious people in my life splashing around like a pair of playful dolphins, reinforced my belief that if I had to do everything over again, I would, just to experience this moment.

Darrol called me at the shop sometime in March to let me know the invitations for the wedding were going out and that he hoped I'd understand why Hania didn't want me at the wedding. The invitation arrived addressed only to Peter and Savannah. As the day drew nearer Peter hadn't mentioned it so I presumed he wasn't going to the wedding, which coincided with his birthday.

We'd planned to go out for dinner that night to celebrate

and I'd made arrangements for Savannah to stay with her sister, Willow, after the wedding reception. Around midday Peter took a shower and came downstairs decked out in a suit and tie.

It was disappointing that Peter couldn't communicate with me about going to the wedding, but I tried to be reasonable. It was an afternoon affair scheduled to finish at 5 p.m., which meant that Peter and I could still have dinner and a night together as planned. By 6 p.m. Peter was not back and hadn't called; the wedding venue was less than ten minutes from our door. At 7 p.m. Peter called to say he was at the Manly Pacific having a few drinks with his family. There was no invitation for me to join them.

When I reminded Peter that we were supposed to be going out for dinner, he said he was having dinner with his family. 'After all, it is my birthday.'

He staggered through the door just after midnight. I'd waited up for him, but he was in no condition to have any kind of discussion. The next morning I moved my things into the guestroom and told Peter I wanted him to leave as soon as possible.

'So I have one night with my family and it's all over?'

'Peter, this isn't about you spending time with your family, it's about you being a gutless coward.'

He didn't attempt to apologise or try to talk me out of my decision, but he didn't seem to be in any hurry to make other arrangements either. He was still living with us on 3 June 1992 when news broke that the High Court of Australia, in the case of *Mabo v Queensland*, had handed down a landmark decision recognising Native Title in Australia for the first time.

'You little ripper!' I said, jumping to my feet.

As the significance of this momentous occasion sunk in, my mind flashed back to a time when my own grandmother, Mamma, went out of her way to conceal our heritage. I was still weeping for joy when Peter came into the room and caught a glimpse of the bare-breasted, ochre-painted women of Arnhem Land dancing in the dirt.

'That's definitely your gene pool,' he said, laughing out loud.

'Yes, and I'm proud of it,' I snapped back.

Throughout my life I'd not made any big thing about being Koori. I never saw the need to be draped in the Koori flag to prove it. But I never denied it, and if anyone took a swipe at my Aboriginality, or stereotyped Aboriginal people in general, they soon learned where my loyalties were. Not even Peter's snide remark could kill the euphoria of this day.

The next morning I told Peter to leave. I didn't really care where he went. He had family, so I told him to give them a call and see if he could stay with one of them.

The house in Canada was sold for less than we bought it for, yet Peter expected to get back all of his investment, with me accommodating the loss. A solicitor in Canada, acting on my behalf, told him this was patently unfair, and Peter threatened to tell the tax office that I wasn't a citizen of Canada. I would have been hit with a massive withholding tax on any money I got back.

'Let him have it,' I said, 'that's all the money he's got in the world.'

If it had gone the other way I imagine Peter would have expected fifty per cent of the capital gain. *A breed's a breed, even if it's only white mice*, I thought, remembering the quirky expression from a cousin of Darrol's when she was trying to allude to the way character traits were often passed on genetically.

In July, Savannah was invited to join her father and his new family on a trip to Hamilton Island. I took the opportunity to visit some friends in Mittagong and go flying. I'd obtained a provisional pilot's permit and was having flying lessons.

'Didn't you have a good time, Possum?' I asked when I saw Savannah's long face when she came home.

'Mum, it was awful.' She burst into tears.

When I asked for specifics I felt my blood pressure rise. Savannah described how they'd been having breakfast in the dining room and Hania and her daughter started talking about someone, but didn't mention any names. Hania was saying what a spoilt and dirty little girl she was. 'She just steps out of her underwear and leaves them on the floor.'

Savannah, who was eight at the time, piped up to ask them who they were talking about. 'We are talking *about* you, not *to* you,' Hania said.

'Where was your father while all this was happening?' I asked Savannah.

'He was doing business,' she sobbed.

'Doing business?'

When I called Darrol to discuss this with him he told me that they were having problems. A few days later he called to say that it was best if Savannah didn't come to his place until things settled down. I left him in no doubt what a spineless bastard I thought he was. Living so close to her father's house and not being allowed to visit was impossible to explain to an eight year old who'd done nothing wrong.

Angry beyond words that Savannah was being pushed out of her father's life, for any reason, I decided to distance us from her father and his dysfunctional new family.

When I spoke to my business partner, Lynne, she told me she'd mortgaged her home to raise enough money to start the business. As I was virtually leaving her to carry on alone I decided the least I could do was leave my money in. If Lynne made a go of it, she could have all the profits, but I wanted out of the partnership; any losses incurred would remain her responsibility.

Rather than winding things up at this stage, Lynne agreed to my offer. I don't think she appreciated that leaving my investment in the business was a gift. Under our partnership agreement I could have just pulled the rug and she may have lost her home.

When I'd gone flying in Mittagong, I'd seen a magnificent property from the air, on a small acreage not far from town. I called the real estate agent in Bowral.

Named 'Oldgate', the thirteen acre rural property loomed large at the end of a quiet country lane. The house was unfinished, but I could see the potential. It was a huge mistake to take Savannah to the inspection. She was in raptures, running around chanting: 'Oldgate, Oldgate, we have to get Oldgate.'

By this stage I was becoming asset rich and cash poor. I was still drawing down an income from Manpower, but I'd also just completed extensive renovations on the Clontarf home, which left me short of the ready cash for a deposit on a new property, so I called Darrol and he agreed to release the money from my director's loan account.

Asking for a six-month extended settlement I made an offer on Oldgate with special conditions. I was only paying a $40,000 deposit, and if I didn't settle on the due date, my liability was limited to the deposit.

When I still didn't have a buyer for Clontarf by the end of November I had to come up with a Plan B. I called Darrol again. He wouldn't agree to giving me a bridging loan from the company to settle on Oldgate by the due date, saying the business was in decline and the money was needed for working capital.

This hadn't stopped him drawing down over half a million dollars that year and dropping it into a term deposit for his private company. With interest rates running at eighteen per cent he earned a tidy $65,000 in bank interest.

It was frustrating that he still had this kind of control over me, while he did as he pleased. The downward spiral of the company since I'd left was also of concern. It couldn't be due to the recession, because temporary labour was always in greater demand during a recession; I knew this from experience. When I asked William what was happening he said once more: 'Darrol doesn't have your vision and drive.'

On Boxing Day I joined Phil Christensen and his partner, Christine, at a friend's place on the headland at Coogee, a great vantage point to watch the yachts in the Sydney to Hobart race. It was here that I first met John Scipione. We hadn't even been introduced when I overheard his surprise at being asked why he had brought his terminally ill ex-wife back into his home and nursed her until she died. 'She was the mother of my children,' he replied.

Anyone with that much compassion was someone I wanted to be able to call my friend. After we'd been chatting almost non-stop for two hours, we exchanged phone numbers.

Just after my birthday in January, Darrol called to tell me that there was a way for me to purchase Oldgate without selling my property in Clontarf.

'I'm listening.'

'You could sell me your shares in the company.'

When the company was at its peak he'd refused the offer to buy my shares, claiming he couldn't afford the book value and goodwill that would apply. Now that he was running the company into the ground and the share value along with it, he wanted to buy me out. The problem was, I was locked into a minority shareholding and the way Darrol was managing the business I could end up with a shareholding in nothing, or worse, a shareholding in a liability.

It was a shrewd offer and given Darrol's history I should have realised there was a hidden agenda. I did some reckoning and concluded that even though the revenue of the company over the past three years had taken a dive, I could still expect my shares to be worth enough to purchase Oldgate with cash to spare.

William, our accountant, was asked to prepare an evaluation of my shares that confirmed this. The book value looked right but no goodwill had been applied and it ought to have been, based on the performance of the company, which had maintained profitability. When I called William to discuss this he said I would need to speak to Darrol about any consideration for goodwill.

Darrol started screaming down the phone, saying that as the company had been in decline for three consecutive years no goodwill would be applied. I told him that my solicitor had calculated that at least $110,000 was applicable.

With only the deposit to lose if I didn't settle by 5 February, I dug my heels in. Darrol started cursing and swearing again, in much the same way he did whenever we attempted to discuss anything of a financial nature.

'You pissed off and left me in the lurch!' he yelled.

I reminded him of what had really happened. 'You thought you could run the company without me, and clearly you can't.'

At that moment I ought to have realised that Darrol had a lot of emotion tied up in acquiring my shares. Unfortunately, my judgement was clouded by the emotion I had tied up in wanting to purchase Oldgate and be rid of him for good.

When I called my solicitor for advice, he told me that I could move to have the company wound up. The implications of that and how it shifted some power back to me made me wonder why he hadn't told me this before. I guess it's the old story. Solicitors take instructions; they don't give advice unless it's asked for.

There was a long silence before William explained the tax

issues that might arise by going down this path. I told him that I didn't care; Darrol was deeper in the hole than I was and any losses would go two-thirds his way. At this point, William asked what my exposure would be if I didn't settle on Oldgate. Not suspecting that he was working against me, I told him. I also told him of the other pressures associated. Having already rented out the Clontarf property, Savannah and I were living out of suitcases at the Briar's Inn, a hotel in Moss Vale, while I was trying to negotiate a deal. What I'd just done was tantamount to playing poker and showing the other guy my hand.

The next day Maurice called to say that Darrol had increased his offer. It was exactly what I'd told William I needed to settle on Oldgate, although it was still short of the goodwill. William and Darrol knew me well enough to know that I'd take the offer, rather than fold the business, putting people out of work and risking incurring massive tax liabilities.

On the settlement day my solicitor told me that the document I was about to sign was 'inter alia', which meant there was no cooling-off period. As he had drawn up the contract I didn't think there'd be anything untoward. I was pushed for time and didn't read every detail.

Matt was present at the meeting in Darrol's solicitor's office. He smiled a half smile, but it was obvious he wasn't at all comfortable being caught up in his father's affairs. After I left Manpower, Matt had been appointed a director, but he wouldn't have had a clue about the documents his father would've given him to sign in my absence.

After completion of the paperwork, Darrol's solicitor handed me a cheque.

'Helena Ricardo!' I smiled, when I saw the signatory.

'Yes, she's my personal banker,' Darrol said, cocking his nose in the air and completely missing the irony. Helena Ricardo of

Citicorp was the first major account I had developed when I joined Manpower. If Darrol had stuck to our original deal of paying me ten per cent of all new business I acquired, that account would have proven to be of more value than my shares in the company.

Darrol and I parted without so much as a sideways glance and I raced back to Bowral to settle Oldgate with only minutes to spare.

The next morning I collected several faxes at the hotel's reception that I hadn't received before I left for the city and signed the deal. One was from William, on his company letterhead, dated 3 February, two days before the deadline to settle. It mentioned several matters that 'ought to be taken into account in the negotiations' particularly 'the goodwill and value in the licensing agreement'.

The licensing agreement! How did I miss that? I felt the blood rush to my face.

A licensing agreement, or franchise agreement as it was more commonly known, is the authority to be able to trade on the parent company's logo and have access to the operating systems. In 1975 Darrol had purchased the franchise from the US to operate Manpower in Australia for $35,000, which at the time had a greater value than his home at Kirrawee.

'How did you miss the licensing agreement?' I asked Maurice, after reading the letter from William.

He became defensive. 'The licensing agreement is only worth something if you can find a buyer.'

I reminded him that we had a buyer. At this point Maurice confirmed the contract for my shares was inter alia. There was no cooling-off period and I got what I settled for.

27

Sue me

It was teeming the day Savannah and I moved into Oldgate. The furniture truck arrived and the driver was surprised when I instructed him to back the truck up to the shed. Most of the furniture I'd purchased after leaving Darrol suited a different lifestyle than we'd enjoy in this rural setting.

Savannah had already started school. When she got home that day she ran wild through the almost bare rooms, sliding around the timber floors in her socks, reminding me of when I was a girl, with jumpers tied to my feet, helping Aunty Daphne polish the wooden floors.

Adam was our first visitor. He helped me get the stuff in the shed sorted, putting his name on several things he said he could use. As we sat having lunch on the back patio, with a view as far as the eye could see, I remembered a day at the house in Harris Park when his father took a photograph. Adam was about eighteen months old at the time, and wearing rags, as he climbed onto the front gate to watch the trains go past. If Adam ever resented the vastly different circumstances of his childhood and that of his little sister, he never said a word about it.

On Mother's Day that first year in Mittagong we got a surprise visit from Matt. Savannah and Matt had not seen a lot of each other over the previous four years. Knowing my penchant for Oriental objet d'art, Matt brought me a lovely blue and white Chinese ginger jar. He stayed the night and left for Queensland the next day. 'Follow your dreams, Matt,' I said, giving him a kiss goodbye. I was very pleased to later hear that he had followed up on his lifelong fascination with reptiles to become a certified snake handler at a wildlife sanctuary.

At the time of her ninth birthday Savannah was still banned from going to her father's house. It had been almost a year since she'd visited her father and to compensate for the disappointment of not seeing him I arranged a party, with a jumping castle, games and prizes for the twenty children in her class.

With three guestrooms we regularly entertained a constant stream of visitors, including Uncle Stan and Aunty Shirley, who presumed I'd done very nicely from the divorce. My time was soon occupied with taking care of the house and garden and getting involved in school activities and various charities – I had never felt so happy or at peace. Savannah was participating in local drama productions, and I'd started to paint again after years without opening my art box . We spent many blissful days sitting at the kitchen table listening to music, painting watercolours and watching the little swallows nesting under the eaves.

'Mum, remember your promise?' Savannah prompted when her tenth birthday rolled around. I made good on my promise and started planning an eight-week holiday touring Italy, France and the UK, with a stop in Singapore on the way home. Naturally, I would be taking her to visit her great-aunts in England, who were now in their nineties. I called Darrol to tell him that we'd be away and that we'd be visiting his mob in Blackpool and Marsden. He told me that he was ashamed of the way they were living. I couldn't imagine what he meant by that and didn't venture to ask.

After touring Italy and France in scorching heat I was hoping for some respite when we reached England. No such luck. Temperatures were in the mid-thirties and people were cooling off in Trafalgar Square fountain. We picked up a car and followed much the same route as Darrol and I had taken previously, this time stopping at more places of interest, including old churches and medieval castles. At Stratford-upon-Avon we lingered at Anne Hathaway's Cottage. I was determined to see Hampton Court if it was the only thing I did in London. In Marsden, Yorkshire, I could only show Savannah the cemetery; there was still no headstone on her grandmother's grave.

Cousin June and Aunty Eadie were retired and sharing a large terrace house in Blackpool. For the life of me I couldn't understand why Darrol felt the need to apologise for them. Perhaps he'd forgotten how ordinary people lived, particularly elderly people on a restricted income. We all went out to dinner and Aunty Eadie wouldn't let go of my hand.

'I am so grateful to our Darrol for doing this. It was so important for him that Savannah connected with her roots,' she said, with tears in her eyes. Far be it from me to shatter an old lady's illusions.

As a little girl, Savannah was a huge fan of Beatrix Potter, and it was a delight to take her to the Lake District and wander around the landscape that inspired the stories of Mrs Tiggy-Winkle, Jemima Puddle-Duck and Peter Rabbit. The stopover in Singapore gave the staff at Raffles a few tense moments to see a child take a seat for 'high tea', although they relaxed when Savannah enquired whether or not they served Darjeeling.

Savannah called her father to let him know she was back. He'd just returned from a cruise on the QEII. I asked her to let me speak to him before hanging up. I closed the study door before taking the call. I relayed how much Aunty Eadie appreciated him arranging the trip because he wanted Savannah to connect with her roots.

'Perhaps as this was so important, you could make a belated financial contribution.'

'You can ask,' he said. His smirk could be felt through the phone.

Playing the country lady was all well and good, but without the income from Manpower, I started to think about unmet needs in the local area, combined with skills I had, with a view to starting a business. My first thought had been to make Oldgate a 'bed and breakfast', but when I'd looked at the council regulations and realised that I would have had to make further modifications to the property, I canned the idea. There was also the concern of having total strangers staying with us on an isolated property. As a single mother with a young daughter I knew it could pose a risk.

Everyone in my family could cook, my grandmother especially, so I learned very early how to get food on the table. From my late teens through to my early twenties I'd worked at the Chevron Hotel in Kings Cross. I started off behind the bar, but I moved on to run the hotel's coffee shop, which also served meals. Serving hordes of hungry troops on R&R from Vietnam taught me to get good meals and lots of them, onto the table fast. It gave me an idea for a business: real food, lots of it, real fast. The catch phrase came before the business plan.

'Aunty Flo's,' I said, when I told Noel Christensen about

my plans to set up a sixty-seat restaurant, with a drive-through gourmet take-away. He was amused that I wanted to use the nickname he'd given me many years before.

After weeks of searching I found the perfect location one afternoon when I was sitting in the kitchen of my good friends, Cathy and Peter, who were living on Bowral Road in Mittagong. I was colour coding all the 3a business zonings on a map when I saw a site exactly where I needed Aunty Flo's to be. 'This is it! I've found it,' I said, pointing to the house they lived in, opposite the twenty-four hour service station owned by Peter and his brother. For some time they'd wanted to sell their house and distance themselves from work. So far the only offer they'd had wasn't enough to swap for a new house without a big mortgage.

'But isn't this is a residential property,' Pete said, doubtfully.

'No, it's in the business zone.' I smiled, sliding the map across the table.

I offered them a fair commercial price and the deal was done on a handshake. I promised Peter that if I ever sold the property, which was once his mother's home, I'd remove the brass door knocker and return it to him.

One evening, a few weeks later, I was working on the development application to council when the phone rang. It was Darrol. In spite of everything, I still tried to maintain some civility; after all, we had a child together and she was not yet twelve years old. He'd called to say that after a six-month separation, he and his wife had gone into therapy. 'They tell me I'm a control freak,' he said, causing me to burst out laughing.

'I could've told you that without you needing to see a shrink.'

As the conversation progressed he dropped in that he'd just bought Hania a new house. 'She wasn't comfortable living in Gordon Street, with so much to remind her of you. The house is at Seaforth. It cost two million dollars, but we didn't have to sell

Gordon Street,' he told me. This vulgar display of wealth, given what little he did for his daughter, annoyed me. I suggested to Darrol that as he was clearly doing so well he should think about increasing the maintenance for Savannah. He told me I could sue him. 'I could bankrupt you in a week,' he boasted.

When he didn't respond to the letter making a formal request that he increase the fifty dollars per week he'd paid since Savannah was six years old, to a further token of one-hundred and fifty dollars per week, I called Maurice. In hindsight, I should have instructed a new solicitor, but having taken a mortgage to get the new business going I was under pressure. The building work had commenced and time was of the essence.

I didn't think for one moment that the matter would go to court, and to ensure that it was settled amicably I told Maurice to advise Darrol that if he pushed this matter I would ask for an amount reflecting the true cost of living for a child attending the most expensive girls' school in the Southern Hemisphere, and that it be paid retrospectively.

Maurice advised that the Family Court had never given a decision in favour of a retrospective payment. I wasn't deterred. 'Perhaps no man in Darrol's financial position has been taken to court for not paying appropriate child support,' I said, instructing him to advise Darrol of the terms.

When no reply came, I filed an application in the Family Court. As part of this process, information came to light that raised many questions I was determined to have answered.

'He seems to have had a considerable betterment since your divorce,' Maurice said as we went over the documents. 'Did he marry someone with money?'

'Not to my knowledge. She lived in a modest home at Manly Vale and flogged advertising space for some magazine.'

I told Maurice I wanted every document, every statement,

every bloody thing as far back, in as much detail as I was allowed to ask for.

'Well, that will be very costly and we have already established Mr Norman's capacity to pay child support,' Maurice countered.

'Please get me that information. When this matter is finalised I will be looking into the possibility of any impropriety concerning past financial dealings with my former husband.'

My invitation to the Christmas dinner for the parents of Frensham Girls' School included a guest. I didn't have a man in my life so I asked John Scipione to come with me. Heads turned when we arrived. John was tall and, I thought, very handsome. John knew how to work a room and before long one of the women sidled up to me and whispered, 'Where did you find him?'

'Hey, Possum, we're on the table with the big wigs. You're sitting next to Sir Waddy-Doddy,' he grinned, before hitting the button in his pocket and activating the lights on the bow tie he was wearing.

Sitting opposite was an insufferable man with a double-barrelled surname and a familiar face. He was name-dropping and happened to mention Russel Harvey, of Nudgawalla, a name I recognised from my past. Seemingly impressed to be sitting opposite someone who knew the Harveys, who were among the highest echelon of Australian society, he asked, 'Did your family own a neighbouring property per chance?'

'No, my grandmother was the housekeeper and cook and I lived with her at Nudgawalla.'

His jaw dropped. John kicked me under the table and out of the corner of my eye I saw tiny lights flashing red and green. There was a break between courses and I went outside with John while he had a smoke. He doubled over with laughter, almost tumbling into the rose garden.

'That was fabulous! He'll never be able to figure out how the granddaughter of a cook could be sitting opposite him at dinner at Frensham,' he said, pulling a handkerchief from his pocket to dab the tears streaming down his face.

'The granddaughter of the Aboriginal cook at that,' I said.

John lost it.

'Actually, I was tempted to remind him of the night I served him dinner at the Chevron Hotel and handed back his twenty cent tip, suggesting he buy a book on etiquette.'

'Oh please, let's go in and remind him of that,' John teased.

When we got home I made us a nightcap. We talked for hours. John loved to chat and it was impossible not to love him. As he climbed the stairs to the guestroom, I felt like I'd been to the ball with Prince Charming, and now everything was turning back into a pumpkin. After that I never called John anything but 'Pumpy' but I never told him why.

One afternoon I was heading home with the last bits and pieces for a dinner party I was hosting that evening. It was going to be formal dress, just for fun. Coming up the lane was a familiar white BMW. It was Myles; he was on his way home from Melbourne and was stopping in for a surprise visit.

'As it happens I'm having a dinner party tonight, it's formal attire,' I smiled.

'How fortuitous,' he said, pursing his lips. 'As it happens I have a tuxedo in my bag, I've just returned from Monte Carlo.'

Myles was an executive with BMW by this time and had just returned from a trip to Europe to visit the German headquarters. He did look dashing in the white tux and held court at dinner that evening, charming the other guests with humorous stories. During the evening he embarrassed me by flirting with a friend, and then couldn't understand why I rebuffed him and sent him to the guestroom that night. The next morning we were having breakfast and I was still a bit cross with him. He came up to me and put his arms around me.

'I love you. Marry me,' he said.

My head fell against his chest. We'd been dancing with, and around, each other for years. There was a time when I would have accepted a marriage proposal from Myles in a heartbeat. But the timing now was all wrong. 'Myles, I can't marry you. I've just bitten off more than I can probably chew and marrying you would really complicate everything,' I told him.

Myles's eyes welled with tears. Then he got angry. 'Okay, but I'll never ask you again.' He got his bag and left without saying another word.

28

Aunty Flo's

Darrol was flanked by two solicitors from a high-profile legal firm. They looked sharp and slick. The blonde in the red power-suit was strutting around. She wrote something on a document and from where I was sitting I could read her lips when she handed it back to Maurice; 'Tell her that's it! That's our final offer.'

Maurice handed me the document that now included a retrospective payment of one year, where I had been asking for six.

'Go back and tell them we're going to court,' I said, handing the document back.

Maurice advised me in the strongest possible terms that this was a very good offer and that a retrospective payment had never been granted in the Family Court. He warned me that if I refused this offer I may be deemed vindictive and costs against me could be considerable.

Given my circumstances I weighed up the risks and relented. After everything was signed and the matter was settled I turned to Maurice and asked him for the documents I'd requested concerning

Darrol's complete financial position. He told me I would only have received those documents had the matter proceeded to court. In that moment, I finally understood why the Family Court put everyone through scanners to make sure no one was carrying a concealed weapon. I was furious, it didn't seem fair. Believing I had no other option, I did the only thing I could. I packed all the documents I had into a box, put it away and tried to get on with my life.

A month before the grand opening of Aunty Flo's I invited the Lavender Hill Mob down to Oldgate for one last bash before life got hectic again. After dinner we sat around the dining table composing and reciting impromptu poems. Around midnight Myles's new fiancée, Lee, announced that she was going to bed. Myles wanted to stay up and talk to me. Usually I waited until all my guests had retired before going to bed, but I was too tired. 'Don't you think you should go to bed? Lee will be wondering where you are,' I said.

'I'm not going to sleep with her under your roof,' he replied.

'Well I'm going to bed. Goodnight.' I gave him a kiss on the cheek and left him in the lounge room.

At about six o'clock the next morning my bedroom door was flung open. Lee was standing there, her eyes darting around the room and her neck straining like a startled chook.

'Where's Myles?' she demanded.

'He's not here,' I replied, annoyed that she thought Myles would be in my bed while she slept across the hall. Myles had crashed out on the lounge. They didn't stay for breakfast.

Three days before Aunty Flo's opened the woman I'd hired for the position of chief cook thought she'd try one on. She hadn't cooked as much as a sausage and was asking for a pay rise. The salary I'd agreed to pay her was more than she'd earned in her last position, and it was way over the award for someone without any qualifications. She said she'd worked out her expenses and the new figure reflected what she needed to live on.

'Okay, I understand. Good bye and good luck,' I said firmly.

She looked surprised. 'So we can't negotiate this?'

'We just did.'

She left in tears and I went around to the local supplier and picked up three chef's jackets in my size. The restaurant was booked out for opening night and during service I made the classic mistake of dropping a cover over a carving knife. I flicked up the towel and the knife went flying into the air. Instead of jumping backwards I reached out and the knife came down, slicing through the thumb joint on my left hand. I put my hand under the running tap and asked my second cook to get the first-aid kit. She helped me wrap a tight bandage around my hand to stop the bleeding. I had no idea if the thumb was severed, but it was hurting like buggery. After the shift I took a look at the wound. It was a deep cut, almost to the bone. I kept my thumb strapped to my hand for a few days and worked in a surgical glove. Being left-handed this was a nuisance and slowed me down.

The next six months saw me working physically harder than I'd ever done in my entire life. I was on the verge of collapse when help finally came in the form of Brendan and his sidekick, Cath. Brendan was a chef, and former owner of 'Poplars', a fine-dining restaurant in Mittagong. Cath had been his 'dish-pig', but he should have called her his guardian angel. She fed him and did his washing and generally made sure he didn't walk into oncoming traffic.

'Right you cunt, you've got four sets of fuckin' tongs and two spoons, that's all you're fuckin' gettin',' she said to Brendan as he tied on his apron to start his first shift. 'If I leave them up there

he'll use them all before he'll rinse a fuckin' spoon,' she told me, grabbing all the remaining utensils from the rack and putting them into the storeroom. Cath's colourful vocabulary was made all the more confronting because she was the sister of the local Catholic priest.

One night, the restaurant was over-booked. People just kept coming through the door and had to be turned away. To top it off, we were short-staffed. Two meals were ready to go out with no waitress in sight.

'Cath, you'll have to take these meals out. *Please!*'

'Fuck me. I'm wearin' me dish-pig dress.'

'Cath, these meals are for the doctors Marsh. They won't care about your dress. They will care if their meal is cold.'

'Oh shit! Doctors?' Cath was intimidated by people with titles, but for the rest of the night she chipped in and ran meals out. She proved to be so good with the customers and helping me get up the salads and desserts that I hired another dish-pig.

One night Cath came back from the dining room spitting chips. 'That fucking idiot on table four asked me if we could do a blue steak and I told him no, all our steaks are red,' she said, grabbing her cigarettes and a can of Coca-Cola and heading out the back for a break.

'You dumb bitch,' Brendan said, 'that's how he wants his steak cooked!'

I was laughing so hard I couldn't speak.

'Well, how would I fuckin' know?' Cath replied, sitting under the tree in the garden, blowing smoke into the air and taking a swig from the can.

Even with the extra help I was spreading myself too thin. Delirious with exhaustion I came home late one night and forgot to hit the remote control and ploughed my car into the front gates, ripping them from the hinges. I had to climb over the mangled wreckage and walk to the house in the pitch black without a torch or a snake stick to pound the ground, and Mittagong was crawling with snakes. Miraculously, the car came away relatively unscathed, but the iron gates had to be replaced.

This incident shook me up and I realised I needed to make some adjustments before I killed myself, or an innocent bystander. But this was not my only concern. When I worked nights, I'd arranged for the daughter of a friend to come and stay with Savannah. She was in high school by then and capable of taking care of herself, but I was concerned about security. One night the sitter wasn't available. Around 9 pm Savannah called, sounding very frightened. 'The dogs are barking and I can hear noises outside, Mum.'

Whipping off my apron, I grabbed my car keys and told Brendan he'd have to close up the restaurant.

By this time I had a mobile phone and called Savannah back, telling her to stay on the phone and keep talking to me. When I got home she had every light in the house on and was quite shaken. She broke down and told me she hated Oldgate and wanted to live closer to Bowral. When we had moved to Mittagong she'd been only eight years old and being close to town wasn't important. But now that she was a teenager she wanted to be able to meet her friends after school, go to the movies and visit the shops.

For months I'd been going around in circles trying to juggle the finances at work and home, and this was the push I needed to make some hard decisions. Oldgate was considered one of the premier properties in the area and if I got the price I wanted I'd net enough to clear the overdraft and still be able to purchase a nice property in Bowral.

Adam brought his new girlfriend, Shauna, to Oldgate for Christmas not long before it was sold. She had a gorgeous little boy called Joshua, from a previous relationship, who was about four years old. A few weeks later, Adam called to say that she was pregnant. There was no talk of getting married but they were going to live together. Adam was living in his father's house, after John had decided to move in with his long-time girlfriend.

Adam had been very sensible with regard to planning his life and finances and there was no doubt that he'd be able to afford to take good care of Shauna and two children. I was particularly proud of my son for not hesitating to accept Shauna's son, by another man, and treat him as he would his own. In my experience that was a rare quality in a man.

I was thrilled at the prospect of becoming a grandmother, and couldn't help but reflect on how much had changed since I had been a pregnant unwed mother. There seemed to be so many more choices than had been available to me at the time that I was pregnant.

After the contracts for the sale of Oldgate had been exchanged I made an offer on Bentham, a charming five-bedroom cottage in Merrigang Street in Bowral. It was already set up to operate as a B&B and just needed council approval; I thought it would provide a back-up option if Aunty Flo's continued to bleed money.

With no time to do the packing I had Bill Hayward, Cath's husband, give me a hand. It took three weeks to pack and the moving day was gruelling. It wasn't until I collapsed on the bed at Bentham around midnight that I realised I'd forgotten the contents of my walk-in robe and other personal items. As the new owners were moving in the next day, I had to rally myself for more heavy lifting and made several trips back to get my things.

Dawn was breaking by the time I walked through Oldgate for the last time, carrying my ubiquitous sewing machine. My footsteps echoed in the lounge room now that the Persian carpets had been rolled up and taken away. Before I closed the door I took a deep breath and felt nostalgia wash over me, a hint of lavender and the scent of beeswax polish from the timber floors wafted through the air. As I drove slowly along the driveway one last time the avenue of flame trees stood tall, having survived a drought and five cold winters while we'd been there. The gates clanged behind me as I got out of the car to leave the spare keys in the letter box, pausing to reflect on all the times I'd packed and left one place or another, too many to count. I longed for the day when I'd never have to pack a suitcase, or pick up my sewing machine and leave. As I looked back at the lovely home, the symbol of a life's work and struggle, I felt a sense of achievement to have succeeded against all the odds. I felt grateful to have had the opportunity to create such a beautiful place to share with my family and friends.

29

It's a girl

The restaurant was fully booked. Brendan and I were in the middle of the lunch sitting when I got the call.

'It's a girl. We're going to call her Kate,' Adam said, when he let me know my first grandchild had been born and that mother and babe were doing well.

'Congratulations, my darling, give Shauna my love. I'm on my way,' I said.

'Congratulations, Grandma!' Cath squealed, when she heard.

During the two-hour drive from Mittagong to Castle Hill Hospital I had plenty of time to think. I'd made some pretty bad decisions as an adult, but as a girl of sixteen I made one of the best decisions of my life: to hold on and not buckle under the immense pressure to give my baby son, Adam, up for adoption.

Adam's father was walking towards me in the hospital corridor. He smiled and greeted me warmly, 'Hello, Kay.'

'Hello, Pop,' I said, giving him a kiss.

My heart melted as Adam lifted the baby out of the cot and

handed her to me. I had a flashback to the night John came to visit me after Adam had been born. Adam was almost two weeks old and John's parents hadn't come to see their first grandchild. At the time, it struck me as strange, but now that I was holding my granddaughter for the first time, it was incomprehensible. I felt myself slip away to a place where words become pointless, even clumsy, as the love for this sweet baby seemed to pour from me and shroud her in a warm light.

The next day, I called Uncle Stan to let him know that his great-nephew now had a daughter. I organised to pick him up as soon as I could and bring him for a visit.

Not long after Kate was born, Savannah and I were having lunch at the restaurant when she dropped into the conversation that she had heard that Poppy Rex, Peggy Gazzard's husband, had died. Peggy and I had not spoken in nine years, but I felt I needed to call and offer my condolences. As it turned out, Rex had been dead for two years. She told me that Rex had bought Jack the property in Nimbin, 'But of course that woman got half when they broke up.' Her voice implied 'I told you so', which I ignored. Instead, I asked for Jack's phone number.

'Hello, Kay,' Jack said, recognising my voice after almost thirty years.

We talked for some time and he told me how proud he was to hear how well I'd done. After talking on the phone every night for several weeks, I arranged for him to come down for a visit. I was hoping, rather foolishly on my part, that we'd be able to recapture what we once had.

The day I picked Jack up from Central Station I knew I'd made a mistake. He looked to be caught in a time warp of the 1970s. He was painfully thin, had lost all of his teeth and a mullet haircut on a man in his mid-fifties seemed rather sad. *What was I to do, tell Jack and his son to get back on the train?*

'He should get down and kiss the ground you walk on,' Peggy said, when we went to visit her after Jack and his son moved in.

Whatever Jack may have salvaged from his share of the property his father bought him, there was no evidence of it. Jack was a vegan and refused to help out in a restaurant that served meat. When I asked if he might like to mow the lawn and tidy up the yard I was told he hadn't come down here to be my 'yard boy'. During the nine months they lived with us, Jack didn't make a single contribution, not towards a new wardrobe or the $4000 needed to get his teeth done.

Things came to a head one evening when Jack was supposed to pick Savannah up from a drama class. Instead, he got stoned and left her to walk home alone, in the dark and in pouring rain. 'She could use the exercise,' was all he said when I confronted him about it.

'That's it, Jack. You put Savannah in danger. Now I want you to leave. As soon as possible.'

When I refused to give him any more money, he called his mother, who coughed up enough for him to get a car. This episode left me drained, but I had no one to blame but myself. If I'd been able to anticipate the effect this situation would have on Savannah, Jack and his son would never have left Nimbin. Rather selfishly, I'd introduced Jack and his son into our lives without any consideration for her feelings. They turned our lives completely upside down, leaving Savannah with deep resentments towards me.

A few weeks after I'd tossed Jack out, I started giving serious thought to where my life was going. I'd lost my enthusiasm for Aunty Flo's and made a decision to sell the business as a going concern. With a bit of luck, I would find someone with deep pockets and the vision to see its potential.

Before putting it on the market I removed the front door knocker and gave it to Peter as promised. Bentham sold quickly, which meant that we had to find somewhere to rent until I could sell the restaurant. We had too much furniture and stuff altogether, so I organised a house moving sale. Adam, Shauna and the children came down to give me a hand. Kate was a real livewire and I realised how much we'd missed living so far apart, with me always caught up in other people's dramas. Adam and Shauna were planning to get married later in the year. I'd rather give my things away to family and friends than sell them to strangers at a loss, so I told them they could have anything they wanted that was going in the sale, and we went around the house and put red sold stickers on the things they could use.

It was difficult finding a house to rent close to town, which would take three dogs. All I could get was a rundown fibro cottage on Bowral Road, two doors up from the restaurant, putting the bulk of our furniture and belongings into storage.

When my friend Simone came to visit we cooked a meal and shared a bottle of champagne. We reminisced about the great times we'd had at Oldgate and her hysteria to open the front door and find her idol, rock star Jimmy Barnes, standing there. Jimmy was a neighbour and his daughter, EJ, and Savannah were classmates. We flicked through some old photographs of the charity ball I had hosted, that required all the lounge room furniture and billiard table to be removed to accommodate the dancing.

'The only difference between you when you had Oldgate and now is that now your parties are smaller,' Simone said, raising her glass.

Simone had been planning a trip to South Australia with her children in the first week of July and asked if Savannah and I would like to join the train at Mittagong and spend a few days in Melbourne with them.

Savannah had withdrawn further into her own world after we left Bentham and wouldn't talk to me about it. I knew it had a lot to do with me bringing Jack into our lives, but there was more to it than that. Since Darrol remarried, Savannah had been pushed out of her father's life in favour of his wife and her children. It had been so long since I'd heard her laughing and having fun and I thought perhaps a holiday together with some good friends, even a short one, might help to restore some of what we'd lost in recent times. When I called Simone to say that we would join her, I could never have anticipated the turn of events that would result from such an innocent expectation.

30

Mea culpa

Melbourne in July that year was inhospitable, with temperatures dropping to single digits. Even so, we were looking forward to our trip to Phillip Island to see the fairy penguins. The day before, I'd eaten a tepid chicken pie. I ought to have known better, halfway through the night I was up and down, alternating between kneeling and sitting in the bathroom. Simone went to the chemist to get me some medication before taking the kids out for the day. By the next morning I'd recovered enough to visit the Victoria Market and then it was time to catch our train home.

We were booked in a first class sleeper and I slept most of the night. After a cup of tea and a soggy muffin, which was served just out of Goulburn, we prepared ourselves to get off at Moss Vale Station. It was just after 4:30 a.m. Savannah was still half asleep as we gingerly made our way to the exit, trying not to disturb the other passengers. I was annoyed that the cabin attendant hadn't come to help with the bags. As I stepped down from the train it started moving.

'Hey, stop!' I called out.

The weight of my suitcase pulled me forward and I lost grip of the handrail, sending me crashing onto the icy platform. When I looked up, Savannah was in mid-air, having panicked and jumped from the moving train, missing a concrete pylon by inches.

'Oh, my God!' Cath yelled, running towards us. Cath had borrowed my car while we were away, on the proviso that she picked us up, as the train from Melbourne didn't stop at Mittagong and there'd be no taxis at that hour of the morning.

The cabin attendant who served our breakfast was hanging out the window of the last carriage with a cigarette in his mouth. 'You stupid bastard! You could have killed us,' I yelled after him as the train sped away. The station master was nowhere to be found.

Shaken after the fall, and reeling by the thought of what might have happened to Savannah, there was so much adrenaline pumping through my body that I didn't feel any pain. Cath drove us home, but by 8 a.m. it hurt to breathe. The doctor in Bowral wrote out a prescription for some painkillers and suggested that I take the day off work. It was a Saturday and the restaurant was booked out. I managed to get Brendan to take my shift.

The next day I took a Valium on top of a painkiller and pushed through the first few hours of the busy lunch sitting. When the drugs started to wear off the pain became intense. Cath had to plate up the meals after I fell down in the storeroom. My lower back was on fire, a searing pain radiating from my toes, up both legs and all the way to the top of my head.

'What can I do?' Cath asked in a panic.

'Do you have a gun?' I joked, trying not to laugh. It really hurt when I laughed.

Cath took me to a doctor in Mittagong. After examining me he said he didn't know how I was standing, much less working. Following X-rays at the hospital I found out I'd crushed two discs in my back, fractured both knees and broken bones in both feet.

Aunty Flo's closed without warning. I contacted all of our customers and cancelled bookings for months in advance, including the lucrative Father's Day and Christmas trade. I was only comfortable lying flat on my back on a hard floor; it was impossible to get up and down without assistance. On one occasion, after Savannah had left for school, I lay there all day in the freezing cold unable to move. Perhaps it was pride, or the fact that I'd never been able to put my hand up and ask for help, but I didn't let on to Adam, or any of my friends, that I was in such a bad way.

Even after two months had passed, although there was some improvement, the simple act of getting out of bed and getting dressed was still a challenge. Some days, the pain in my back was so sharp it overrode everything else. I resisted taking painkillers, except when things reached a point where I thought about throwing myself into the path of the express train that whizzed behind the house every morning.

Savannah was only fifteen, and didn't seem to process what was happening, often expressing anger that I couldn't help out with simple tasks or drive her to school. Rather than shop and cook meals, which I was unable to do, we lived on take-away from the convenience store across the road. Savannah would take her meal to her room and I wouldn't see her until the next morning.

On the October long weekend she was surprised to get an invitation to visit her father in Sydney. It had been at least a year since she'd seen him. Unable to drive, I booked her a ticket on the CountryLink train that went straight through to Central Station where Darrol would pick her up. She called to let me know she'd arrived safely and that Hania was in New Zealand. I told her that I hoped she'd stay there and to have a good time with her dad.

The next night she called to say that Hania was back and there'd been a big fight. Her father was bringing her home immediately.

'It's midnight!' I said, surprised.

'Yes, he told me to get packed. We're leaving now.'

About thirty minutes later the phone rang. It was Hania. She was drunk and we had a heated exchange. I was about to put the phone down when she screamed, 'You were nothing in that business, Darrol did all the work!'

I laughed and told her she'd been talking to the wrong people, but I was quietly enraged by her comment. A few years earlier I'd been prevented from obtaining the documents that may have explained how Darrol's assets had increased exponentially after our divorce. Now I wondered if perhaps I had given up the fight too soon. Crawling on my belly, I pulled out all the documents still stored in boxes under my bed. For the next few days I went through everything, making notes and compiling lists. After hiring a wheel-chair and swallowing enough painkillers to numb me from the neck down, I travelled to Sydney and Canberra to search documents with ASIC, the Australian Securities and Investments Commission, and the Land Titles Office. I intended to dig up as much information on Darrol's personal and business assets as possible. I was determined to piece together the mystery of how his financial circumstances improved so soon after our divorce and especially after he purchased my shares in the company; it just didn't make sense.

There were some startling revelations, not the least of which was an exchange of contracts to purchase a $3.5 million resort at Airlie Beach in Queensland on the same day he settled with Manpower US for a buy-back of Manpower Australia, which saw him pocket a handsome consideration for the licensing agreement. Among other matters of interest was the amazing turnaround of revenue that jumped from $8 million in 1992 to a whopping $22 million by 1995. More remarkable still was the result of the company, owned solely by Darrol, which he claimed had no assets in 1988 but had assets in excess of $3 million by 1995. It seemed everywhere I looked there were zeros.

Working on a hunch, I called Manpower's head office in Sydney and spoke with the manager. Using the name of a former employee, it was very easy to convince him that I knew the inner workings of Manpower and had worked with Mrs Norman on developing IBM/Manpower partnership agreement in the 1980s. The manager was more than enthusiastic to share with me the success of the company since they'd introduced the Skillware program and partnered up with IBM. 'We've since moved across to Compaq,' he told me, 'but we still use the systems adapted by Mrs Norman. We haven't been able to better them.'

He also confirmed that Manpower Australia had signed a lucrative contract with the Australian Defence Force and was now turning over $100 million per annum.

That night, when I called John Scipione to tell him about this he laughed. 'Darrol was to Manpower US what Alan Bond was to Kerry Packer, an opportunity that comes along once in a lifetime.' He was referring to the consideration for the licensing agreement for a paltry $7 million for a company that was turning over more than $100 million within three years of purchase. It appeared that I'd been well and truly had.

Having recently purchased a laptop computer for Savannah I started to put together a history of my marriage to Darrol and our business association. I sent it to a solicitor in Bowral at the same time that I sent off the financial documents to my accountant.

'Your property settlement was manifestly unfair,' my solicitor confirmed, before telling me something which, up until that point, I had not been aware. 'The superannuation funds were not taken into account and they ought to have been, given the income for you and your husband. Your one-third shares ought to have been adjusted to fifty per cent to reflect your position as his wife. This could all be settled under section 79a of the Family Law Act.'

'What will section 79a of the Family Law Act do?' I asked.

He explained that if successful, the original Consent Orders signed in 1988 would be turned over and we'd have to renegotiate a settlement based on our assets today. Every time he opened his mouth I heard a symphony playing.

John Scipione encouraged me to get a second opinion and set up a meeting with a solicitor friend of his. I was deterred from pursuing the matter in the Family Court; I was told that certain documents had been retrieved from the court that quashed my chances. 'It's all here,' the solicitor said, handing me a large brown envelope. 'But we won't waste time going over it now.'

Instead, the matter took a different turn and I had to prepare a new statement for a firm of commercial lawyers with a greater emphasis on my business partnership with Darrol. A year passed as they tried to obtain the documents I needed to go forward. William, Darrol's accountant, refused to give us access, claiming he had not had instructions from his client to do so. When it became clear that we weren't going to get what we needed, I then instructed a forensic accountant to review all of the records we had in order to determine if there was sufficient information for me to proceed. It took them several months to prepare a very detailed report. 'Mr. Norman is just going to have to give you back some money,' I was told, which raised my hopes.

'Give yourself an uppercut, Possum. How did Darrol get away with this, without you having a clue what was going on?' John Scipione asked me, when I called to discuss the forensic accounting results with him.

'*Mea culpa*. I trusted him without question.'

'Well don't be too hard on yourself; you had every right to expect that you could trust you husband.'

'You know what really irks me about all of this?'

'Apart from having lost millions of dollars?' John chuckled.

'It's the realisation of what I suspect were the motives behind Savannah being banned from going to her father's home between July 1992 and September 1993,' I said, pausing to compose myself. In the light of evidence now at hand it seemed very plausible that Darrol had banned Savannah from his home after they'd come back from Queensland, where he'd been doing business in July 1992, because he didn't want her overhearing his dealings with the sale of the company. To have sold his interest in Manpower on the same day that he exchanged contracts to purchase a multimillion dollar resort at Airlie Beach suggested to me that he was already in negotiations with Manpower before he purchased my shares.

'You're probably right, and if you are, you'll be able to go after him,' John said, encouragingly.

When I next met with the commercial lawyer, I could barely see him over the files piled high on his desk. 'You can't take the marriage out of the business, the business was the marriage,' he said, when I told him that I saw my marriage and the operation of the business as a single entity and had trusted my husband without question. I told him about my theory regarding Darrol's negotiations with the US for a buy-back of the franchise.

'If you ever discover that your former husband was negotiating to purchase your shares, at the same time he was negotiating with the US, you'll be able to revisit this matter,' he said, confirming what John had told me. 'But as things stand, without access to the general ledger and other financial details I can't recommend that you initiate proceedings.'

By this time Savannah and I were living in Ultimo, having relocated back to Sydney after she completed Year 10. She had enrolled into Sydney Church of England Girls Grammar School and was settling in nicely, winning a major short story writing award and being shortlisted for the *Sydney Morning Herald* Young Writer of the Year. I had written to Darrol to let him know, and Savannah soon received an email in reply. When she passed it on for me to read, I could see that she'd been crying.

Although he lived only fifteen minutes away Darrol had not seen or spoken to Savannah since we moved back to Sydney. The email opened with a brief note of congratulations on her 'achievements' before berating her for a comment from her maths teacher on her half-yearly report. Then he launched a scathing attack, reminding Savannah that it was a privilege to be attending a private school: *A privilege neither me or your mother, or your brother and sister had.* The second page of the email was addressed to me. It concerned the account for miscellaneous school expenses. Savannah had tossed the receipt out with the box containing her school shoes; he'd deducted this amount with a note: *'No receipt, no pay.'*

By this time I had spent almost two years pursuing the legal case and had parted with a staggering amount of money. At times I found myself wondering if it was worth it. Following Darrol's email I was again reminded of the years of hard work I had put into the business, especially the years I had lost with my son, while I had put my husband's interests, and those of his kids, first. I knew nothing could give me back the time I had missed with Adam, but the magnitude of the injustice gnawed at me.

With this in mind, I sat down and reviewed all of the information I had gathered thus far in relation to the case. I was gobsmacked when I realised that the advice I'd received from John Scipione's mate was erroneous. He'd misread the date on the documents from the Family Court, which left open the possibility that I may still be able to pursue the matter. By now I was getting increasingly suspicious of lawyers generally, and I thought it would be wise to obtain my files from my former solicitor, Maurice. When I called him he sounded nervous to hear my voice. 'We don't keep the files here; they are archived and take time to retrieve,' he said.

When I went to collect them his secretary was off-handed and told me that as the statutes had passed, all of the files regarding my matrimonial property matter and the sale of my shares had been destroyed.

'What about my personal journals?' I asked.

'Everything in the files has been destroyed,' she said.

'You had no right to destroy my private diaries.'

Just then, Maurice came into reception. He looked startled to see me.

'I am disgusted with you, Maurice,' I told him. 'I was relying on you to advise me and all you did was to wait for instructions.'

'Would you have listened to anyone?' he mumbled sheepishly, before scurrying to his office.

As I was now living in Sydney, it didn't seem practical to go back to the solicitor in Bowral, a decision that would cost me dearly. After briefing four legal firms, one who made Dennis Denuto of the *The Castle* look competent, my matter was finally filed in the Family Court in 2002.

At the first hearing, I was asked to wait in a private conference room at the court. 'This is just a preliminary discussion,' I was told. 'Your attendance isn't required.' I later learned why my solicitors were keen for me not to witness the proceedings. They had not followed my instructions and, as a result, my matter had been completely compromised. It was a devastating blow that placed me in a difficult situation. If I withdrew, Darrol would have been

in a position to wipe me out and I had no doubt that he would have
done so. I sacked the entire legal team and, refusing to pay their
account, I approached the court for an adjournment. I was now
faced with the challenge of trying to find new legal advisors, who'd
be willing to take my case knowing it had been seriously compromised. I was relieved that I would have six months to regroup
before the second hearing.

31

Letting go

Moving back to Sydney had not done much to improve my relationship with Savannah. What had been a total breakdown in communication had escalated to an atmosphere of open hostility. Things reached boiling point one day and I lost my temper, slapping Savannah on the face for the disrespectful way she spoke to me. Frustrated by my inability to reach out to her and ashamed by my lack of control, we agreed that the best possible solution to ease the pressure on her and resolve the ongoing tensions was for us to live separately.

Savannah was in Year 12 and working towards her HSC. SCEGGS didn't take boarders and there was no question of her going to live with her father, so we found her a one-bedroom apartment in a secure building opposite the school and less than ten minutes by car from where I was living. The week before her eighteenth birthday we went to an auction and bid successfully on some nice furniture to make it comfortable. 'Happy birthday, my darling,' I said, when I paid the cashier.

A bank transfer was set up for Savannah to receive the maintenance from her father. As she had no rent to pay it was more than adequate for her to live on. Savannah moved into the apartment the day before her birthday. When I returned home that afternoon I went up to her old room and lay down on her bed, breathing in her unique scent. Clutching one of the teddy bears she'd left behind, I reflected on the previous eighteen years. Like a sentimental old movie on late-night TV, memories flashed through my mind: her first kick, the sound of her first cry, the daisy kisses and all the beautiful cards and drawings she'd given me, still kept in a safe place. My fondest memories of us were at Oldgate, sitting at the table in the kitchen with the log fire crackling in the background as we'd painted watercolours and watched the swallows nesting under the eaves. We were so happy then; I was her world and she was mine.

'Look Mum, the babies have hatched,' she'd say excitedly, as the tiny heads poked up from top of the nest squawking for food. Each day we'd watch their progress. The mother bird used to take her chicks down to the wire fence. She'd fly around and come back to keep a lookout for predators while her chicks took their turn. Then one day all the chicks flew off, leaving the mother bird sitting alone on the fence. For several minutes she sat there, looking forlorn, then she too flew away.

'How sad,' Savannah said, 'now she's all alone.'

'That's her purpose,' I replied.

I felt that had been my purpose, too. Now I just had to have the courage to let my little one go.

By August 2002 I was able to dispense with the wheelchair but I still needed a walking stick. I booked a ticket to the US to meet up with friends at the Lyons Folk Festival in Colorado. Savannah would sit for the HSC exams at the end of September and I was intending to get back before then.

The night before I flew out, John and I went to see Savannah's HSC drama performance. 'She's amazing! You could have heard a pin drop,' he said, wiping away a tear after watching her breathtaking portrayal of Martha in *Who's Afraid of Virginia Woolf*. We had dinner at the Balkan Restaurant in Taylor Square and as we kissed goodbye at the traffic lights he wrapped his arms around me in a big bear hug. He had a bad cold and I chided him about smoking. 'Those bloody things will kill you,' I joked.

I'd been away for about three weeks and was staying with friends in New Mexico when I logged on to my email. My friend Christine had sent me a message. I had to read it several times before it sunk in: *I am sorry to have to tell you in an email, but John Scipione died suddenly this morning, a heart attack.*

On the long flight home I thought about the all-round best mate John had been to me and Savannah. He always took an interest in Savannah's life and was happy to attend her drama performances and award presentations. In my darkest hours he was the one who sensed that I needed help and offered it without being asked. He was my confidant, with a keen insight into human behaviour and an ability to decipher legal terminology to help me get to the heart of a matter.

The church was packed for his funeral. His coffin was draped in regalia from his beloved 'Swannies', the Sydney-based AFL team, and a Hawaiian shirt from his extensive collection. As I watched the casket move slowly towards the curtain I clutched Gabor's hand for support. John had been my rock. It was hard not to feel a sense of abandonment by his sudden death. It was as if he'd jumped onto a fast moving train and left me stranded.

The wake was held at the Yarra Bay Sailing Club. Spinning in a hurly-burly of jetlag and grief, I walked past a group of women discussing a current affairs program that had recently aired. 'Abos get all of those special perks – houses and cars – it's just not right,' I overheard one woman say.

The group nodded their heads and mumbled in agreement. I stopped to listen more closely, intrigued by their complicity. The implication was that Aboriginal people were lazy drunks who trashed everything and didn't respect the things they were given. When I'd heard enough of the racial stereotyping I laughed out loud to get their attention. 'When you find out where this gravy train leaves from let me know, I want to be on it,' I said.

A woman turned to face me when she heard my voice. 'You're not an Aboriginal,' she stated.

'I most certainly am, and proud of it,' I declared.

'So do you get welfare?' she asked, snickering.

'Do I look like I'm on welfare?' I replied. 'Let me ask you, do you know whose land we are standing on today?'

Her face was blank.

'This is Darug country and if you gave every surviving Darug person a house, a car and a block of flats in Bondi, you'd still owe them for the land that was stolen from them.' I walked away in disgust – my pent-up emotion cutting through my fatigue.

Myles and his wife, Lee, were sitting together at a nearby table. Myles was already slurring his words. 'You look bloody sensational,' he said when I sat down. 'Dior?' he asked, motioning to my outfit.

Still spitting chips, I told Myles what I'd overheard in the previous conversation and how I'd reacted.

'Well I'm not a proud Indigenous person,' he said, shocking me with this admission and causing his wife's eyes to widen in disbelief.

'Well you ought to be. Your mother was a decent, hardworking woman, who had it bloody tough in order for you to be where you are today.' I was struggling to keep my voice down.

'Myles isn't Aboriginal,' Lee gasped, as if he was admitting to having some kind of disability.

'He most certainly is,' I snapped, 'and that he isn't proud of it is a bloody disgrace.'

Losing one of my best mates wasn't the only brick wall I hit that year. When my matter had first been heard in the Family Court I had been curious about how Darrol's legal team knew to sub-poena my solicitor in Bowral, who hadn't been mentioned in any affidavits submitted as part of my application to the court. The mystery was solved at the second hearing when I realised that one of Darrol's legal representatives had had a lengthy discussion con-cerning my matter with my Bowral solicitor in 1999. How much this compromised my case I couldn't be sure, but from where I was sitting it appeared to be a conflict of interest.

Even so, I took the opportunity to subpoena William, our former accountant. Darrol claimed that all files that exceeded the statute had been destroyed, but I had a hunch that William may have held back some important files I'd been trying to get my hands on for years. I was particularly interested to discover how my director's loan account had sufficient funds in August 1988 for me to purchase a property worth $400,000 in Avalon, but by December had been reduced to $122,000 as shown on the consent orders.

'Your loan account was in credit for $534,000 as at August 1988,' my accountant said, when he inspected the files William had sent to the Family Court.

'So where did the rest go?' I asked.

He pointed to other entries where significant amounts had

been taken from my account and transferred to the company owned wholly by Darrol.

'Can he do that?' I asked, looking at these entries with disbelief.

'To do so without your knowledge or consent is a very serious matter,' he said. 'It's no different from having taken money from your bank account.'

The implication of this was almost too much to take in. In 1988 I had received a matrimonial property settlement of $425,000. This was approximately the same amount as the funds that had been transferred to Darrol from my director's loan account into Darrol's company. It appeared from these transactions that Darrol had used my own money to pay me out. Initially I was excited by these discoveries, and hoped they might strengthen my case, but when my solicitor advised that I could no longer submit new evidence I was devastated. This was the coup de grâce. Fourteen years had passed since our separation but I felt as beaten as I imagined any battered wife could feel.

32

Settling old scores

Savannah did herself proud in the HSC, making the Honour Roll for Advanced English and Drama and having her English paper published by the New South Wales Board of Studies. She was the first person in my family, and Darrol's, to complete high school and go on to higher studies. Although he'd been invited, Darrol didn't attend the valedictory dinner.

Savannah decided to take a gap year before starting university. Under the child support agreement I'd seen to it that Darrol had to continue to support her throughout her education. My solicitor advised that this would cease if there was a break in the continuity. I let Savannah know this, but her mind was made up. The payments from Darrol ceased immediately and until Savannah found a job I had to continue to support her. As rent alone, for the two of us, amounted to $800 per week I sent all my furniture to storage. I moved into a nice unit in Harbord with my friend Julie who was looking for a housemate. This reduced my outgoings significantly and gave me some time and space to consider my future. It was also comforting to have the company of an adult female friend while I struggled to fill the yawning gap that losing John had left in my life, and adjusted to the fact that both of my children were adults and off living their own lives.

Almost three years after I fell from the train, I filed a claim for negligence against State Rail. Unlike the other legal matters I had been battling this one was based on a no-win, no-pay arrangement. I was required to obtain witness statements and agree to numerous medical examinations to determine the extent of my injuries and how they may impact on my future. It was dragging into a lengthy and heavily contested case, with State Rail claiming I had pre-existing injuries. They put a private detective on my tail. I found this out when a neighbour alerted me to a dodgy-looking bloke in a suit who had been asking questions about me and taking photographs of my car.

'The tapes of the CTV cameras from the station that day are missing, and the death certificate of their only witness is on the table,' my solicitor called to tell me, sounding elated.

At the hearing, the legal representative for State Rail tried to make an issue of me purchasing a new Mercedes. Since the fall from the train I had bought a later model sedan as the two-door coupe sat too low. It was easier to get the wheelchair in and out of the back seat, rather than lift it in and out of the boot.

'What does it matter if Ms Howarth owns a Rolls-Royce?' the magistrate asked, clearly annoyed.

Then they tried to assert that I had been in such a hurry to get back to my business that I'd jumped from a moving train.

'It was 4:40 a.m. and my fifteen-year-old daughter was behind me,' I said. My barrister tried to suppress a laugh.

When that didn't work they tried to establish that I had a

pre-existing condition. They sifted through a bundle of medical records going back years and pulled out one where I'd been to see a doctor after straining a muscle – I'd been lifting a heavy oil can.

'Just one month before the fall from the train I passed the aviation medical with Dr Tinning at Mittagong,' I said, nodding at the documents in his hand. 'Surely you have that report?'

'Alright, I've heard enough,' the magistrate interjected. 'We'll recess for thirty minutes.'

'You've won. It's just a matter of by how much,' my solicitor reassured me as we sat in the waiting area.

Although I received a six-figure payout it went nowhere near compensating for the financial loss of having to close my business and being left with a thirty per cent permanent physical impairment, which would only get worse with time. This win lifted my spirits, but unfortunately a good chunk of the money went directly into paying off various legal accounts that were still outstanding.

When Julie sold her unit at Harbord I found a house-sit at Newport for a couple who were going to Europe. They were less concerned about their multi-storey mansion than the need to have someone take care of Daisy, their much-pampered King Charles spaniel.

One evening, while enjoying the spectacular sunset across Pittwater, with the hypnotic sounds of metal rigging echoing up from the moorings at Prince Alfred Yacht Club, I experienced déjà vu. I recalled the night long ago when I had sipped my first liqueur only a stone's throw from where I was now living and marvelled at how quickly time seemed to have passed. For more than fifty years my life had been at full throttle. Now, I couldn't see into next week, and it seemed my only purpose was making sure Miss Daisy's ears were clean and her claws were clipped.

Although I was living in a waterfront mansion, strictly speaking, for the moment at least, I was homeless. When Savannah came up to visit she was clearly uncomfortable being in someone else's house. I felt like I had let her down by risking what would have been a considerable inheritance. Although I had no idea, until I was in too deep, that the odds were stacked so heavily against me, I hoped that in time she would understand that I couldn't let her father walk all over me without putting up a fight. I hadn't received the outcome I felt I deserved, given how hard I'd worked, but I could learn to live with the financial loss.

I filled in my time plugging away at the manuscript I'd started some years earlier. None of my good friends, except for Simone, lived close by so we didn't get to catch up often and I missed their company. It was hard to admit that for the first time in my life I felt lonely. I started thinking about finding a companion, a lover even, to bring some fun and purpose into my life. Having turned fifty-three I wasn't comfortable with the notion of putting myself out and about, so I got onto an internet dating website, knowing that the humiliation of a knock-back would only be witnessed by me, and that I could also do some picking and choosing of my own. The response was immediate and overwhelming. Most of the replies I politely discarded. I met up with a few different men for coffee, went on a couple of lunch and dinner dates and was about to pack it in when I saw a contact from someone with an interesting face.

It was evident from the way he'd written his profile that he was educated, and the picture showed a tall man, dressed in black leathers, standing beside a gleaming red Honda motorcycle. My curiosity was piqued, but when I saw he was living in Colorado in the US I wrote and told him that the distance was too great. His name was James, and he asked if we could become pen pals. I tentatively agreed. We progressed to speaking on the phone and

279

then started chatting on Skype. Like me, James had known the heartache that comes with making bad choices and his need for love and affection seemed as urgent as mine. We were two lonely people, drawn together by a mutual longing to fill the void. I found myself quickly sucked in to the romance of it all.

For six months we spoke on the internet every day, sometimes for three or four hours at a time. James had taught high school, but something had happened involving a female student, which he said was a frame-up that cost him his career. He was currently operating a small handyman business and had to continue working, so we decided I would make the trip to the US. He didn't offer to meet me halfway with the costs, but I wouldn't have to pay for accommodation when I got there, so I felt alright about it.

Magnificent autumn colours spread across the landscape like a patchwork quilt as I flew over Colorado towards Denver airport. James stood out from the crowd as I walked down the exit ramp. He looked nervous. I was worried that I wouldn't measure up to the fantasy he may have built up over the months we'd been talking. 'Are you disappointed?' I ventured to ask, quite prepared to get on the next plane and go home if necessary.

'No Katie, you are beautiful and just as I expected,' he said, before bending down to kiss me. I could taste the tobacco on his breath, even though he'd told me he quit.

James was handsome in a rugged kind of way. When we had spoken on Skype the lighting at his end was always subdued and I never noticed the deep scar along the left side of his face; he told me he got it when his mother accidently pushed him through a glass door when he was a little boy. It must have been some injury because even as a grown man the disfigurement was significant. None of this mattered to me, but I thought it helped to explain why he wasn't as confident in person as he had been when we spoke online.

'Nice car,' I said, as James put my bag in the back of a spotlessly clean SUV. 'It belongs to a buddy; my pick-up had to go to the mechanic yesterday.'

On the drive to James's house he took a detour to a scenic outlook with a view to a quaint village nestled between the snow-capped peaks in the heart of the Rocky Mountains.

'What's that?' I asked, pointing to the massive construction that seemed to cover about one-third of the town.

'That's Walmart.'

James fumbled in his shirt pocket and then got down on one knee, taking my hand. 'Katie, will you marry me?' he asked, with tears in his eyes, before slipping something onto my finger – it looked like three pieces of wire twisted together in a makeshift fashion.

I wasn't sure if I should take him seriously, so I said nothing.

'You don't want to marry me?' He looked devastated.

'Of course I do,' I said, stroking his forlorn face.

When we picked up his car, the ashtray was overflowing and I had to clear the junk from the passenger seat before I could sit down. Faint warning bells, which had been ringing since I'd arrived, cranked up in volume when we got to his house.

'Gee Katie, I'm so embarrassed,' he said. 'It's been hard on my own. I've kinda let the place go,' he explained, handing me a sand-wich on a paper plate. We had to eat it on the floor because the only table was covered with model aircraft that couldn't be moved until the glue dried.

Our first night together didn't go well. James had two bois-terous dogs that scratched and whined at the bedroom door until he relented and let them in. The next day he took me to meet his oldest and closest friends, Clayton and Mandy, at 'The Ranch', which is what Clayton called the property perched on a rocky outcrop a few miles out of town. Apparently James had done a lot of the work on their house, yet they treated him like a servant. It was as though he was beholden to them for something, and until the debt was paid they owned him. They insisted that James finish the hanging pot rack that he had started, which took a day out of the time we had together. James took it like a lapdog.

After some discussion it was decided that James would sell up and relocate to Australia. While he went to work I busied myself cleaning his house, which couldn't be put on the market in its present condition. One morning, he came back early. 'The pick-up's packed it in,' he said, 'and it really ain't worth fixin'.'

He told me a friend of his had a nice station wagon 'going cheap', but until the house sold he didn't have the money.

'Why don't you sell the bike?' I asked. His Honda was worth more than the car and if he was intending on coming to Australia it made sense to sell it.

'The bike belongs to Clayton; he just lets me borrow it.'

James's profile picture on the internet dating site had shown him standing proudly beside the bike, which I'd presumed was his and not a prop he'd borrowed for the occasion. 'I'll pay you back when the house sells,' he smiled, giving me a hug and taking the money I gave him to get the car.

Clayton offered to show me around while James was working. He arrived in a pick-up truck, complete with a rifle in the gun rack and boxes of ammunition stashed behind the seat. He was wearing an orange vest and cap, and handed me a similar set to put on.

'What's this for?' I asked

'They're regulation,' he said, explaining that it was hunting season and the Texans coming across the border would shoot anything not wearing an orange vest. Clayton seemed anxious to give me the low-down on why James was no longer teaching. It was a vastly different version of events from the story James had told me when we first met. Then he surprised me further by telling me that James's ex-wife had left him because she didn't want to catch AIDS.

'James isn't a homosexual,' I said, shocked and offended by the remark. We didn't speak the rest of the way home. Not wanting to repeat a mistake I'd made with Darrol, I told James what Clayton had said, which he emphatically denied. I was left to wonder why a friend of thirty years would say such a thing.

When I returned to Australia I was too embarrassed to tell anyone that I was engaged to marry someone I'd met on the internet. It would be many months before James would be able to join me, and anything could happen in that time. I made up my mind to leave Sydney and try to find a quiet place in the country. If it worked out with James, I thought, we'd both be happy in that environment. If not, I'd still be more content in a rural setting, where I intended to finish the book I had started.

'Bombala's too hot and dry – and too many bloody snakes,' my mate Peter said, when I stopped in at Mittagong and told him I was taking a road-trip south to find a place to settle down.

I stopped at Myrtle Mountain lookout, where the view took my breath away – rolling hills with cattle and sheep grazing as far as the eye could see. I knew I'd found the place I'd been searching for. As I drove into the village of Candelo in the Bega Valley the sign into town declared a population under 350 people. Every building in the main street could have been heritage listed. It was as though time stood still. Outside the white-painted timber post office, a couple of old blokes wearing Akubra hats were sitting on the long bench against the sunny wall, reading their mail and complaining about the weather. The petrol station, formerly the blacksmith's shop, owned by a chatty bloke called Eric, doubled as a museum for old farm equipment. The general store looked like something out of Dodge City, selling everything from a piano to a pin. The deciduous trees on the village green, ablaze in vivid autumn colours, would have been saplings when the foundation stone of the Candelo Hotel had been laid in the 19th century. I continued on to Bega and called into the real estate agents to enquire about rural properties in the area.

'We have a farm nearby,' the agent told me.

I was filled with enthusiasm and wanted to see more of the countryside. We crossed the Candelo Bridge and drove for a few more kilometres, when the agent pointed to a cottage perched on a hill. 'That's it,' she said. 'That's Model Farm.'

The charming weatherboard cottage, circa 1889, had a wrap-around veranda with stunning rural views in every direction. A fuel stove in the large eat-in kitchen and a log fire in the lounge room gave it a rustic appeal. There were four large bedrooms, with high ceilings, and a huge shed for James, who was keen to make furniture. The orchard out the back was a real bonus. After completing all the paperwork I headed back to Sydney to arrange for the move.

Two trucks were needed to transport all my belongings, some of which had been stored since I left Bowral. Fortunately, I had several months to unpack before James arrived. Working my way through the boxes I ruthlessly culled and sorted stuff to give to friends or send to St Vincent de Paul. The process was slowed as I unpacked a file containing some old news clippings, and came across one Uncle Stan had given me many years before. At the time I had been in such turmoil I hadn't even bothered to read it. It was a half-page article in the *Sydney Morning Herald* dated 7 September 1985 with a headline: *The Soft Touch Capitalist of Cobar*. It wasn't until I saw the name Arthur 'Pop' Burgess that I realised why Uncle Stan had wanted me to see it. Growing up, I'd always been told that my father was Ray Burgess, who played for the Western Suburbs Rugby League team. As Pop Burgess was his father, this meant I could be looking at my paternal grandfather for the first time. Given what I now knew about Jack McCarthy, Aunty Daphne's husband, I'd much prefer to think that Uncle Stan knew more than he let on. To be honest, I doubted that even my mother knew for sure.

As I scanned the face of this spritely old man I felt a strong connection to his story. He was said to be the stuff that fables are made of; an entrepreneur, a compulsive hard worker and a generous man who gave money away as fast as he made it. Reading this story restored my faith in the goodness of people, and helped me realise that in spite of my experiences, men like Pop Burgess were out there changing people's lives and touching their hearts. It was nice to think that the King of Cobar may have been my grandfather. It made me feel hopeful about the future.

Once I had settled into life on the farm I had one more item of unfinished business with Darrol and our former accountant. In the previous legal battle I had finally gained access to the director's loan account files but at the time decided not to launch into something that would involve more solicitors. Now I felt ready to revisit the matter and find out if there was any possibility of recovering some of the money that had been lost to me. It wasn't about the money itself, which in the scheme of things was trivial compared with other losses I'd sustained, it was more for my own peace of mind. Darrol had mocked me once by saying, 'You got what you settled for,' but I didn't agree. It wasn't fair and I wasn't going to settle for it. I'd received so little, by comparison, for the years of hard work I'd put into the business and the marriage, and I was looking forward to finally being able to confront Darrol and ask him why he felt he had the right to do what he did. Was it just because he was a man, and he felt entitled? Or did he really not value the contribution I'd made for all those years?

The senior detective at Bega Police Station was more savvy with complex financial matters than most of the legal minds I'd dealt with in the previous few years. He told me that it was a matter for the major fraud squad in Sydney. He photocopied all of the relevant documents and prepared a detailed statement for me to sign.

While I was waiting to hear back from them, I called William and made an appointment to see him in his office. He didn't even ask me what it was about.

'How much do you want?' he asked, as I took a seat in the boardroom.

'I've done the sums, William, and with interest applied it's around $19 million dollars. Can you get that for me?' I asked, trying to hide my surprise that his approach was virtually an unsolicited admission that I'd been ripped off.

While some of the losses I'd sustained were due to poor legal advice, others had been due to my own naivety or having made bad decisions in difficult emotional circumstances. The information contained in the director's loan account file was another matter. I told William that I required a term deposit, in Savannah's favour, for the total amount that had been transferred from my loan account to his client in 1988 or that his client agree to purchase a property in her name of equal value.

'He has thirty days to agree, or this will go forward,' I said.

'I'll speak with him,' he assured me.

As I got up to leave I said, 'Oh, and if I ever discover that Darrol was negotiating with the US at the same time he was negotiating to buy my shares in the company, he won't get off so lightly.' I didn't think I needed to add, 'and neither will any of his associates.'

*

Shortly afterwards Savannah called, sounding very excited. Her father was buying her a unit in Manly.

'That's wonderful, darling,' I said, 'but please let me see any documents before you sign them.'

When Savannah mentioned this to her father, he told her she was 'looking a gift horse in the mouth'.

33

'Do I look pretty in this?'

James arrived in Australia on 4 July 2004. He was late getting through customs and said that after they found his set of handcuffs they conducted a thorough search.

'Handcuffs?' I raised my eyebrows.

'Yes, I told them they belonged to my fiancée,' he laughed.

We spent a few days sightseeing in Sydney and catching up with friends before heading down the coast. James was nervous about driving on the left-hand side of the road.

'Lay back and relax. I've never been involved in a car accident,' I said, turning on some music. It was an eight-hour drive and while James slept in the passenger seat I had time to reflect on my feelings for him. I can't say I was madly in love, with the heated passion I once had for Karl, or even Darrol at the beginning, but I felt we had something to build on. James had a quality that tugged at my heart strings. At times he was like a little boy who wanted a mummy to fix things. It felt nice to be needed.

James loved the farm and I think he was more than a bit surprised by some of the lovely things I had collected over the years. After we had dinner on our first night at home, I thought we needed to get some housekeeping issues out of the way. Talking about money was something I hated doing, but I wanted to work out a budget for the wedding, and the honeymoon we were planning in Tasmania. 'May I suggest that I pay for everything to do with the wedding, and you sort out the trip to Tasmania?' I asked, figuring that if I catered for the thirty guests and we held the ceremony and reception at the farm the costs would be about equal.

'I haven't got any money,' he said, unable to look at me.

'So you haven't settled on the property in Colorado?'

'Oh yes, but after the mortgage was cleared there wasn't much left, I just had enough to pay for the wedding rings and my airfare.'

The wedding rings were fashioned from three gold rings containing diamonds and rubies that I had given to James; he only had to pay the jeweller to make them.

When we'd been in Sydney it struck me as odd that James never offered to pay for anything, although I never asked about it. He'd paid for his own ticket and I thought *fair enough*.

But now I was starting to worry. 'What happened to the car?' I asked, realising that he'd never offered to pay that money back.

'I left it with Tim,' he said. Tim was James's nineteen-year-old son, who lived with his mother.

'You've come here with no money at all?' I was flummoxed. 'Why did you wait until you got here to tell me this?'

'I was afraid you'd dump me,' he said, with tears in his eyes.

If James hadn't come all the way from Colorado this would have been a deal-breaker. His lack of finances was going to be a problem, especially as he wouldn't be able to work until his visa for temporary residency was granted, and that could take years. However, it was the lack of courage, and even dishonesty, not to tell me about his situation earlier that was of greater concern.

'James, we have to be totally honest with each other or this isn't going to work for me,' I said sternly.

'I am sorry, Katie; I just didn't want to lose you.'

Most of the country had been in the grip of a severe drought and the skies decided to open up on our wedding day. I'd made my own dress and James wore a grey suit that looked like it might have fit a shorter, less heavy-set man, before he found it in an op-shop.

Over the years, issues harking back to Adam's childhood had kept resurfacing, causing conflict. We had recently patched up one of our rifts and I was thrilled that my son was going to be giving me away, and Kate was to be my flower girl. The wind was almost blowing us down the hill as he walked me over to where the ceremony was taking place. He looked so handsome in his black suit and gold tie, which complemented my dress perfectly. My granddaughter, Kate, looked angelic, and the image of her Aunty Savannah at the same age. Savannah looked elegant but refused to be called the matron of honour. They were a handsome mob and I was so proud of them.

We'd booked into a B&B in Candelo for the wedding night so that Adam and his family and Savannah could stay at the farm. The next morning, James went to get some wood organised so they wouldn't be cold. This kindness towards my family put James well ahead of any partner I'd had to date.

As soon as we were married we commenced the application for his permanent residency. The immigration department required thousands of dollars deposit and we had to produce details of our joint bank account, which we'd set up after selling some paintings and two custom-made guitars, to show that we had sufficient funds to support him until his visa was granted. After the paperwork was finalised James had to attend a series of medical appointments to make sure he was in good health. Over the following twelve months they poked their noses into every corner of our lives.

'Next they'll be asking to see videos of us naked in bed,' I joked.

To ease some of the financial strain, I took a part-time job as a cook at the Candelo Pub. The casual hours suited me, as I wasn't sure how my injuries would hold up. To ward off boredom and homesickness for James I sold my car. I bought two vehicles and all the tools he needed for a 'man shed' to keep him occupied while I worked. I also started researching the local market for business opportunities that could make use of James's handyman skills, when his visa was finally granted. I soon discovered an unmet need, especially in Merimbula and Tura Beach, where the economy was driven by demand for real estate.

'That's a brilliant idea, Katie,' James said when I discussed the idea with him, which would provide a service with a practical application. We'd advise vendors on the best way to present their property to optimise the selling price, and James would complete any of the work necessary to spruce up the properties.

Within a year James received a work permit and I got cracking, designing a logo and getting the company and business name registered. I put together a marketing campaign targeting every real estate office in the area, as well as direct mail-outs to individual property owners and advertisements in the trades section of the local papers. Pretty soon, the phone started ringing and faxes from the real estate offices covered the floor.

'What happened?' I asked, when James came home shortly after he left the house to do his first job.

'I left my tool box at home.'

The next time he had to come back to get his mobile phone.

Work orders from the real estate agents were mostly small jobs, as they were still trialling our service, but we soon got a big job involving an upmarket home at Tura Beach. I went with James to quote on the job and discovered that I knew the owner, who also had a property in Mosman, where I used to live. This seemed to clinch the deal. There was a tight deadline to get the property ready to go on the market, and one morning James didn't look like he was going to work. He was playing around on his computer when he ought to have been on the road.

'Aren't you going to work today?'

'No, it's raining. I can't go to work when it's raining, Katie.'

He was working indoors and I told him the client would expect to see him there. I was starting to feel like a nagging mother.

James made the deadline with a fine margin but the finished job was of such a poor standard that we didn't hear from the real estate agent again, and news in a small town travels fast. James made no attempt to look for other work. This meant I had to increase my shifts at the pub, and start popping painkillers again. Fortunately, I still had a number of valuable assets in the form of jewellery, artwork and Persian carpets that I was able to send to auction, but it was hard not to feel resentment at having to let them go. Especially when it came to selling my custom-made left-handed guitar for a fraction of its worth.

It started with stockings and a suspender belt, which looked odd on a man of James's stature, but I thought, *whatever floats your boat.* Then it was a pair of ladies' panties, which progressed to a full teddy, then a bra. It presented me with some serious challenges. I'd come a long way since my sessions with Haig Masters and considered myself to be sexually confident and, within reason, open to new experiences. But getting into bed with my husband wearing women's underwear just didn't turn me on. I knew James was buying items on eBay using my debit card, which I thought was stuff he wanted for the shed. Then I noticed that some of the purchases were from an online adult shop. One night he handed me a spiked paddle and wanted me to spank him and draw blood. I couldn't do it, I didn't see myself in the role of dominatrix. The woman that James wanted to be started taking over, and he was asking things of me in the bedroom I wasn't comfortable with. It got to the point that every night, before he came to bed, he'd spend an hour in the bathroom making the transformation.

When he appeared one night with artificial breasts glued to his shaved chest I knew it was time for us to talk. The next evening I was serving dinner when I heard footsteps behind me. At first I thought the lambs had found their way inside.

'Do I look pretty in this?' James asked in a voice that I barely recognised. I turned around to see him towering before me in a pair of stilettos and thick pancake make-up. 'Well?' he probed, fidgeting with the synthetic red wig that he'd paired with a shocking pink taffeta dress. He'd shaved his moustache and the red lipstick looked like it had been slapped on with a bread and butter knife.

It was pointless being anything but honest: 'James, there's only room in this marriage for one woman.'

He burst into tears.

I had no issue with homosexuals or transsexuals. What I had an issue with was that he thought that it wouldn't change the dynamic of our marriage; that I would just go with the flow, slap on a strap-on, and carry on as if everything was normal.

'I'm sorry, Katie, but I can't help it,' James cried.

'I know you can't help it but this isn't something that's just over-taken you,' I said, remembering my conversation with his friend Clayton, who'd clearly been trying to warn me.

Sometime during the night I heard noises and thought James might be watching a late movie. I needed to go to the toilet and had to walk past the study. James was wearing headphones and didn't hear me come in. Just hours earlier my husband had wept in my arms and begged me to let him stay. Now, he was wearing his wig, make-up, a black leather bustier and talking in hushed tones to someone on the computer. I went to the bathroom and back to bed without saying a word. The next morning, I called a travel agent.

James had no money of his own, as far as I knew, so I went to town and withdrew several thousand dollars so he wouldn't land back in the US with nothing. He was happy to take it. In the days before his flight, however, his moods vacillated. He was morose one minute and aggressive the next. I was grateful to be in Australia, and not the US, where he could just pull a loaded gun from his drawer. I called my friend Peter, in Mittagong, to let him know what was happening. He asked if I wanted him to come down. I told him I was taking James to the airport the next day. That night I barricaded myself in the spare room.

The next morning James packed two bags. He tossed them into the car and was about to get into the driver's side. 'James, I'd like to drive please,' I said, holding my hand out for the keys.

'No, I'm driving, get in the fucking car or I'll go without you and dump it at the airport,' he threatened.

'If you drive away in my car I'll call the Merimbula police and report the car as having been stolen. Now give me my car keys!'

The landscape was dry and brittle after another hot summer, but even at its worst the Bega Valley is hard to beat for scenic beauty. We didn't speak on the forty-two-kilometre drive to the local airport. Although James still had three hours before his departure, I waited just long enough for him to collect his bags and when I heard the boot close I drove off in a cloud of dust, catching a glimpse of him in the rear-view mirror. When I got home there were three plastic garbage bags in the spare room, containing James's man clothes. It made sense. Limited by weight on the flight he'd decided to take the ladies clothes he bought on eBay, which would be harder to replace when he returned to live with his mother in a small town in Michigan. I couldn't help but think of the raised eyebrows he would get going through US customs if his bags got searched again.

Dry as a bone, I made a cup of tea and sat on the veranda. It was a beautiful clear day; lambs frolicked in the paddock and ewes grazed nearby. My hands started to shake and I felt a slow trembling coming from somewhere deep inside. The cup rattled against the saucer as I put it down. I couldn't hold back and let out a loud agonised howl, the kind a cat makes when someone takes its kittens. My head fell into my hands and the tears started to flow. I thought I was made of titanium, able to withstand anything that life threw at me, but this episode with James left me completely shattered, emotionally and financially. It was as if I'd grown old and bypassed maturity. I was still a kid picking up strays and taking them home without calculating the risks. I was totally spent when I finally went inside and collapsed on my bed. James's cologne still hung in the air.

It was at least a month before I could bring myself to tell anyone that James had gone back to the States. In recent years my friend Simone had become my closest confidante. I shared personal information with her that I didn't share with anyone else. When I called to tell her what had happened, I was feeling uncharacteristically maudlin.

'Kate, you're frightening me,' she said. 'I've never heard you talk like this before.'

It wasn't the first time in my life that I had contemplated suicide, but I think it was the first time I really went close to acting on it.

I wrote to Savannah who was studying in England. She came back with a loving and sensitive reply. Adam couldn't get his head around James wearing a dress. I was having trouble with that myself, but once I'd contacted the kids I started to turn a corner. No matter how bad things got for me I couldn't do that to my children.

I found myself praying again. It seemed a ridiculous thing to be doing, but sometimes it's all you have.

34

All mothers are important

For the previous year I'd hardly put a word down on the page and it was beginning to feel like I'd never get my story finished. After reading the first rough draft John Scipione had asked why I'd glossed over the time I'd spent in St Margaret's Home for Unwed Mothers, back in the 1960s, when I was pregnant with Adam.

'I kept the baby,' I told him. 'Where's the story in that?'

In his wisdom John had told me about a New South Wales parliamentary inquiry into adoption practices that had taken place some years earlier. Before he died, he sent me the link to the government website but I hadn't gotten around to downloading it until now. I'd lit the fire in the kitchen and was settling down with a pot of tea, having printed out 'Releasing the Past', the final report from the NSW Parliamentary Inquiry into Adoption Practices between 1950 and 1998. Reading the report stirred memories I'd kept buried for forty years.

'The rotten bastards!' I screamed, loudly enough to unsettle the sheep for miles around. I was shocked to learn that financial support for unmarried mothers had been available since the 1920s and it was not something introduced by the Whitlam government in 1973, as most people believed. Had I known of the availability of this financial assistance when Adam was born, how different my life – and his – could have turned out. Thinking about the years of our forced separation and the pain we both had to endure, I became incensed.

Then I thought of the young women I knew who had lost their children to adoption because they were badgered into believing they were evil to even think about keeping a baby they couldn't support. The 'Releasing the Past' report and the research conducted by Dian Wellfare, the founder of Origins, the support group for those affected by adoption, uncovered an almost unbelievable truth: financial assistance for single mothers had been available but was kept hidden. The implications of this seemed wicked. The report claimed adoption practices, and the treatment of unmarried mothers, was not only unethical, but at times illegal. This dark chapter in Australia's social history had been buried for decades because the young mothers, who'd been labelled as heartless sluts who didn't want their babies, had been traumatised into silence.

The report went on to say that the inquiry was unable to take evidence from a single mother who had kept the baby. It seemed I may be the only person who could tell the story of the treatment, which was tantamount to torture, a young mother suffered when she refused to surrender her child for adoption. Suddenly, a story that I'd been struggling to tell had real meaning and purpose. I put my head down and got to work.

When Savannah returned from Europe for a couple of months in 2007 she came down and spent some time with me at the farm. I'd contacted the Bogan Aboriginal Corporation about obtaining my

Certificate of Aboriginality, a process that required me to travel back to my family's country and get the signature of six community Elders. Together, Savannah and I set off on a road-trip to Nyngan. I was looking forward to catching up with members of my mob who I hadn't seen in decades. A cousin of mine, Ted Greenaway, was an Elder in the community, while Aunty Lorna, my grandmother Biddy and her mother Lizzy Higgins, had been well-known and much-loved identities.

We arrived on a crystal-clear July morning and in the distance I could hear the sulphur-crested cockatoos squawking along the Bogan River. I sat beside the fire in the garden at Tommy Ryan's place having a yarn with my cousin. 'I'm writing a book, Ted, but it's not just any book,' I told him. 'My book is going to kick up some dust. I want to be recognised as a Koori writer and I don't want any bullshit.'

Ted and Tommy both nodded. They understood what I meant. When I was a kid I had been scorned and called a half-caste bastard. I was buggered if I was having anyone tell me, now that I was an adult, that I wasn't black enough.

On the return journey we'd planned to catch up with Myles, who was living in the Blue Mountains. Myles and I had been talking on the phone and exchanging emails for some time. He and Lee had divorced and she'd gone back to her home country of New Zealand. He was still complaining of a bad back, which had plagued him for years. After every kind of alternative treatment he said the only thing that gave him any relief was having his little dog, Buttons, sleeping in the small of his back. 'Buttons, understands,' he said, patting his little dog affectionately.

We had dinner at an Indian restaurant in Katoomba, where Myles still called Savannah 'The Junior Princess'. After I got back to the farm Myles called to ask if I'd go and live with him. It wasn't a marriage proposal and for that I was grateful, because I had to knock him back again. I still hadn't finished writing my story and Myles was accustomed to me waiting on him hand and foot. He had no clue about the time I'd spent as an unmarried mother and why I felt compelled to get the story written. I could foresee clashes, where I'd want to write for ten hours a day, as I often did, and he'd feel neglected and be wondering what was for dinner.

'Myles, I have to get this book done. This is not just about me. It's a much bigger story. Please, let's just see each other when we can for the moment,' I tried to explain.

He got angry and hung up on me.

For almost two years I'd been attempting to write the story about my early life but I had been coming at it from an adult perspective and it wasn't working. As a child I had no analytical ability, I had been flat out trying to out-run the brown leather strap or dodge a pair of scissors being hurled in my direction. Then I realised that I had to try and tell my story through the eyes of the child I had been. This presented considerable challenges, which I overcame by reading the work back to myself to make sure that the naive voice of young Kate remained at the fore.

The process of digging into my past in order to retell it was, I imagined, a lot like giving myself an autopsy without an anaesthetic. As the jigsaw puzzle of my life started to come together I could see a much more complex story emerging, one that was going to shine a very uncomfortable spotlight, not only on members of my own family but also on a society whose children had no voice, and where women were treated like chattels. I found myself having to confront events that I'd blocked out concerning the abandonment from my mother, and the indelible marks it left on me. Ultimately, I was left to reflect on the effect this had on my own experiences as a mother. For the first time in my life I was making a connection between never having known my father and the mistakes I seemed to keep repeating in my relationships with men. At the outset, my motivation for writing the story was to address the injustice done to my son, and others in a similar situation, and maybe help to heal their pain. As it was turning out, the one being healed was me.

On 13 February 2008 I got dressed and tied red, yellow and black ribbons around my neck in a big bow. There was a mob of local blackfellas milling around a big screen that had been set up outside the Bega Council Chambers to broadcast the speech being made by newly elected Prime Minister Kevin Rudd. He was going to fulfil an election promise to say 'Sorry' to the Stolen Generation, which had involved the removal of tens of thousands of mixed-blood Aboriginal children from their families for the stated intention of 'breeding out' the blackfella.

'G'day Aunty Rita,' I greeted a local Elder.

'G'day Kate,' she said, taking my hand.

We stood together and shed silent tears as these long overdue words were spoken. Rudd continued to tell the story of Nanna Nungala Fejo, a Warumungu woman who had been snatched from her mother as a child, never to see her again. Rudd asked her what she would have him say. She replied, with profound wisdom, simply: *All mothers are important.*

By March 2008 I thought I might have had enough story down for a manuscript appraisal, at least enough for someone to tell me if I was wasting my time. I'd gone back and included the details of my experience at St Margaret's Home for Unwed Mothers, just as John had encouraged me to do. At this point the story had a working title that didn't fit the narrative. Then it occurred to me that the prayer I'd recited throughout my life was the key. The Hail Mary is the prayer of penance and forgiveness following confession, and ten Hail Marys are said if the sins are great.

I was encouraged to enter the manuscript into the David

Unaipon Award – a literary award that recognises unpublished Indigenous writers. To my amazement, two months later I got a call advising that my story had been shortlisted. At first I was jumping around like I'd just won Lotto. Then I was bawling my eyes out with gratitude and disbelief.

When I received an invitation to the award ceremony in Brisbane, where the winner would be announced, I was bursting to tell someone. Savannah had returned to Europe and Adam and I were going through another period of not speaking, but I'd maintained contact with my granddaughter, Kate, via the internet. Kate was twelve years old and an excellent English student. I thought it would be an enriching experience for her to come with me to Queensland for the award ceremony. 'Way to go, Nannio!' she squealed with delight.

We got to Brisbane in time to do a little shopping and I bought her a nice handbag to go with the lovely dress and shoes her mother had bought her for the occasion. Walking across the bridge on the way to the State Library we stopped to admire the city lights. 'Kate, I have to tell you that I know I haven't won this award,' I told her, not wanting her to be too disappointed.

'Oh no, Nannio, you'll have won for sure!' she said, her beautiful face beaming with pride.

'No darling, I know I haven't won, they've already told me, but I wanted to come and thank all the people who put me in the winner's circle. The worst I can do here tonight is a bronze, and that's worth coming for.'

Kate cheered when she saw my name on the big screen announcing the shortlisted entrants. At the after-party she worked the room, charming the boots off some of the most influential and talented writers in Australia. I couldn't have been more pleased with having my granddaughter with me to share my success.

*

'Hello, you,' I said, when I heard his voice.

'Hello,' he said, rather coldly. Myles never spoke to me like that.

Ignoring his gruff attitude, I told him that I'd called to tell him that my book was going to be published.

'That's nice,' he said.

'Myles, cut it out. What's the matter?'

Any excitement I'd been feeling drained away as he told me that he had terminal cancer, with only months to live.

'Yeah, anyway you pissed me off, so that's that,' he said, hanging up on me.

I was devastated. Myles was dying and he was going to shut me out.

By November I had made the decision to leave the farm. I found a house at Tura Beach that would, I hoped, make me feel less isolated. It was Myles's birthday at the end of that month. I hadn't missed calling him on his birthday in almost forty years and I wasn't going to let it go by unnoticed.

'It's your birthday, you can't tell me to piss off on your birthday,' I told him.

He laughed, which I took as a sign of forgiveness. 'And besides, you can't die yet; you still owe me $500. Remember our bet?'

'What bet?' he replied indignantly, as if he never welched on a bet.

'You bet me $500 that Gai Waterhouse would never train a group one race winner,' I challenged.

'Ah, she got lucky,' he said.

'Have you got everything you need? Is there anything I can do?' I asked, relieved to be back on solid ground.

'Phil and Christine are champions, and Gail's a saint,' he said. Gail was his first wife, who was also the mother of his two boys. She and Myles had been divorced for more than twenty years, but after learning of his illness, Gail attended to his every need.

'That's a true measure of a very decent person,' I said.

Myles spoke of his regret for not having been a better husband and father and was humbled by how his family and friends had rallied around him. As much as I wanted to be with Myles during those last days, I didn't feel it was my place. It was more appropriate that he spent as much time with his sons as he could.

That Christmas, Savannah came home and brought her best mate, Simon. Having their company helped take my mind off the impending doom that Myles would soon be gone forever. By mid-January he was very weak and often couldn't take my calls. In February, aged sixty-four years, Myles lost his battle with cancer. His death hit me hard and I didn't want to share my grief with anyone. I couldn't make the nine-hour drive to attend his funeral but when I spoke with Noel Christensen, he said the wake was very 'upbeat'. Myles would have liked that. He was a big, colourful personality and would be remembered for his robust sense of fun and his ability to spot what he called a 'mug punter' from a mile away. He had also earned a reputation for a laconic wit, like when he told motorcycle champion and multiple Bathurst winner, Tony Hatton, that he'd be happy to show him the *'fast way'* around the track.

Phil told me that Myles's ashes were scattered in two places: at Pinchgut, the former penal prison sitting in the middle of Sydney Harbour, also known as Fort Denison, and in the stream running near the Jenolan Caves in the Blue Mountains. I knew the exact spot. Myles and I had sat beside that crystal-clear stream many times watching the trout swimming in the shallows. It was there that he first told me that he loved me. At the time I was flippant and had suggested that the eucalyptus in the air had gone to his brain.

'You're probably right,' he'd said, chuckling.

Although I tried my best to conceal it, getting around was very difficult, and I still needed a walking stick. I'd been talking with Savannah, who'd sold the Manly unit and bought a cottage in Katoomba. She'd left for Germany and I was concerned that being out of the country and relying on real estate agents to take care of the place was a risk. I suggested that I rent the cottage for a while. She needed the rental income, and I needed to be better placed to travel around after my book was launched.

With too many possessions to accommodate I had another house moving sale at Tura Beach, but trying to cram my stuff into a two-bedroom cottage was still a tight squeeze. The second bedroom was already packed to the rafters when I got an email from Savannah telling me that her father was clearing out his storage unit and that he was arranging a truck to deliver her things to the house the following week. When the boxes arrived they were split open at the sides and I had to unpack and sort out her belongings so nothing would be ruined. In the process of doing this, I came across a file with bank statements and all kinds of paperwork in a terrible mess.

'A bastard to the end,' I said out loud, when I saw the documents relating to the purchase of the Manly property, which Darrol had led Savannah to believe was a gift. Although the deed for the property had been in Savannah's name, it wasn't a gift. It was a debt. The documents showed that Darrol had lent Savannah the money to purchase this property, and providing there was no provision to waiver the debt following his death, somewhere along the line there'd be a settling day for Savannah.

After getting the house sorted I contacted the Aboriginal Culture and Resource Centre in Katoomba and was pleased to learn that they held regular Elders' lunches, general 'yarn-ups' and daytrips to places of interest. Although they were mostly local Gundungurra and Darug people, they welcomed other First Nation People to their country with open arms. On the night my book was launched they loaded up the community bus, collecting Uncle Stan and Aunty Shirley on the way, and all lobbed in to help me celebrate the event.

When I attended the writers' festival in Katoomba, Uncle Graeme Cooper did the Welcome to Country, which he said was the first time he could recall an Elder being asked to do so. Uncle Graeme's family had lived in The Gully and when they had been told to leave, to make way for the Catalina Raceway, he told me the story about his grandmother who had refused to leave her Humpy. Her home was then bulldozed with her still inside. No charges were laid.

In the months that followed I received a steady flow of letters from women, and some men, who had been affected by adoption. They thanked me for telling my story. It was a very humbling experience to know that I had done something to ease the burden they had carried in silence for too long.

In November 2010, Rachel Siewert, a senator for Western Australia and member of the Greens Party, kicked off a national Senate inquiry into past forced adoption practices. I gave evidence at the inquiry, along with hundreds of women across the country who were finally ready to come forward and share their harrowing stories.

It wasn't until early 2013, however, that Siewert gave a heart-rending address in Parliament House when she tabled the findings of the inquiry. This was followed by an apology from then Prime Minister, Julia Gillard, for the Commonwealth's involvement in past adoption practices that had seen over 150,000 babies taken from their mothers and sold to couples waiting to adopt. Further apologies ensued from the Catholic Church and other organisations. While for many of the mothers, fathers and children affected by such practices an apology will never be enough, for others, an apology was all that they required.

Later that year I was given the great honour of planting a tree, with my name to be added, at the Elders' Grove in Wentworth Falls. The wind got up and the fragrance from the eucalyptus took me back to a place not far from there and memories of Myles, who had never found any pride in being a Koori. How I wished he'd lived long enough to see this day.

Savannah had arranged her life so that she spent six months of the year living and working in Australia, and the rest of the year in Berlin. When she returned to Australia in November I moved out of the cottage and found a place at Ettalong Beach. A month later she came over and we enjoyed our traditional Christmas Eve dinner and gift giving, followed by a picnic at Pearl Beach on Christmas Day. It had been decades since Savannah and I had been swimming together and I marvelled at her power and grace as she sliced confidently through the water. Savannah had a big show on in Sydney and would be tied up for months, so we made plans to invite my granddaughter, Kate, to come and stay for a couple of days in May, to coincide with Aunty Savannah's twenty-ninth birthday.

When the day arrived I made a special effort to make it memorable for all of us. Kate and Adam's wife, Shauna, told me they'd been working to try and repair the rift that had stubbornly persisted between Adam and me. I felt I'd done all I could do to fix things between us and wasn't sure what more there was I could say or do.

Shortly after our birthday lunch, Kate called me from the car. She was travelling to Melbourne with her father.

'Nannio, I'm in the netball finals! Dad wants to know if you're coming to watch me play?'

'Tell him I wouldn't miss it.'

'Yes!' she squealed, and I could almost see her pumping the air as though she'd scored a great victory.

On the day of the game, I saw Adam before he saw me. I tiptoed up behind him and without me even needing to speak, he turned and said, 'Hello, Mum,' and leaned down to kiss me. As we linked arms and cheered for Kate's team from the sideline I wanted to cling onto Adam and never let go. It didn't escape my notice that Kate was now the same age that I had been when her father was born.

Kate's team won their game and we all went out for a celebratory lunch. Adam and I didn't feel the need for recriminations as we talked and laughed together, and it felt as natural as if we'd never spent a day apart.

As I observed Adam with his family I was overcome with pride. He'd raised Joshua as his own son, and the love and respect Joshua had for the man he called 'Dad' was evident.

As we were leaving, Adam put his arms around me and said, 'I love you, Mum.' That night, when I checked the messages on my phone, there was a text from Adam. He told me how proud he was of me and Savannah, and what great role models we were for Kate. He thanked me for showing him the real meaning of unconditional love. In that moment I knew I finally had my son back.

Acknowledgments

My story may never have been told if not for the work of Dian Wellfare and Lily Arthur, who lost their children to forced adoption in the 1960s. Together they formed Origins Inc, an organisation that offers support to people affected by adoption in the ongoing fight to put lives back together.

In my life I have been blessed with a solid core of friends. Some are gone, and some are living, but I love them all and will be forever grateful that they have been a part of my journey.

To my children, grandchild and extended family, who have not stood in judgement of the mistakes I have made – thank you.

Thanks to Dr Janet Hutchison for her insights and gentle guiding hand, and to Jacqueline Blanchard of University of Queensland Press, who encouraged me to dig deeper than I may otherwise have had the courage to do. To my partner, Bruce, for his love, encouragement and support.

Names of some individuals have been altered to protect their privacy, but events in this story are true, and retold as close to my honest recall as possible.

TEN HAIL MARYS
Kate Howarth

Winner – Age Book of the Year (Non-fiction)
Shortlisted – Victorian Premier's Literary Award (Indigenous Writing)

In January 1966, Kate Howarth gave birth to a healthy baby boy at St Margaret's Home for unwed mothers in Sydney. In the months before the birth, and the days after, she resisted intense pressure to give up her son for adoption, becoming one of the few women to ever leave the institution *with* her baby. She was only sixteen years old.

What inspired such courage?

In *Ten Hail Marys*, Kate Howarth vividly recounts the first seventeen years of her life in Sydney's slums and suburbs and in rural New South Wales. Abandoned by her mother as a baby and then by 'Mamma', her volatile grandmother, as a young girl, Kate is shunted between relatives and expected to grow up fast. A natural storyteller, she describes a childhood beset by hardship, abuse, profound grief and poverty, but buoyed with the hope that one day she would make a better life for herself.

Frank, funny and incredibly moving, *Ten Hail Marys* is the compelling true story of a childhood lost, and a young woman's hard-won self-possession.

PRAISE FOR *TEN HAIL MARYS*

'This compelling story is an important part of Australia's social history. It teems with pathos, energy and insight.' *Books + Publishing*

'A powerful memoir, without the self-pity of the "misery" genre. It is a harrowing read.' *Sunday Age*

ISBN 978 0 7022 3770 6

BOY LOST
Kristina Olsson

Winner of the 2013 Queensland Literary Awards
Shortlisted for the 2014 NSW Premier's Literary Awards
Shortlisted for the 2014 Victorian Premier's Literary Awards
Shortlisted for the 2014 Stella Prize

Kristina Olsson's mother lost her infant son, Peter, when he was snatched from her arms as she boarded a train in the hot summer of 1950. Yvonne was young and frightened, trying to escape a brutal marriage, but despite the violence and cruelty she'd endured, she was not prepared for this final blow, this breathtaking punishment. Yvonne would not see her son again for nearly forty years.

Kristina was the first child of her mother's subsequent, much gentler marriage and, like her siblings, grew up unaware of the reasons behind her mother's sorrow, though Peter's absence resounded through the family, marking each one. Yvonne dreamt of her son by day and by night, while Peter grew up a thousand miles and a lifetime away, dreaming of his missing mother.

Boy, Lost tells how their lives proceeded from that shattering moment, the grief and shame that stalked them, what they lost and what they salvaged. But it is also the story of a family, the cascade of grief and guilt through generations, and the endurance of memory and faith.

PRAISE FOR *BOY LOST*

'The writing is beautiful and Olsson's ability to capture a person or a moment is stunning – but it's the fierceness and restraint she demonstrates in this memoir that makes it so moving.' *The Conversation*

'Moving and insightful ... a devastating portrait of 1950s Australia.' *The Age*

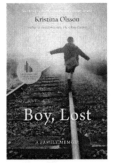

'A powerful memoir. Olsson's prose is lyrical and heartfelt.' *Books + Publishing*

ISBN 978 0 7022 49532

CPSIA information can be obtained at www.ICGtesting.com
Printed in the USA
LVOW06s0913200715

446771LV00002B/10/P